WHEN IVORY TOWERS WERE BLACK

WHEN IVORY TOWERS WERE BLACK
WERE BLACK
A STORY ABOUT RACE IN AMERICA'S CITIES AND UNIVERSITIES

SHARON EGRETTA SUTTON

Empire State Editions
An imprint of Fordham University Press
New York   2017

Fordham University Press has no responsibility for the persistence or accuracy
of URLs for external or third-party Internet websites referred to in this
publication and does not guarantee that any content on such websites is, or will
remain, accurate or appropriate.

Fordham University Press also publishes its books in a variety of electronic
formats. Some content that appears in print may not be available in electronic
books.

Visit us online at
www.fordhampress.com
www.empirestateeditions.com

Library of Congress Cataloging-in-Publication Data
available online at http://catalog.loc.gov.

Printed in the United States of America

19 18 17   5 4 3 2 1
First edition

To the memory of
J. Max Bond, Jr., FAIA, Columbia University's first
black professor of architecture and the "dean" of
African American architects

Contents

Foreword

The 1960s and early 1970s were socially and politically disruptive and divisive times, eerily, and sadly, almost identical to those this country is currently experiencing. In *When Ivory Towers Were Black*, Sutton explores the history of race and power at one of this nation's most distinguished universities.

On December 17, 1972, a fire burned our family out of its home. Coinciding with this was my beginning tenure as the fifth dean of the School of Architecture at Columbia University. That day I went from fire to fire.

A few of the dramatic events that occurred just before and during these early days of my tenure defined the context of these turbulent times.

In 1968, nineteen days after the assassination of Dr. Martin Luther King, Jr., as the nation quaked with the fear of race riots, the first confrontation of the student-led "revolution" at Columbia University occurred.

In 1969 the military draft was authorized, Richard Nixon's swearing-in as president initiated four years of covert bombing in Cambodia, and an unprecedented flood of African American students entered the academy, including at Columbia's School of Architecture.

In 1970 the massacre of unarmed students at Kent State University took place, sparking student strikes at hundreds of universities, colleges, and high schools across the nation.

In 1971 a half million people (my family among them) marched in Washington, D.C., to oppose the Vietnam War. Shortly thereafter, the *New York Times* fueled national outrage by publishing portions of the *Pen-*

tagon Papers, which disclosed secret communications about U.S. involvement in the war.

In 1972 the clandestine and sometimes illegal activities of the Nixon administration, known as the Watergate scandal, began to be covered by the media (and would dominate the news for the next few years).

In 1973 the Paris Peace Accords brought a formal end to the Vietnam War. That same year, after the United States supported Israel in a war with Syria and Egypt, Arab members of OPEC (plus Syria and Egypt) announced an oil embargo. The embargo doubled the price of crude oil, caused massive shortages and a cascade of devastating recessions, and seriously weakened the economy-dependent practice of architecture.

Clearly this was a difficult time to assume the deanship at Columbia. Fragments of political unrest remained on campus and in the architecture school, particularly within the community of African American faculty and students. I was not yet aware that architecture schools within academic research universities were misunderstood and treated like second-class citizens, as were the minority students.

Architectural education as a discipline was first created at the École des Beaux-Arts in Paris, while in the United States architecture study was often located in schools of engineering. The first freestanding school of architecture was at MIT, followed soon after by ones at the University of Illinois, Cornell University, and then Columbia University. From those beginnings, the profession of architecture evolved into an elitist, predominately white pursuit dependent for patronage on both private financial power and social prestige. Almost one hundred years later this situation has not materially changed.

Early in the fall semester of 1974, six representatives of the Black and Puerto Rican Student, Faculty, Administrators Organization visited me. Given the context and the recent history, I should not have been surprised. It quickly became apparent that I was to be tested in regard to various grievances and the call for long-sought structural changes within the school. At this time I did not understand that a dean is part of the "establishment" and as such is ultimately responsible to the trustees of the institution. It became clear to me that a political collision between the school administration and its minority community was inevitable.

While I shared many of the opinions expressed by the minority students at this first meeting, I was still a midwestern, upper-middle-class, Caucasian male and academic amateur. I had no conception of how to move forward. But move I did.

Over the coming months I received approval from the Provost's Office to add "graduate" to the school's name. I was also able, with considerable difficulty, to see that a doctoral program was created in the Urban Planning Division, and to allow the Historic Preservation program to grant master degrees. As a result, the school eventually was renamed the Graduate School of Architecture Planning and Preservation.

While the name change did not necessarily solve all problems, it was a symbolic triumph that publicly emphasized the intellectual achievements of the school's three divisions. Even my harshest critics would likely agree that the school moved toward a significantly brighter future during my tenure. Sadly, for a whole host of reasons, the cohort of African American students who flourished in the school during its brief revolution did not survive to partake of this future.

Sharon Egretta Sutton's achievement in documenting the appearance and disappearance of her minority classmates at the School of Architecture is far more than a work of exquisitely crafted historical scholarship. *When Ivory Towers Were Black* could not have been created without her living through racial injustices as a student, observing them as a faculty member, and working to change them as an activist architect.

James Stewart Polshek

Prologue

This book tells the story of how I got a free Ivy League education. The odyssey commenced on my sixty-fifth birthday in February 2006, when I began thinking about what a privileged life I had led. As I entered the home stretch of my racecourse, it occurred to me that I should somehow pass along all the privileges I had received to the next generation—which actually had a lot to do with my getting this free Ivy League education. A few weeks after my birthday, I had my first idea: thanking the person who had paid for my education, which incredibly I had never done. I knew who it was. Vincent Kling, a Columbia University trustee who owned a large corporate architecture practice in Philadelphia, paid for my education. I knew he paid for my education because I had received, just before I graduated, a letter he wrote me saying that he was my benefactor and that he would like to offer me a job in his Philadelphia office. Hah! I was too full of myself in those days to consider working in a run-of-the-mill corporate office. Being the sensitive artistic soul I was, I deserved, and got, a job with Alex Kouzmanoff, a Columbia faculty member who had a small boutique design office in Midtown Manhattan.

So I turned up my nose at Vincent Kling's job offer and never even replied to his letter. In 2006, shuddering at my astounding rudeness (and looking at the file of treasured thank-you notes graduating students had written me over the years), I tracked down my benefactor through the development office at Columbia. He was ninety at the time and living in a suburb of Philadelphia. Choosing my words very carefully, I wrote:

Dear Mr. Kling:

As you know from [the development officer at Columbia University], I have been looking for you to deliver a really long overdue THANK YOU!!! I do not have a satisfactory excuse for why I waited thirty-three years to contact you, but in truth your name had gone out of my consciousness until the morning of March 5th when I woke up thinking, "Oh my goodness. Vincent Kling paid for my education at Columbia, and I never thanked him."

Well, it was his turn not to answer my letter; I never heard from him. Vincent Kling died seven years later in 2013, hopefully having forgiven me.

My next idea was to set up a scholarship for an architecture student in my will. I spent some time debating with myself whether to establish an endowed architecture scholarship at the University of Michigan, which gave me the opportunity to become the first black woman in the nation to be promoted to full professor of architecture, or to Columbia University, which gave me the privilege of an Ivy League education. As it turned out, the University of Michigan's College of Architecture and Planning was not terribly interested in my endowed scholarship, having just received a $30 million gift from the billionaire real estate tycoon A. Alfred Taubman. So, by default, I chose Columbia University, and in 2007 I began working with my attorney and the development officer at the Graduate School of Architecture Planning and Preservation (GSAPP) to craft the terms of my will. As we were ironing out the details, I started thinking, "Hmm . . . This is nice, but it's not very satisfying, because it will only happen after I'm dead." Fortuitously, these conversations were occurring just prior to the fortieth anniversary of Columbia's infamous 1968 student rebellion—which I had always assumed was the main reason for my being able to attend the university's School of Architecture.

You see, the rebellion had closed down the university for an entire spring and summer, and part of the negotiations for reconvening classes was that the university had to recruit some black students. At the time, I was working as a musician in the orchestra of the original cast of the Broadway musical *Man of La Mancha*, playing "The Impossible Dream (The Quest)" on my French horn over and over, eight times a week. As an antidote to that mind-numbing sameness, I had begun taking interior design classes at Parsons School of Design during the day (since I mostly worked at night). But in August, in the wake of the student rebellion, I received a call from the secretary for Romaldo Giurgola, a famous architect who was then chairman of the Division of Architecture. One of my teachers at Parsons worked in Giurgola's architecture office and had told him about this black woman who was in his class. And that's how I was recruited to the School of Architecture. The secretary invited me to come to the school for an interview with Giurgola; I showed him my portfolio from Parsons and got an instant admissions offer. So, I quit my job, sold my French horn, and by September was enrolled in Columbia University. Perhaps you can see why I assumed that the rebellion, and the negotiations to end it, were the main reason for my presence at Columbia. As the fortieth anniversary of the rebellion approached, and I still had not found a satisfactory way to pass along my privileged life, I had my third idea: I would tell the story of how the 1968 student rebellion made it possible for me, and a lot of other black students, to get a free architecture education at a world-class university.

One day, when I was having lunch with the alumni relations officer to discuss my endowed scholarship, I mentioned this idea of a book to her and inquired about whether she could put me in touch with the black and Puerto Rican students who had attended the School of Architecture just before and after the rebellion. She, of course, agreed, but we also began talking about having the rebellion be the focus of GSAPP's annual alumni event that year. Many events on campus would be dedicated to fortieth anniversary remembrances, so the idea seemed perfect, and Mark Wigley, the dean of the school, later agreed. My classmates and I would be the featured speakers, and we would share our experiences of attending the school during this momentous period of upheaval. The 2007 GSAPP Alumni Symposium took place in October and turned out to be a joyous reunion of a small group of ethnic minority alumni, with a fabulous private party hosted in the architecture office of J. Max Bond, Jr., our distinguished mentor—whom some of us had knighted as "the dean" of African American architects. By the end of that weekend, I had dug into the memories of Max and my classmates to compile a fairly complete list of ethnic minority architecture and planning students who had attended the school immediately before and after the student rebellion. And that is how the research for this book began.

In the years since, I have slowly unraveled a story that has turned out to be quite unlike the one I had always assumed to be true. In fact, it was not the student rebellion that made possible my attendance at Columbia University, though the rebellion was a very important catalyzing moment. Rather I learned—quite by accident one Sunday as I was squirreling around the Internet—that the funding for the affirmative action recruitment effort came from the Ford Foundation, two years *prior to* the rebellion. Without that funding, I seriously doubt that there would have been any recruitment effort as part of the negotiations to get classes back up and running. The rebellion just happened to have occurred as university officials were trying to figure out what to do with Ford's $10 million grant, which was to be used for "urban and minority affairs." I also learned that it was the Division of Planning and not the Division of Architecture that was the leader in the recruitment effort and in the most forward-looking curricular changes that occurred in the School of Architecture. As an architecture student, I had not actually paid much attention to the planning students—architecture was the center of my universe. But I discovered the story of the planning students and their brilliant chairman, Charles Abrams, in the course of retrieving many seemingly untouched file boxes from the bowels of Butler Library, where Columbia stores its magnificent archive of rare books and manuscripts. Sifting through endless folders filled with yellowing paper and disappearing onionskin copies, I learned that the Division of Planning was at the leading edge not only of recruiting ethnic minority students to the School of Architecture, but also of transforming the school's curriculum and shaping it into the humanistic, justice-oriented architecture education I received.

You see, mine was not an *ordinary* Ivy League architecture education; rather, it was an architecture education dedicated to realizing the black power revolution that was exploding nationally, and especially in the streets of Harlem, the country's premier African American ghetto and Columbia's next-door neighbor. Mine was an architecture education dedicated to giving voice to the disenfranchised, to leveraging design to improve the human condition, to bringing about a diverse and inclusive profession of architecture. As a student and not knowing otherwise, I assumed that my architecture education at Columbia University was the norm. As I proceeded with my research, writing and rewriting the book as new information surfaced, I began to realize that it was not only the scholarship money but also the orientation to how I teach and think about architecture that is the privilege I need to pass along to future generations.

In truth, the gift of a free Ivy League education has been more than a little onerous. Columbia exposed me to a transgressive approach to teaching and practice that has forever placed me outside the mainstream and created no small degree of contradiction within my career. As a faculty member in top-notch professional programs of architecture and planning, I am undeniably deep inside the mainstream, charged with equipping already-advantaged students with the technical skills and the ways of being that will enable their even-greater advantage within the dominant society. Yet deep down, my heart rejects those skills and ways of being; my heart beckons me to teach and practice in a way that gives voice to the disenfranchised, that leverages design to improve the lowliest human condition, that seeks to bring about a more diverse and inclusive profession. Over the years, my not-too-disguised passion for social justice has betrayed me, time and time again. Some students have accused me of being too radical, too black, too feminist, too narrowly focused upon inequity; some deans have declared me unfit to serve as an administrator, said I am not really an architect, said I would ruin the curriculum, promote too much community service, and polarize faculty and students; some awards panels have pronounced my work unworthy of recognition, said its social mission outweighs its contributions to architecture education and practice.

And yet there are those few students and colleagues—mostly women and persons of color but also some white men—who have seen me as their guide into the murky waters of transformation. They say I have shown them a way forward in their own quest for revolutionary social change, uncovered truths and shortcomings about the architecture and planning professions, brought the voices of disadvantaged children and low-wage workers into planning and design decisions, and equipped indigenous students with non-Eurocentric tools to redress the unsafe, unsanitary slum conditions that plague their homelands. Like it or not, Columbia's gift demanded that I embrace two contradictory missions: that I simultaneously attain a privileged status within the mainstream of my profession and also seek to change that profession.

To manage the crazy-making contradictions of this outsider-within role, I sometimes channel a Native American fable about a storm rolling in—out west somewhere, where it can be seen for miles because the terrain is absolutely flat; out west somewhere where Native Americans were banished so African-descended slaves could turn their stolen lands in the Deep South into the cotton-producing wealth that underpins my privileges. But I digress; back to the fable. Out on this flat terrain where you can see for miles, the domesticated animals—the cattle—turn sideways when they see the storm approaching, averting their eyes from the threat. With the problem out of sight, they continue grazing, unperturbed even though the storm is, most assuredly, rolling in. The wild buffalo behave differently. Blessed with wide shoulders and sturdiness, they turn unblinking to face the storm; with the entire scene in full view, they prepare to stand their ground. My Columbia gift has helped me behave like the wild buffalo. Encouraging me not to avert my eyes from injustice, it helped give me the courage—and the Ivy League credentials—to stand unblinking and face the storm that is, most assuredly, rolling in. This book tells the story of how I learned to behave like the wild buffalo. It chronicles Columbia's recruitment effort and also the changes in the curriculum and pedagogy of the School of Architecture that made the recruitment effort successful not only for the ethnic minority students, but also for the surrounding Harlem community—and for the disadvantaged communities most of the ethnic minority alumni chose to serve throughout their careers.

Many people made this odyssey possible. The faculty, staff, and administrators who welcomed me and my ethnic minority classmates into Columbia's School of Architecture are named and recognized within the pages that follow, and I have already made my mea culpa to Vincent Kling. Here I thank those who facilitated the research itself, beginning with the twenty-three of my classmates who provided rich oral histories that, along with my own, narrate first-person perspectives on our school days and the careers that followed. According to the terms of my contract with the University of Washington for conducting the research, pseudonyms appear in the book, but the real names, degrees, and graduation dates of all fifty-nine ethnic minority students who attended the school during this period appear in the back matter along with the biographies of those who provided oral histories. Thanks go to my dearest mentor Max Bond, now deceased, who was an encyclopedia of information about the school and its recruits. Max persistently urged me to collect oral histories from the white students who had been leaders in the rebellion and its aftermath so I would have a comparison group—but I, too, persisted. The white students' story has already been told; mine is the untold story of the ethnic minority students.

Thanks go to GSAPP's Office of Development and Alumni Relations, an official collaborator on the research, and the many different alumni relations officers who provided support over the years. Thanks go also to the University of Washington's College of Built Environments for the sabbatical it provided so I could mine the Columbia archives. Thanks go to the librarians at Columbia University's Rare Book and Manuscript Library and at Avery Library's Department of Drawings and Archives, who were especially helpful, including making small adjustments to their rules after I broke my right hand during the first week of my sabbatical. Thanks go to Nancy Hadley at the American Institute of Architects (AIA)

Archives and Records and Randall R. Vosbeck, who helped me piece together AIA's civil rights–era activities.

Thanks go to New York colleague Magda Bogin and Seattle colleagues
Susan Kemp and Victoria Kaplan, who patiently advised me on my many
different schemes for framing the book over the nine years of its gestation. Thanks goes to doctoral student Elizabeth Circo, who collected the
oral histories—some as early as 5:00 a.m., others as late as 11:00 p.m.—
recording and then transcribing the sometimes too-loquacious narratives
from me and my classmates. A special thanks goes to former architecture student extraordinaire Pamanee Chaiwat, who worked with me via
Skype from her home in Thailand, expertly crafting all the graphics for
this book.

Finally, a big thanks to all my students—the ones who are in my classes
and the ones who are missing from them due to the lack of affirmative
action in today's supposedly color-blind society—young people who
continually inspire me to tell the story of how I learned to behave like
the wild buffalo.

WHEN IVORY TOWERS WERE BLACK

Introduction

Institutional transformation requires a major social dislocation, or even a series of dislocations, "before the anger that underlies protests builds to a high pitch and before that anger can find expression in collective defiance."[1] Following an insurgency, as protesters attempt to fend off institutional efforts to reestablish normative conditions, the power imbalance between them and the institution almost certainly assures a return to the status quo. Yet, in that brief moment between the coming and going of collective defiance, concessions can be and are won. This book tells the story of an institutional transformation that occurred at an elite school located adjacent to the nation's premier black neighborhood in an urban mecca of civil rights and black power activism. It asks you to trace an evolutionary arc that begins with an unsettling effort to eliminate the exercise of authoritarian power on campus and in the community, and ends with an equally unsettling return to the status quo.

This turbulent encounter with the forces of social change takes you to New York City to Columbia University's School of Architecture; it occurs between 1965 and 1976, mirroring the emergence and denouement of the black power movement. You will begin your journey as deadly race rebellions boil over nationwide, sparking frantic efforts to remedy the crisis; your journey will surge ahead during a university-wide student rebellion on Columbia's campus in 1968; it will drift into obscurity by 1976 as America loses its passion for upending inequality. Your journey will follow the ethnic minority affirmative action recruits who walked through a door of opportunity in between the coming and going

1

of insurgency. Reading their oral histories, you will learn about the experiences and legacy of the mostly low- and lower-middle-income recruits who received the gift of an Ivy League education. In reading the untold story of the recruits, you will also learn about a surprisingly little-known era in America's educational, architectural, and urban history when substantial transformations occurred in city-making pedagogy and practice. Some of these transformations have lasted unto this day, as you will see, but you will become one of very few people who knows their origin.

Your journey will also follow two university units that steered the School of Architecture toward an emancipatory approach to education early along its evolutionary arc. One was the Division of Planning, a unit within the school whose legendary chair, Professor Charles Abrams, had worked as an antidiscrimination lawyer; the other was the university-wide Urban Center, established with Ford Foundation monies to carry out "new work by Columbia in the field of urban and minority affairs."[2] Buoyed by the era's civil rights and black power activism, these two units used Ford's deep pockets to open the ivory tower to a cadre of ethnic minority recruits, involving them and their revolutionary white peers in learning to improve Harlem's slum conditions. As you might imagine, their separate but overlapping pursuit of a community-based social justice agenda put these units on a fatal collision course with the university's assured return to the status quo.

This particular story of institutional transformation can tell you something about contemporary struggles for racial and economic equality— struggles within the university and within the distressed communities in which many urban universities are located. Back then, in the post–World War II era, multiple disruptions occurred in the social fabric. They were due to civil rights and black power activism, urban renewal, deindustrialization, and the Vietnam War, among other extraordinary conditions; layered one on top of the other, ultimately these disruptions led to mass student defiance of the status quo at Columbia and elsewhere. No doubt, you will agree that such extraordinary conditions are infrequent,[3] as are opportunities for winning the kind of concessions they create—however briefly. You know that similar disruptions are occurring today as a result of income inequality, homelessness, chronic unemployment, mass incarceration, and a host of other social ills. For example, earning a college degree, the presumed ladder into America's middle class, has become increasingly unattainable as tuition and textbook costs rise, while high-paid administrative and low-paid contingent faculty positions proliferate and custodial workers make do with poverty-level wages. And despite the stunning election and reelection of the nation's first African American president, perhaps you will agree that "a racial caste system [is] alive and well,"[4] made even more insidious by the prevailing thrust toward color-blindness.

These and other injustices are occurring against a backdrop of extreme distrust of politicians "just standing around with their arms folded"[5] in the face of outrageous state-sanctioned violence against people of color, especially black people. These disruptions in "the threads that have been holding the system together"[6] since the 1970s may well be paving the way for a huge outbreak of collective defiance, as the raucous racial uprisings that have been occurring across the country suggest. In embattled cities from coast to coast—in Ferguson, Baltimore, Salt Lake City, Milwaukee, Minneapolis, Baton Rouge, and New York, among many other cities—reaction to police killings of black men "did not so much draw outrage for the deaths alone, but for the systemic problems that have so many black people feeling hopeless."[7] When the outrage finally explodes, perhaps this book's first-person portrayal of how a transformative process got reversed in one particular university and school can help extend the period of experimentation and reform that a mass defiance of the status quo generates. Perhaps it can help reopen the door of opportunity to ethnic minority students, who are still in strikingly short supply in elite professions like architecture and planning.

The remaining pages of this chapter prepare you to trace the full sweep of the School of Architecture's evolutionary arc; they outline in miniature the entire story, summarize the methodology, and introduce the ethnic minority recruits who provided the oral histories that narrate the book. The chapter ends by providing you with an overview of the book. Now for the whole story so you will know where you are going.

The Arc of Insurgency

Columbia's arc of insurgency began in 1965 as civil rights and black power activism turned violent during the Watts race rebellion and gained steam during the "long hot summer" of 1967 when a racial Armageddon seemed certain.[8] In response to surging urban tensions, the Ford Foundation provided the university with a $10 million line of credit to address problems in Harlem,[9] and the Division of Planning mobilized to take action. A critical milestone along this evolutionary arc was a university-wide student rebellion in April 1968 that included Avery Hall, where the School of Architecture was housed. The rebellion ended in a violent bust by the police, igniting among the insurgents in Avery a fierce commitment to social justice; the raw display of power fueled their determination to make a wholesale change in the school's approach to education and to the surrounding ghetto community. The group commenced a three-year, ever-changing experiment in democratic governance and education that about half the faculty fervently supported, and the other half overtly or covertly sought to upend. Overseeing the resultant experimental operation was the enigmatic Dean Kenneth A. Smith; loved by some, despised by others, he was the school's only official administrator despite the faculty's adoption of interim rules, which—in total violation of university statutes—gave students and teaching staff roles in school governance.

Insurgents in the Division of Planning, who assumed leadership of the transformation, decisively situated learning in the surrounding community. In particular, their curriculum engaged students in offering technical assistance in the Puerto Rican communities of East Harlem and Morningside Heights through the East Harlem Planning Studio and later the Community Development and Planning Studio. As a complement to these community-based studios, the division's Urban Action and Experimentation Program (UAEP) undertook community-focused brick-and-mortar projects, which created an ideal client base for students. In a win-win, the Urban Center used its Ford monies to support the supervision of students' service work, thus keeping down the cost of UAEP projects while providing a superior learning experience.

Insurgents also co-designed and implemented a new approach to student-centered learning, called the *platform system*, in which self-selected groups organized to study particular problems. Occurring primarily in the Division of Architecture, some platform system problems were community-based, but many related to problems typically studied in architecture school, like adaptive reuse. Alongside for-credit community-based studios were paid internships, many provided by the Architects Renewal Committee in Harlem (ARCH) or the Real Great Society in East Harlem (RGS/Uptown). Architecture and planning students offered technical assistance through these internships, blurring the line between education, service, and employment—a line further blurred by the fact that community organization staff sometimes had teaching assignments in the school.

Believing that the urban crisis could best be solved by indigenous city-making professionals who would have the cultural competence to facilitate the redevelopment of ethnic minority communities, the School of Architecture, especially the Division of Planning, set out upon an audacious effort, financed through the Ford-funded Urban Center, to enroll black and Puerto Rican students. The recruitment effort was one of the most successful university-wide and arguably the boldest among the country's architecture and planning schools. It reflected national efforts among city-making professionals to tackle both the urban crisis and the lack of indigenous professionals who could address the crisis. The effort was initiated right after the rebellion through the cleverness of the school's few existing ethnic minority faculty and students and their revolutionary white peers. It gathered speed when the Urban Center funded an assistant to the dean for minority affairs, who tenaciously pursued his charge to catalyze an ethnic minority presence in the school. As the recruitment progressed, the membership of the Black and Puerto Rican Student-Faculty-Administrators Organization (BPRSFAO) grew, and so did its influence; BPRFSAO members became widely respected for their academic performance as well as for their devotion to student recruitment and mentoring, faculty and staff hires, and curricular reform.

The arc of insurgency at the School of Architecture began to peter out when a sequence of bad things happened in the Division of Planning. First was the weakening of an already too small teaching staff that occurred when the charismatic Charles Abrams took a leave of absence and then died, his replacement was denied tenure, and a third chairman was promoted without strong university support. Second was the university's torpedoing of the Urban Center, its linking of the center to the division's "potentially explosive" social justice mission, and its capturing of center funds for a new, sanitized urban studies agenda, which effectively defunded ethnic minority recruitment and community-based teaching. Third was central administration's anointing of a division chairman from the Law School, rumored to have had a run-in with a black community, who was to help the division articulate its role within the university's new urban studies agenda.

Then the School of Architecture was dealt a crushing blow when its centerpiece, the professional program in architecture, received only conditional accreditation, primarily due to the university's longtime disinvestment in the school and a byzantine administrative structure that comingled the university's top-down statutes with the school's democratic interim rules. Intensifying its assaults upon the Division of Planning, the university assigned an external administrator, who had been key in developing the Urban Center torpedo strategy, to oversee all the school's daily operations (which he referred to as the "agonies in Avery"). With the Division of Planning weakened by internal interference, the Division of Architecture facing external censure, and the entire school under surveillance, the arc of insurgency was on a sure course toward extinction, especially since student interest in participatory democracy was fading as were the ethnic minority recruits. In the wake of the accreditation report, Smith resigned and university administrators put on hold plans for renovating the school's aging facilities.

Jolted into action, faculty members conceded their contested interim rules, replacing them with ones that maintained the spirit of democratic participation but within the constraints of the university hierarchy. Faculty members' adoption of these new rules officially terminated the school's experimental operation almost exactly three years after it began. Within two years, a democratic search process—the first in the school's history—yielded a new dean, James Stewart Polshek, who took the helm with strong university support for fixing the school's serious malfunctions. After achieving full accreditation for the architecture program, he hastily implemented sweeping changes, converting architecture's undergraduate program into a graduate program, firing and hiring faculty, eliminating the Division of Planning's two applied research centers, and renovating the school's facilities. The rapidity of these changes—captured in a new name, Graduate School of Architecture and Planning (GSAP)—naturally caused some consternation on the part of students, faculty, and even central administration. Overall, however, positives outweighed negatives as the school returned to normalized operations.

Still, two residual and interconnected problems remained that would drag on for several years: one related to the school's rapidly vanishing cohort of ethnic minority recruits, the other related to the Division of Planning's ever more unpopular social justice mission. As recruitment efforts lagged, the BPRSFAO and the assistant to the dean for minority affairs went on the offensive, registering complaints with school and university administrators, and once even engaging the services of a politically connected Harlem attorney. Even though some of the complaints proved baseless, Polshek (with the guidance of an assistant dean who was trained as a social worker) proved particularly adept at negotiating BPRSFAO's demands to the satisfaction of all involved, their vanishing numbers bringing finality to the conflict. The problem with the Division of Planning was not so easily resolved.

A complaint from the assistant to the dean for minority affairs unfortunately shone a spotlight on the PhD in Urban Planning program, his complaint sparking a review by a Graduate School for Arts and Sciences (GSAS) committee that oversaw the program. The review began collegially enough but turned vicious when the primary senior faculty member in the PhD program resigned. GSAS halted admissions and appointed a different committee that insisted upon reorienting the program from an applied social justice perspective to an abstract theoretical one. Characterizing the division's social justice mission as a threat to the university's search for truth, the committee rejected its choice for a new senior faculty member, condemning her as a political advocate rather than a researcher. Outraged, Polshek accused GSAS of stifling GSAP's development through a perverted use of university statutes. He demanded—and received—an apology from central administration, but in the long run the Division of Planning had to bend to the will of GSAS on all counts in order to reopen its doctoral program, now unfunded and with few students wanting to enroll.

Meantime, the broader sociopolitical context changed as backlash against reforms wrought by civil rights legislation grew. Fearful of violent civil rights activism and their own downward mobility, middle-class whites bought into President Richard M. Nixon's law-and-order agenda, which replaced social programs with mass incarceration. At the same time, conservative politicians, particularly two congressmen from Arkansas, discredited groups like RGS/Uptown while tightening the purse strings of the Ford Foundation, an unabashed supporter of civil rights activism. Federal disinvestment in public housing was assuredly the last milestone along the school's evolutionary arc. When combined with an energy crisis and related fiscal crisis, a cycle of urban disinvestment began that dashed the hopes of the newly minted ethnic minority alumni for utilizing their skills to improve the living environments of poor ethnic minority communities. As they exited school to find the doors to their careers all but closed, an accrediting team returned to review the new graduate program in architecture, finding its mostly white, well-to-do students overly invested in heroic architecture but passive on social issues.

Thus did the arc of insurgency—graphically illustrated by the rapid increase and decline of cohort members entering and graduating from the school (see Figure 1)—vanish into obscurity, but its outcomes have persisted unto this day. As you will see, its legacy lived on in the achievements of the ethnic minority alumni and in the educational innovations in community-engaged learning, both of which have contributed to advances in city-making practice and education. These successes notwithstanding, the militancy that catalyzed Columbia's insurrection has reappeared on the national and global horizon in reaction to the race-based

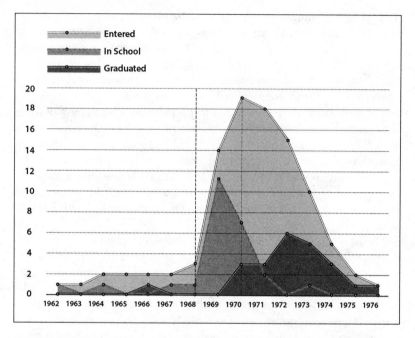

Figure 1. This chart of the rapid increase and decline of cohort members entering and graduating from the school between 1962 and 1976 offers a graphic illustration of the arc of insurgency.

injustices of corporate capitalism. These perilous times call upon students and faculty to engage anew in the impassioned dialogue that sparked transformation at the School of Architecture beginning in the summer of 1968.

The Methodology

The initial investigation—collecting oral histories from the affirmative action recruits—began in 2007 prior to a symposium for the school's alumni. My research assistant[10] utilized a two-part protocol: the first part collecting biographical histories, the second part delving into career histories and thoughts about improving cultural diversity in architecture and planning.[11] Working from audiotaped recordings, she produced the verbatim transcripts utilized in this book,[12] spending a full sixteen months to complete her work instead of the planned two months. The time period extended primarily due to the busy lives of the interviewees, who were working overtime as the Great Recession reduced their staff and increased their search for clients.

A parallel review of primary and secondary archival materials provided a context for the oral histories. Also begun in 2007, its point of departure was the school's centennial publication titled *The Making of an Architect, 1881–1981: Columbia University in the City of New York*.[13] In 2008, a weeklong review of the minutes of the Faculty of Architecture (dating back to 1931) and of the transcripts of interviews done for the centennial publication enlarged this evolving picture of the institutional context. Then in 2013, a monthlong visit to the archives uncovered documents that had been confidential at the time of the centennial research and led to a complete reframing of the book. These documents revealed the Division of Planning's pivotal role in the insurgency—a program not mentioned in *The Making of an Architect*, which deals solely with the Division of Architecture[14]—and the Urban Center's role in funding the division's work. They also provided new insights into the school's evolving governance system and the university administration's paternalistic relationship with the school.[15]

This book triangulates published sources and archival data with the oral histories of the ethnic minority recruits to convey to you, as accurately as possible, the events occurring during the School of Architecture's evolutionary years, acknowledging the author's tenuous position as both documentarian and member of the cohort that narrates the story. Also acknowledged is that cohort members had varied experiences depending upon their enrollment in particular degree programs. Most (fifteen of the twenty-four cohort members) were in the professional degree program in architecture,[16] the longest and most externally regulated of the school's programs and the one with the strongest Eurocentric roots. Of the remaining nine members, seven (including one doctoral student) were earning degrees in urban planning, the most community-engaged, justice-oriented program, with two people earning degrees in specialized programs that were largely unaffected by the community-engaged, student-centered experiments (see Figure 2). Despite these differences in the programs—and despite the dynamic evolution that was in progress within the school—cohort members' oral histories demonstrate a remarkable consistency, as you will see.

The Oral History Cohort

You will read the oral histories of twenty-four of the architecture and planning alumni, this author included, who attended the school just

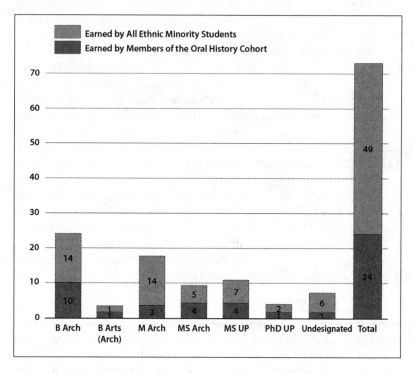

Figure 2. This chart of the degrees earned by cohort members and by all ethnic minority recruits indicates that more architecture than urban planning recruits graduated in both groups due to the much larger size of the architecture program.

before and after the student rebellion. The list began with just eight or nine names but expanded to forty-six persons (including forty-one who had graduated) during a gathering of ethnic minority alumni at the 2007 Alumni Day symposium of what is now called the Graduate School of Architecture Planning and Preservation (GSAPP). Eliminating alumni who were deceased, incapacitated, or had no contact information left a potential pool of twenty-nine; just five persons in the pool declined, which created an oral history cohort of twenty-four persons. The cohort's enrollment years overlaid onto a historical timeline of events that shaped their student experiences defined the period of investigation as 1965 to 1976, though one cohort member did not graduate until 1978 (see Figure 3).

Several years after completing the oral histories, the 2013 search

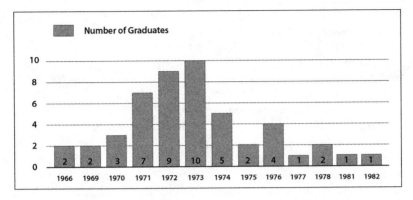

Figure 3. This chart of graduation dates indicates that ethnic minority graduations peaked in 1973, reflecting the exceptional recruitment efforts occurring in 1969 and 1970; graduations declined to pre-experiment levels after 1976, reflecting the curtailment of those efforts as the resolve to achieve educational equity waned nationally and within the school.

through archival records revealed the names of another thirteen persons, of whom eight had graduated. You see, in a student body that ranged from about 300 to 350, the School of Architecture had a groundbreaking total of at least fifty-nine ethnic minority students in attendance during its evolutionary arc, including forty-nine who graduated. However, the oral histories you will read are from the original group of twenty-four.[17]

This group, including ten women and forty-nine men, formed the only significant group of historically marginalized students to attend GSAPP unto this day. You should find their educational and professional achievements impressive; they earned a total of fifty-six degrees from Columbia, including thirty-one master's degrees and three doctoral degrees. After graduating from Columbia, eight earned a total of eleven advanced degrees from other institutions; at least twenty-one are licensed architects in the United States, with four being fellows in the American Institute of Architects (AIA);[18] at least two are licensed planners, at least one is a licensed interior designer, at least two have foreign certification, at least two are distinguished fine artists, and at least one is a college president.[19]

The school's recruitment of ethnic minority students was so success-ful that, up until 2007, Columbia University had graduated more African Americans who became licensed architects than all but the historically black colleges and universities (HBCUs)—a total of fifty-seven persons, or 4 percent of all the licensed black architects in the United States and

6 percent of all those educated at over 117 majority schools combined.[20] As of 2006, 35 percent of Columbia's black licensed architects were enrolled during the short period under investigation, a remarkable statistic since, until then, the School of Architecture (founded in 1881) had produced just five black architects—Hilyard R. Robinson (*Columbia* 1924), John Louis Wilson (*Columbia* 1928), Beverly L. Greene (*Columbia* 1945), Norma Merrick Sklarek (*Columbia* 1950), and Jeh V. Johnson (*Columbia* 1958)—three of whom achieved fellowship status in AIA.[21]

As you will see, members of the oral history cohort have thrived in all sectors of the workplace, achieving distinction as firm principals, administrators, planners, academics, and fine artists. They used their Ivy League education to overcome discrimination and fiscal crisis, ultimately carving out singular careers and winning the respect of fellow city-making professionals. And practically all continued to seek an improved quality of life in disadvantaged ethnic minority communities.

The Book

Your journey begins with a chapter on the national and local dislocations that occurred post–World War II up until 1965 as Negroes migrated from the South to midwestern and northern cities that were soon ravaged by urban renewal, suburbanization, and deindustrialization. You read about a simultaneous movement to achieve educational equity that featured black students who advanced a community-engaged notion of higher education. You read the stories of the oral history cohort members that relate their experiences during this period. You see how the movement gave black students access to the Ivy League, including at Columbia, where aggressive urban renewal in Harlem charged race relations. Finally, you read about the School of Architecture's decades-long marginalization by university administrators, who selected a parade of weak leaders and kept faculty salaries among the lowest in the university.

You continue your journey in Chapter 2 by reading about mounting racial tensions in the nation's metropolises during a period bracketed by the 1965 Watts rebellion and the 1967 Newark, Detroit, and Harlem rebellions. You read about responses by professional organizations in architecture and planning—responses so conservative that a radical group called Planners for Equal Opportunity formed, drawing the FBI's attention. You learn about mounting racial tensions in New York City as angry residents descended upon Mayor John Lindsay to protest housing conditions, and you are introduced to two community groups (ARCH and RGS/Uptown) that responded to these conditions. You also learn about mounting conflicts between Columbia and its neighbors, the Ford Foundation's paradoxical response to the conflict, and cohort members' reactions. Finally, you learn about the School of Architecture, its administration, and its response to the conflict.

In Chapter 3, you focus upon the explosions of 1968 when violence was omnipresent both nationally and in New York City. You read about the spectacles of the Vietnam War, the King assassination, and the ghetto war, these spectacles almost perfectly matched by a freewheeling counterculture. You also learn about the anger that finally built into insurgency at Columbia, catalyzed by the university's construction of a gymnasium in a Harlem park, the Vietnam War draft, and the university's support of the war. You learn that, after the insurgency exploded full force, insurgents gained control of five university buildings, including Avery Hall, which housed the School of Architecture. Finally, you learn that a violent police bust cleared all the buildings on the eighth day after the first occupation, but also set in motion a more determined insurgency.

In Chapter 4, you read about a counterforce of incredible creativity that the display of brute police force ignited, including faculty support at the School of Architecture for a university-wide boycott. You learn about the faculty's adoption of the "May 17th Resolution," which contained illegal interim rules that set in motion the school's experimental operation. You also learn that, during the following summer, student-led groups began meeting to hammer out a completely transformed curriculum that established new modes of learning and a new relationship to the surrounding community. Finally, you learn about the all-out search for ethnic minority students that began with just three ethnic minority students and faculty and then snowballed as news of the effort spread.

In Chapter 5, you experience the steepest part of the school's arc of insurgency, occurring when an unparalleled crop of ethnic minority recruits walked through Avery's oak doors. You see that the recruits have fearlessly transgressed institutional norms so that what is outside in the community has come inside into the school, and vice versa. You also see that they have gained access to Avery's inner sanctum, the design studio, where revolutionary students have disrupted the off-putting traditions of studio instruction. You read how a growing body of recruits helped open up the studios to the community through for-credit courses and paid internships sponsored by the Division of Planning. Finally, you read about the projects the recruits completed, which were wide-ranging and frequently practical in nature.

In Chapter 6, you learn about the recruits' brief sojourn at the apex of the arc of insurgency as the school sprinted ahead of national affirmative action efforts. Then you read about the descent that ensued as widespread conservatism unraveled the school's experimental operation. You read about battles between the school and university that attracted an external administrator's scrutiny as the planning division took the lead in the downward trajectory. You see how the university stripped the Urban Center of its funds, eliminating the planning division's major source of support for its recruits and their community-based work. You see how the descent sped up when the architecture program received a conditional accreditation, prompting Dean Smith's resignation and the external administrator's threat of receivership should a replacement not be found immediately. You see how BPRFSAO and the assistant dean for minority affairs went on the offensive when ethnic minority enrollment plummeted. Finally, you learn that the faculty adopted new rules in May 1971, ending the school's experimental operation.

In Chapter 7, you learn that, when James Stewart Polshek became dean in July 1972, he undertook a slew of changes, some of which had devastating consequences for the recruits. You learn that, in addition to securing full accreditation and funds for Avery's expansion, Polshek eliminated architecture's undergraduate degree and planning's community engagement programs. You learn that BPRFSAO fought declining recruitment efforts, with Polshek's evenhandedness calming the battle and the recruits' plummeting numbers bringing finality to it. You also learn that university administrators eliminated the division of planning's social justice mission and rejected its choice for a well-known senior faculty member as a nationwide fiscal crisis devastated poor communities. Finally, you see that as the devastation spread, the school turned toward educating affluent students who were concerned more with heroic architecture than with social reform.

In the final chapter, you see how a fiscal crisis overshadowed the beginning careers of the ethnic minority alumni. You learn how conservative policies eliminated the work many had planned to do, isolating them as lone individuals within an all-white world. You learn how, during their early career years, they navigated the difficult transition to work from school, passing in unusually high numbers the Architecture Registration Exam. You learn how, during their middle years, they continued progressing primarily by overachieving and by benefiting from affirmative action and emerging city-making trends. You see that the alumni came into their own amid a booming economy, securing significant professional recognition while maintaining their grounding in social justice. Finally, you read a call for faculty and students to follow the School of Architecture's insurgents, and you receive closing instructions for transforming today's institutions of repression in a manner that can thwart a return to the status quo.

You conclude your journey with an epilogue that issues a first-person call to action—to you and to transgressive faculty at today's institutions of higher education—a call to join me in becoming "intellectual freedom fighters"[22] as the extremely perilous social disruptions of a new insurgency come into view.

1
Pre-1965 Context

This story is complicated—fascinating but complicated. You see, its subject matter lies at the potent intersection of race, urban development, and higher education; its backdrop is New York City and its historically African American neighborhood of Harlem, where such issues come into exaggerated relief; its time period is the 1960s when the potency of race, urban development, and higher education turned to passion and protest. Ultimately the story will take you to Columbia University's School of Architecture where a bold experiment in affirmative action took place that few people have ever heard about. To get inside the school—to receive the experiment in all its passionate potency—you first need to step back and see both the national and the local scene in which this untold tale takes place.

The foundations for the story were laid during the outbreak of World War II, a turning point in America's history of the Big Three (race, urban development, and higher education). Two things happened. First, blacks migrated from the South to fill the country's need for manpower in factories and on the battlefield, radically reshaping urban development patterns in the North and Midwest. Second, blacks who had participated in wiping out racial supremacy overseas became determined to end racist practices at home,[1] igniting a civil rights struggle led by students that eventually transformed the country's higher education system. These two interdependent racial disruptions played out across the country, including throughout New York City and in Harlem specifically, with black migra-

tion catalyzing a momentous change in urban development patterns—
and setting the stage for the experiment.

Black Urbanization

After World War II, as more than five million black migrants surged into
already congested urban ghettos in search of "the promised land," they
found instead racial restrictions that paralleled the southern Jim Crow
system. On the one hand, the socioeconomically diverse enclaves that
resulted from the enforced separation of blacks from white society created
unique black spaces—within churches and voluntary organizations, dance
halls and honky-tonk clubs alike. Offering a stage for political activism,
these spaces-apart were especially vibrant in large cities that attracted
black artists, activists, and intellectuals, such as Chicago's Bronzeville, Detroit's Paradise Valley, Philadelphia's Black Bottom, and especially New
York's Harlem. One of the members of the oral history cohort who
narrates the first-person story of the experiment, Laura Marie Swain,
described growing up in a space-apart in the Midwest where poor and
well-off families lived side by side in a spirit of cooperation and sharing.
While her more affluent neighbors saw to it that she had the resources
for developing her musical talents, she also was charged with assisting an
invalid neighbor. Most important in her depiction was the mobility she
enjoyed:

> Growing up in my neighborhood is what started my interest in
> cities. It had so many different kinds of houses and people. One
> apartment house had these dirty raggedy kids playing in a yard—no
> grass. Then there was a dead-end street with men dealing drugs
> where my mother dared me to go (laughs). And across the street
> was the white nurse who always wore a starched white uniform.
> I remember she bandaged my knee the day I fell. . . . And there
> were the two women with beautiful houses where I could practice
> on a baby grand piano. They'd leave the key and I'd go inside
> and open the lid on the piano and practice my lesson. Of course I
> didn't dare touch anything—just go in, open the piano, practice,
> close the piano. . . . We had two little stores I could walk to or
> I'd ride my bike to a nicer one. I walked to elementary school, I
> walked to high school, I walked to piano lessons, I walked to the
> Conservatory of Music, about forty-five minutes each way carrying

heavy stuff. Sometimes I took food to a woman who'd had a stroke. Her door would be open and I'd just walk in. I walked all over the neighborhood.

Laura Marie Swain

On the other hand, the mobility Swain experienced within her neighborhood did not extend to other areas of the city where law or custom circumscribed access to public facilities, as another member of the oral history cohort, Craig Shelton, explained:

> When I was born in D.C., it was—and still is—the nation's capital, but it was a segregated city at the time. I was born before the U.S. Supreme Court's historic 1954 *Brown v. Board of Education* decision. So, I was born into a segregated society, where my parents couldn't even go downtown to see a movie in a movie theater, or go to a restaurant downtown, or stay at a hotel downtown, or even shop at certain department stores, because all those facilities were segregated. And this was in the nation's capital no less!

Craig Shelton

Living conditions within segregated neighborhoods reflected pervasive structural racism. In major metropolitan areas such as Atlanta, Boston, Chicago, Cleveland, Detroit, Philadelphia, Los Angeles, and Washington, D.C., formerly all-white middle-class neighborhoods became black as whites—often provoked by unscrupulous real estate investors—sold their property and headed for outlying areas. Absentee landlords then haphazardly converted single-family homes into apartments and boarding houses, filling them with tenants who paid exorbitant rents but received few services.[2] And though blacks constituted the largest single American-born ethnic minority population, they competed for housing with an expanding group of ethnic minority immigrants who joined longtime Native American and Mexican American residents—all crowded into racialized, deteriorating neighborhoods.[3] Despite these realities, migrants continued to be drawn to large urban areas by the promise of educational, professional, and economic opportunity, often relocating their families bit by bit over a period of years. Another cohort member, John LePoi, was from just such a family:

> I was born in Trinidad, 1946. My father moved to the United States when I was three years old . . . to try to make a better life for himself

and his family. Then my mother moved to the United States as well a few years after. So I lived with my brother and sister in Trinidad with my aunt and uncle until I was thirteen. So in 1960, myself and my brother and sister moved . . . to Brooklyn. This is when I started the life, you know, the experience of the United States.

John LePoi

Two federal subsidies had a hugely negative effect upon inner-city neighborhoods. One subsidy for highway construction and another for home mortgages helped middle- and upper-class white families relocate to spacious, racially homogenous suburbs while still having easy access to downtown employment. To make way for highway construction, states maligned black enclaves as "places of shame and dysfunction,"[4] and then targeted them for wholesale bulldozing under the guise of slum clearance. In countless U.S. cities, new federally funded highways obliterated block after block of black commercial and residential districts, grassy embankments and concrete walls rendering the deteriorating remnants of these districts invisible to white suburban commuters.[5] Using the power of eminent domain to purchase and raze properties for redevelopment, the largest public works project in U.S. history indiscriminately shattered about 1,600 African American communities during the 1950s and 1960s.[6] Urban renewal turned functioning black neighborhoods with their churches, schools, political clubs, newspaper offices, and jazz clubs into wastelands. Among the fatalities were the nation's most vibrant black spaces in Chicago, Detroit, and Philadelphia.[7] Close-up experiences of urban renewal were both positive and negative for the affirmative action recruits, deeply influencing their outlook on city making. For example, highway construction provided Jimmie Lee Jacobs with a great childhood attraction:

It was fascinating at the time when the interstate system . . . was just beginning to be implemented. Here I am, a boy at—I think it was 1955, 1956 they started the interstate system—so I'm six, seven years old, and I'm seeing all this construction going on. At Coney Island, Brooklyn, New York, we had the Verrazano Bridge, I saw that being built. I could see it from . . . the Coney Island Bay. Just watching that go together and I was fascinated by all these buildings that were going up in this world city of New York, and it was fascinating.

Jimmie Lee Jacobs

But for Laura Marie Swain, urban renewal spelled a loss of home place and memories:

> Urban renewal destroyed all three of the neighborhoods where I grew up. That's how I got interested in architecture—seeing all the places I lived get wrecked and wondering who'd dream something like that up.

> I played the last performance in the old Metropolitan Opera House before it was demolished for an incredibly ugly office building. The old Cincinnati Conservatory of Music was also demolished for something totally ugly. Unfortunately, these architectural fatalities were not isolated events—the feds called this period of all-out destruction "urban renewal."

Laura Marie Swain

As urban renewal decimated African American communities and the strong kinship networks that sustained them, highway construction combined with new technologies to reduce job opportunities. Highway construction reduced jobs by shifting the dominant mode of transporting goods from trains, which depended upon centralized urban freight yards, to trucks. Trucks traveling on new highways could access outlying areas, so industries dispersed to cheap, virgin real estate, free from land-use regulations and the demands of a unionized workforce. At the same time, new technologies reduced jobs by automating the low-skill labor that black migrants once provided. Ironically, just as large numbers of African Americans entered the urban industrial workforce, urban industries were not only dispersing to (mostly white) suburban and rural locations, and automating entry-level jobs, they were also moving overseas to Asia, the Caribbean, and Latin America.[8] Depleted by a combination of urban renewal, suburbanization, and deindustrialization, urban black enclaves became "stagnant centers for joblessness and despair,"[9] their deteriorated physical conditions confirming stereotypes of black inferiority. In Harlem, the backdrop for this story, this process followed a similar path but with Columbia University's expansion, not highway construction, driving urban renewal.

Black Student Activism

With the scene of black urbanization in place, you can now move onto the civil rights struggle that heated up in the South over educational equity. *Civil rights* as a concept came into being after the war's end under Harry Truman, the president who finally banned a segregated military. Truman ordered a report on how to combat the racism that was infuriating him—and blighting the nation's image on the world stage.[10] The so-called Truman Commission produced a controversial six-volume report deriding the discriminatory practices of colleges and universities, thus setting in motion a slow trajectory toward equal educational access.[11] Mounting grassroots and legal activism in the postwar 1940s and 1950s became the bedrock of full-blown 1960s civil rights protests, including those in New York City, both in Harlem and on Columbia's campus.

Students were key players in these protests, many having participated in Freedom Rides, voter registration drives, and teach-ins in the South, some possibly from Columbia's School of Architecture. Many of the student protesters believed that "after witnessing firsthand the ugliness of racial discrimination and oppression . . . it was their obligation to change society, and that they could start with the universities."[12] Inspired by such activists as Dorothy Day, Paul Goodman, Martin Luther King, Jr., Bayard Rustin, Abbie Hoffman, Stokely Carmichael, and Tom Hayden, these idealistic revolutionaries joined forces to demand student power and self-determination; they wanted to end military recruiting on their campuses, transform irrelevant curricula and the competitive way they learned, and eliminate deference to faculty and administrators.[13] Simultaneously embracing individual creativity and collective action, they would overcome racism, poverty, imperialism, and authoritarianism; replace the hegemony of institutionalized power with democratic participation; put their faith in youth, the poor, workers, and other disenfranchised groups; and—like Robin Hood—share the resources of their institutions so these groups could solve their own problems.[14]

Taking center stage among the revolutionaries were black students, their protests set in motion by the Supreme Court's *Brown v. Board of Education* decision that outlawed racial segregation in schools—preceding by just two years (and perhaps spawning) the legislation subsidizing highway construction. Two crucial moments punctuated their activism. The first took place on February 1, 1960, when a sit-in by four black college students at a drugstore lunch counter in North Carolina touched off a twelve-year national civil rights movement in which thousands of black students and their sympathizers staged sit-ins, marches, and boycotts to gain equal access to public facilities.[15] The second occurred almost exactly nine years later on February 13, 1969, when thousands of black students zeroed in on higher education, disrupting campuses all across the nation—a watershed day that "had been in the making for more than one hundred years and changed the course of higher education."[16] In the interim, police and vigilante brutality against nonviolent protestors in both the South and the North attracted national television coverage and captured the imagination of many black students and their supporters.

Black student protests began at historically black colleges (HBCUs) but quickly spread to white colleges and the Ivy League as the tone of protest transitioned from nonviolent resistance to calls for black power and solidarity with oppressed people worldwide.[17] Unlike the courteous, business-attired black student protesters of the early 1960s, those of the late 1960s were defiant, assertive, and decked out in African-inspired clothing and hairdos.[18] Along with white, Hispanic, Native American, and Asian students, they disrupted nearly one thousand campuses in every state except Alaska, demanding a relevant non-Eurocentric curriculum that would equip them with "the intellectual tools to fix a broken society."[19] Using black student organizations as their base, they demanded increased recruitment of black faculty and students, increased social and financial support, black studies curricula, black dormitories, and even student-controlled black universities;[20] they also united with neighborhood residents to demand a reversal of university expansion policies and provision of affordable housing and other supports for nearby communities.[21]

Many members of the oral history cohort described being involved as high school students in both mainstream and radical organizations, including the National Association for the Advancement of Colored People (NAACP), the Student Nonviolent Coordinating Committee (SNCC), the Northern Student Movement, the Students for a Democratic Society (SDS), and the Black Panthers, as well as in churches and civic and community groups. For example, Kirk Bowles told of working with the Black Panthers and of advocating for economic justice:

> I was in high school in the sixties. I remember the desegregation issue in Little Rock, Arkansas, all the desegregation issues around the country; the court cases, the Supreme Court decision. . . . I spent time working with the Black Panthers, getting involved with their local chapter. Throughout my life, particularly when I was in high school, I was aware of the inequities existing in our society. . . . In high school, we participated in marches for job equality and a host of other causes. We marched across the Brooklyn Bridge and protested in front of the Board of Education building in New York.
>
> Kirk Bowles

Bruce Fenderson described being involved with the Northern Student Movement and with SDS, which he characterized as a white Ivy League organization with connections to the HBCUs:

> I knew all the people who started a group called Students for a Democratic Society. I used to go hang out with them all the time. Eventually, it went off to kind of split between the white students and the black students. The white students were kind of all more in the privileged campuses and the black students were much more interested in the community and the struggles in the South. But I joined an organization called the Northern Student Movement, which was a little-known organization. . . . There were really grave problems in the cities of the North that were not receiving attention. But I was also active with the early development of the Students for a Democratic Society, which was a predominantly white organization not only on the Columbia campus, but in the Ivy League schools around the country, including Harvard, Yale, there were a lot of people from University of Michigan. And then we also had relationships with some of the historically black colleges.
>
> Bruce Fenderson

Cohort members referred to participating in the March on Washington but also in many other marches, boycotts, rallies, sit-ins, and poetry readings, with several reporting sustained involvement in the Black Student Movement on white campuses during their undergraduate years. For example, August André Baker referred to being involved in a rebellion at Vassar College that resulted in improved conditions for black students:

> We had just finished taking over and shutting down Vassar College. . . . We were trying to get Vassar to do some of the same things that the Columbia students had been trying to do—increase recruitment of black students from the private schools and the inner-city public schools, increase financial aid to black students, establish a black studies program. . . . We wanted a black dormitory, which we got by the way, and it was closed down 'cause it was against the law. But anyway, we had it for two years. Our thing was, well hell, all these schools had predominately white dormitories and a place like that wasn't against the law. But in any case, we wanted black tenure-track faculty, we wanted a black counselor,

and so on, and we got almost everything out of that package that we wanted.

August André Baker

Similarly William Manning described working to improve conditions for black students at Wesleyan University:

I was coming from an undergrad school where we were very active. Wesleyan University was a majority school; it wasn't a historically black college or anything like that, but there was a very strong social consciousness among the African American students. As a matter of fact, we were very instrumental in working with the administration to make the curriculum and accommodations more relevant to minority students.

William Manning

And Craig Shelton described working with black architecture students at the City College of New York to secure a tenure-track African American faculty member:

When I first entered City College's School of Architecture . . . they didn't have any full-time African American faculty. So, we formed a group and had meetings with the dean and the faculty and were instrumental in getting the school to bring on their first full-time tenure-track African American faculty member. And that person was Arthur L. Symes, a graduate of Howard University's School of Architecture.

Craig Shelton

As the oral histories convey, black students advanced a community-engaged notion of higher education. In contrast to the mostly middle- and upper-middle-class Negro students of an earlier era who tended to ignore or avoid any association with impoverished blacks,[22] the mostly working-class 1960s advocates of black power embraced this group. Rejecting the notion that "their personal advancement up the American ladder of success advanced African Americans as a whole,"[23] these students put forth a vision of black studies that not only focused upon the histories and cultures of African-descended people but also called for "a constant stream of young black people from the colleges and the universities helping ghetto dwellers to achieve black power and to transform their neighborhoods."[24] This vision drove the experiment at the School of Architecture that you will eventually receive. However first, you need to move from this national scene to encounter Harlem, the immediate backdrop for the experiment.

New York City's Harlem

Columbia University is strategically located within the Harlem/Morningside neighborhoods (see Figure 4). Towering over the nation's premier African American neighborhood, the university set out to revitalize these neighborhoods through New York City's largest and most racially fraught urban renewal program. Harlem was, without question, the nation's foremost black space-apart, endowed with a network of "churches, political clubs, jazz clubs, and speakers' corners" that attracted "assertive, race-conscious, and politically engaged" Negros.[25] Southerners had moved to Harlem during the first migration between 1910 and 1930, increasing the area's already majority black population. Then, during World War II, the black population surged even higher with some migrants overflowing into the once exclusively white neighborhood of Morningside Heights, also known as the "Acropolis of America" because of the galaxy of elite institutions located atop a hill.[26] Formerly the preserve of Columbia's faculty and students, the neighborhood underwent a 700 percent increase in its black population between 1950 and 1960.[27] At the same time, large numbers of Puerto Ricans were relocating from the island, most settling in East Harlem but some also moving into Morningside Heights. Puerto Rican immigration, middle-class white flight, and an influx of greedy real estate speculators combined to further the decline of Morningside Heights just when institutions on the Acropolis were seeking to expand.[28]

As slum landlords divided large apartments into SROs (substandard one-room units), and crime and overcrowding increased, Columbia, St. Luke's Hospital, the Cathedral of St. John the Divine, and others banded together and engaged the services of a preeminent Chicago-based architecture and planning firm. The coalition ordered up New York's grandest urban renewal scheme and then lobbied the city to secure federal monies for it.[29] Specifying the removal of more than six thousand people from six hundred acres of land,[30] the scheme gave Columbia and its sister institutions carte blanche to "reduce overcrowding, rehabilitate run-down edifices, remove dangerous and uninhabitable buildings, and create housing options for people of different economic backgrounds."[31] In short, the scheme pitted the institutions' needs for expansion and for having an attractive environment for their privileged constituents against

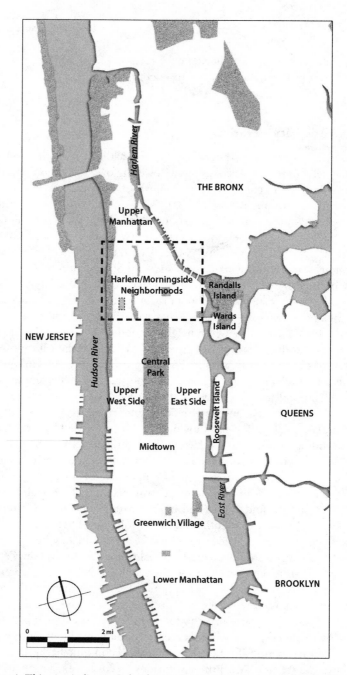

Figure 4. This map indicates Columbia University's location on the Upper West Side of Manhattan at the northern edge of Central Park and within neighborhoods broadly identified as Harlem/Morningside.

the needs of those who would be dispossessed by the inevitable onslaught of evictions.

Morningside residents directed much of their anger toward the area's mega builder, Columbia University.[32] The conflict between Columbia and its low-income neighbors was set in motion as early as 1957 when the university cleared out about thirty-five of its properties to make way for married student and staff housing.[33] By 1961, Columbia announced a $68 million expansion plan, including $8 million for an undergraduate gymnasium to be built in Morningside Park.[34] As the university eliminated more and more of the low-rent housing that lay in its path of growth, a virulent, racially tinged town-gown conflict took shape, providing a charged urban development context for the experiment. Now that you understand this context, you need to know something about the Ivy League to which Columbia belonged—and about that body's legacy of racism—so you can understand what the experiment was up against.

The Ivy League

Columbia University is one of "eight institutions in the Ivy League—an athletic conference established in the early twentieth century."[35] In addition to Columbia, the Ivy League includes Brown University, Cornell University, Dartmouth College, Harvard University, the University of Pennsylvania, Princeton University, and Yale University. With the exception of Cornell, all these elite academies were founded during the colonial era, deeply "rooted in the slave economies of the colonial world"[36] and funded by the profits of the slave trade. While some of the distinguished white men who led these academies were abolitionists who condemned human bondage, others were enslavers who realized that such bondage was essential to their own success and to the flourishing economies of college towns like Princeton, New Jersey.[37] Having built the Ivy League with their forced labor, perhaps you can see what a journey it would be for blacks to even get inside the ivory tower, let alone help cook up Columbia's experiment.

Blacks and the Ivy League

Though named as a coalition of sports teams, the Ivy League became known for academic excellence and selectivity in admissions. Until the 1920s, these prestigious schools admitted students almost entirely on the basis of scholastic performance. However, as the number of Jewish students began to swell, they adopted a new policy that empowered gate-keepers to exercise personal judgments about whom to admit or reject and its centerpiece was "'character'—a quality thought to be in short supply among Jews but present in abundance among high-status Protestants. . . . Inherently intangible, 'character' could only be judged by those who had it."[38]

In the wake of the postwar mobilization against anti-Semitism and racial discrimination, a New York City councilman zeroed in on this gatekeeping policy, sponsoring a resolution to investigate Columbia's possible discrimination against Jews and Negros. Threatened with loss of its tax-exempt status, Columbia's administration forcefully declared that "Columbia University has always been, and now is, strongly opposed to any discrimination whatever against any person by reason of his race, color, or creed."[39] Other Ivy League schools took notice and hastily issued similar declarations, and yet de facto policies remained firmly in place that favored affluent, Anglo-Saxon prep school boys. Only the Black Student Movement and widespread rebellions against racism—including nationwide urban riots—were powerful enough to shake loose the old values that buttressed Ivy League notions of meritocracy and white supremacy,[40] producing frenzied recruitment efforts.

The pressure to recruit black students was especially intense at Columbia, Harvard, Penn, and Yale due to their callous expansion into poor and working-class ethnic minority neighborhoods. Harvard started ahead of the game, recruiting impoverished black students from southern schools as early as the 1940s and providing them with scholastic and financial support. Throughout the 1940s and 1950s, Harvard enrolled more African Americans than any other Ivy League university—though admitting on average only about six in entering classes of well over one thousand.[41] However, as recruitment intensified across all the Ivy League universities, Harvard's lead in attracting black students shrank. In 1961, Yale moved to the fore of the recruitment frenzy, establishing relationships with high schools that served gifted blacks students. Princeton, known to be so inhospitable to black students that few even applied, "announced for the first time in its history that 'Princeton [was] actively seeking qualified Negro applicants.'"[42]

As acute racial tension spread across campuses, the eight male Ivy League institutions and their female counterparts, known as the Seven Sisters schools, joined together in an unprecedented effort to bring talented black men and women from the South, making recruitment trips to meet with high school guidance counselors, teachers, and students, and sending undergraduate students "to spread the word that there [were] places open and waiting at their alma maters for able Negro students."[43] Yet, the national recruitment pool of black students was tiny, given the structural inequities in secondary education that, in turn, produced discrepancies in SAT scores. If the elite private schools were to admit significant numbers of black students, they would have to change their notions of who was "fit" for an Ivy League education. At Yale, with disorder on the rise owing to its encroachment into predominantly black neighborhoods and "the reckless behavior of the police forces on and off campus,"[44] the admissions office finally acknowledged that the academic profile of African American applicants was linked to their earlier opportunities and thus "made it standard procedure . . . to seriously consider the possibility that SAT scores might reflect cultural deprivation rather than lack of intelligence."[45]

In response to this new perspective on qualifications, Princeton created a special category for black applicants similar to what it had always used for alumni sons, prep school boys, and athletes. Harvard hired its first black admissions officer, enlisted its black students in recruitment efforts, and altered its admissions criteria to take greater account of the background of economically disadvantaged black candidates, maintaining that the presence of these students would enrich the campus culturally and intellectually.[46] Columbia, however, rejected the kind of institution-driven recruitment effort that Yale, Princeton, and Harvard pursued, despite New York City's significant black population—at 14 percent, about twice that of New Haven in 1960. Thus Columbia was in no way on the cutting edge of affirmative action.

Architecture and Planning in the Ivy League

To understand why the experiment took shape in the way it did, you need to know something about how the fields of architecture and planning got started in relation to the country's ongoing racial drama. Architecture took off as a profession after the Civil War when the nation was growing at a phenomenal rate; more people were living in larger cities and more wealth was taking the form of property, which a decreasing percentage of the population owned.[47] Architects were needed to design the structures of an elite class of white property owners dizzy with the profits of industrialization, and the Ivy League rose to the challenge. Except for Brown and Dartmouth, all the Ivy League universities established architecture programs during this period (Penn in 1868, Cornell in 1871, Columbia in 1881, Harvard in 1895, Yale in 1916, Princeton in 1919). Adopting Beaux-Arts style instruction that drew upon antiquity and aligned architecture with the arts, these schools prepared their affluent, white male students to design the grandiose spaces of a Gilded Age whose opulence stood in stark contrast to urban poverty. Located in a city of extraordinary industrial wealth produced by black and immigrant sweat, Columbia's School of Architecture especially reflected the contradictions of the era.[48]

Planning, on the other hand, organized as a profession after World War I in a society seeking to solve the social and economic fallout from rapid industrialization; with Harvard taking the lead in 1923, four of the Ivy League universities added planning programs. These small sister programs were more socially conscious than their architecture big brothers, making students aware of the plight of the poor, but both fields conceived their professional responsibilities through a lens of white privilege. For example, during the period after World War II, when 43 percent of all Negroes lived in older cities that were hemorrhaging the profits of industrialization, planners were scrapping inner-city neighborhoods clean for the construction of highways; at the same time, architects were designing the regional shopping centers, homes, and schools of brand-new suburbs. These companion professional agendas served white privilege and, in return, earned planners and architects professional status within the dominant society. For example, almost half of the design awards conferred in 1954 by a prestigious architectural journal went to suburban buildings.[49] All this context is provided so you will understand just how bold the experiment at Columbia's School of Architecture was and, more to the point, why the Division of Planning took the lead. Now for some background on the school itself.

Columbia's School of Architecture

The School of Architecture traces its gestation to February 1881, when the trustees authorized a course called "Architecture and Sanitary Engineering." A formal program did not come into being until 1896, and the Faculty of Architecture did not form until 1931. Critically important to this story, university statutes specified that the president, vice president, provost, and dean of faculties (of the university)[50] and the dean (of the Faculty of Architecture) formed the school's official administration. This statutory structure explains the school's heavy-handed management by university administrators that you will observe throughout this story. For example, faculty meetings were chaired by one of the administrators, most often the president, who was (and is) the statutory chair of the

Faculty of Architecture. Internally, the dean was the chair of the School of Architecture, charged with managing a faculty and teaching staff that had many practitioners with reduced-load tenure, adjunct, and lecture appointments, some with little commitment to, or understanding of, academia.[51]

Within the School of Architecture, planning evolved over a period of fifty-three years from a single course to a distinct, but tiny, unit offering three degrees to about a quarter of the school's students.[52] This evolution culminated in 1965 when the administration—motivated by the possibility that a proposed research institute could attract external funding[53]—divided the school into three divisions: architecture, planning, and architectural technology, each with its own chairman. As hoped for, the following year the Division of Planning established the Institute of Urban Environment with its own director and research staff. Though this administrative structure of four units with four heads was spelled out in the internal faculty rules, it was not acknowledged in the university statutes, which specified departments, not divisions, as administrative units within schools. The School of Architecture was too small to divide into departments so its divisional structure was off the record. Official appointment letters from the university to the new chairmen bore only their professorships and salaries so as not "to create by statute any regular departments within the school."[54]

Accordingly, the only official administrative appointment (and the only one with fiduciary responsibility) within the school was the dean—an important fact you should keep in mind. A related fact was the imbalance of power within the Faculty of Architecture, as set forth in the statutes. At the top of the hierarchy were the university administrators, with titles, doctoral degrees, handsome salaries, and a vast knowledge of statutes that were so unaccommodating of a small unit like the School of Architecture. Toward the bottom were the teachers, many part-time non-academics, many with undergraduate degrees—at the time, a bachelor degree was typical in architecture—and salaries that were well below the already-low university average. At the very bottom were the students who, regardless of social class, lacked any say in school affairs. Shuttling between the top and bottom rungs of the hierarchy was the dean, who had to curry favor with university administrators to access the resources that would placate the underpaid teachers and their students. While many of the teachers aligned with the students, some teachers and students set their sights upward, leapfrogging over the dean to seek support directly from university administrators. In short, the statutory structure of this tiny, rather insignificant school encouraged the exercise of authoritarian power by university administrators and the dean, which encouraged petulant resistance to authority among teachers and students, who in turn attracted an even greater exercise of power.

A Disrupted School of Architecture

As you learned, the societal context in which the fields of architecture and planning came into being played into the nature of Columbia's experiment, but long-simmering problems at the tiny and structurally subservient School of Architecture provided its incubator. You see, university administrators managed the school with the same heavy-handed tactics they exhibited in their dealings with the Harlem/Morningside residents, giving faculty little or no say in issues affecting them. In particular, university administrators—their stunning ignorance of planning and design proven by the banal buildings they developed in the 1950s and 1960s[55]—had historically excluded faculty from the important process of selecting the school's leadership. Consulting only with an inner circle of well-to-do alumni and owners of large architecture firms, their paternalistic management style surely nurtured a childlike dependency among the school's factionalized faculty and contributed to its invisibility in the national discourse on architecture practice and education that was ongoing at Harvard, Penn, and Yale, and in Europe.[56]

The school's stagnation began in 1933, when the university administration selected Joseph Hudnut (*Columbia* 1917) as dean. Hudnut jettisoned the Beaux-Arts instructional method faculty had used since 1881 and then quickly resigned for a better job at Harvard, leaving the school in a state of considerable confusion.[57] Then the administration selected Hudnut's former assistant Leopold Arnaud (*Columbia* 1919), characterized as more of a "head clerk" than a leader. Arnaud held onto the deanship for almost a quarter century, the school drifting at sea between Hudnut's reform and the Beaux-Arts curriculum he jettisoned.[58] When Arnaud finally resigned in 1960, the administration appointed Charles Colbert (*Columbia* 1947), who escalated the ongoing internecine warfare among the faculty but also awakened some new ideas about education that would find their way into the experiment. With a rank and file consisting of about sixty largely part-time faculty and teaching staff and just 150 students, Colbert—like Hudnut—attempted to purge architecture's out-of-date Beaux-Arts pedagogy. He instituted in its place a modernist interdisciplinary and collaborative approach that engaged students in taking on "real world" projects. At the time, "the idea of students working on complex, mixed-use, urban projects was still relatively new, and

Colbert's changes introduced to the school the concept that architectural practice could take new directions."[59]

Colbert's real-life projects consisted of studies for Columbia's South Campus, Harlem's Community Planning Board, and the central business districts in Worcester, Massachusetts, and Dallas, Texas. Though some faculty and students complained that these projects inappropriately blurred the line between professional and academic pursuits,[60] they established a precedent within the school for providing clients with planning and design services that would reappear with much greater potency in the experiment. Colbert also made alliances with Teachers College, the School of Public Health and Administrative Medicine, and the School of Journalism, and then created one-year master's programs that linked to those alliances. In addition to concentrations in urban design, restoration and preservation, and general design, students could specialize in school design through Teachers College and hospital design through the School of Public Health and Administrative Medicine.[61] As you will see, the school's specialties in housing, urban design, and especially school design became the backbone of the experiment.

Sabotaging Colbert's innovative approach to education was his ruinous absence of tact. Perceiving many faculty to be incompetent, he first complained about their poor performance to university administrators, and then he made his dissatisfaction public at an alumni gathering,[62] setting into motion a sibling-like squabble among the various factions of the faculty. First one faculty member wrote a letter to university administrators protesting Colbert's behavior, and then many other faculty and students wrote letters, some supporting Colbert, some supporting the protesting faculty member. The letter-writing campaign set in motion an investigation by university administrators, who concluded that Colbert was incapable of leading the faculty, organizing and administering the school, or working within a university framework.[63]

In an audacious break with the university's patriarchal management style, Colbert took it upon himself to subpoena the entire faculty and staff (including the secretarial staff) of the school to a meeting to discuss his deanship.[64] First university administrators asked Colbert to cancel the meeting; when he refused, they blocked any possibility for frank discussion by engaging a stenographer to transcribe verbatim what was undoubtedly the lowest moment in the school's history. With the administrators playing the part of authoritarian parents, the faculty squabbled about whether the problem was the dean's speech or the faculty member's letter, their squabbling punctuated by infantilizing remarks about the female secretaries (who remained totally silent).[65] As the bickering wore on, the administrators blocked motions for giving the dean a vote of no confidence or, alternatively, for censuring the protesting faculty member. Needless to say, the meeting ended without the discussion Colbert had hoped to have.[66] Afterward, as the letter writing wore on, university administrators settled the fight, ousting Colbert and delegating authority to Associate Dean Kenneth A. Smith, an engineer who had joined the faculty in 1935.

In July 1963, university administrators appointed Smith acting dean and charged a trustee, Vincent Kling (*Columbia* 1940), with securing a permanent dean. Kling established ambitious performance criteria and recommended two men for the position; the tenured faculty, emboldened by winning the Colbert battle, added to Kling's slate a popular adjunct professor and Yale alumnus. University administrators ignored the faculty's nomination, and Kling's recommendations were not interested in the position because, according to university policy, they would have to abandon professional practice but could neither accept university commissions nor even "have an effective voice in matters of campus expansion."[67]

Holding fast to their policy even in the face of a failed dean search, university administrators elevated the "businesslike, judicious, and well-liked"[68] Smith to the deanship. At the same time, they created three disciplinary divisions to be led by chairmen who were distinguished in their respective fields but who would have no statutory position in the administrative hierarchy. Having created this bizarre management structure, university administrators declared that the school would be regilded "with the real gold of a new plan, a new dean, new heads of the divisions and expanded staff, and rationalized offerings within each."[69] In the coming years, Smith, who did not "possess an architectural philosophy or pedagogical goals . . . administered the school without really shaping it to a vision of his own. . . . Leadership fell to the chairmen who did not, however, control the budget. Thus, the chairmen, who were the sources of innovation in the program, had limits on their abilities to enact changes involving budgetary expenses."[70]

In short, the School of Architecture stumbled through three-plus decades as university administrators dominated its dean selection process without providing the conditions that might have attracted—and retained—a dynamic leader. Nor had they begun planning the new facilities the school desperately needed or improved the faculty's salaries, which remained among the lowest in a university with well-below-average faculty salaries overall. These problems, demoralizing though they were, made a perfect incubator for the experiment.

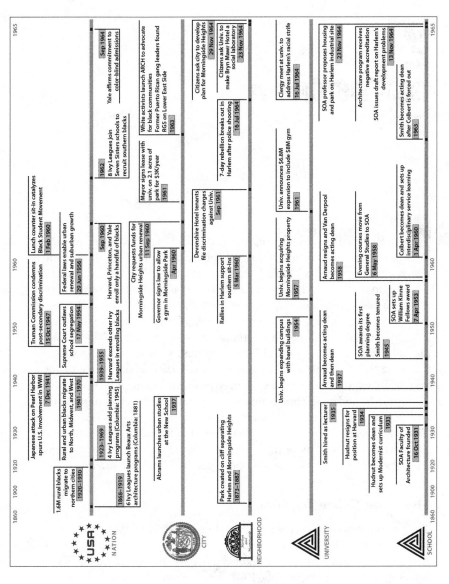

Figure 5. This timeline schematizes the events occurring before 1965 in the nation, city, neighborhood, university, and School of Architecture. (For a larger version of this image, download the file at http://fordhampress.com/media/mconnect_uploadfiles/s/u/sutton_art_1.zip.)

2

1965–1967 Context

By 1965, the potency of protest had vastly increased. You see, the lack of progress in addressing the intersecting problems of race and urban development had fueled a deepened anger—in the nation as a whole, and in New York City in particular. As anger boiled over, various organizations and people stepped forward with new ideas for addressing these problems, including at Columbia's School of Architecture. You will need to continue following this complicated story in order to understand the full extent of the crisis, and the experiment's embedded-ness within it. Along the way, you will discover some key themes that came to the fore in the experiment: interdisciplinary problem solving, blurring of institutional boundaries, community participation in the planning process and (going a step further) planners' advocacy of community-generated plans, and—above all—indigenous control of indigenous neighborhoods. You will also meet a few of the key players in the experiment who inject these themes into the race/urban development/Columbia drama.

Mounting Urban Tensions

The period of time you are journeying through, 1965 to 1967, was bracketed by some of the most virulent race rebellions in twentieth-century America. It opened in August 1965 with a six-day rebellion in Watts, Los Angeles, and closed in July 1967 with a three-day rebellion in East Harlem and five-day rebellions in Newark and Detroit, including deadly clashes between black and Puerto Rican residents and the police, the

National Guard, and the U.S. Army.[1] The rebellions in East Harlem, Newark, and Detroit were among 163 uprisings in what was dubbed the "long hot summer" of 1967. Typically provoked by some incident of police racial profiling, these major civil disturbances resulted in thousands of casualties among both civilians and law enforcement, along with millions of dollars in property damage. They were so violent that police departments underwent mob training in preparation for a racial Armageddon.[2] Televised worldwide, the uprisings catalyzed public attention and produced a plethora of editorials and congressional hearings that sought to nail down their cause, resulting in more than $100 million in research funding from both public and private sources.[3] As you will see, some of this money found its way into the experiment and into the pockets of the ethnic minority recruits.

Response by the Architecture Profession

The extent of the urban crisis—and the dollars dedicated to resolving it—roused even the primary professional association for architects, the American Institute of Architects (AIA), from its typical devotion to elite clientele to consider the poor. Early in 1967, AIA swung into public policy mode, offering advice to the U.S. Department of Housing and Urban Development on including design professionals in rebuilding initiatives[4] and establishing a committee on urban design to act as its authority on urban issues.[5] In addition to advocating interdisciplinary problem solving and testifying before a subcommittee of Democratic Senator Abraham A. Ribicoff,[6] the committee held numerous workshops to explore how professional schools, firms, and the government might design better neighborhoods for the poor. These workshops produced such recommendations as encouraging corporate investment in ghettos, promoting scholarships for Negro architecture students, and establishing internship programs "in city slums" so architects and planners could develop the empathy to "interpret the needs of the people."[7]

A shining star among these initiatives was unveiled at an AIA Board of Directors meeting by Jules Gregory, a prominent architect of modernist private homes set in idyllic East Coast landscapes. Seeing slums as a new market, Gregory challenged "the institute, as a whole, to reevaluate, reorient, and reorganize its directions and purposes."[8] After delivering an impassioned explanation of the urban crisis and the "unprecedented demands of, and opportunities for, the profession" it produced,[9] he shamelessly estimated the number of man-years needed to remedy the crisis.[10] Moved by Gregory's speech, the AIA Board voted for several measures that would increase architects' participation in the urban crisis, including setting up local community design centers (CDCs) and lobbying for revisions to labor laws to allow greater use of prefabricated products.[11] Though in the 1960s CDCs did become a primary "staging ground for professionals to represent the interests of disenfranchised community groups,"[12] overall AIA's self-serving approach did not go very far to assuage the anger that had built over the race/urban development crisis.

Response by the Planning Profession

Planning was most assuredly in the epicenter of the urban crisis. Accustomed to working from statistics and abstract principles to mandate physical interventions in "blighted" areas, the field was now "pushed to the front of the battle against poverty, injustice, decay, [and] ugliness"[13] in an explosive and changing society. A widespread distrust of expert, top-down planning grew during this period as urban rebellions reinforced the notion that planners had done little to ameliorate—and may have even caused—the abhorrent conditions in cities. Planning had two organizations at the time: the American Institute of Planners (AIP) for professionals and the American Society of Planning Officials (ASPO) for laypersons associated with planning. With its greater historical investment in urban space and urban society than architecture, changing elitist practices in these organizations might have seemed easier than in AIA. However, so conservative was the 1960s stance of AIP and ASPO that an interdisciplinary group of activists created an outsider-within organization to advance the cause of civil rights.

Organizing during a 1964 AIP convention—before the urban uprising fully erupted—representatives of the fields of housing, planning, architecture, and social work founded Planners for Equal Opportunity (PEO). The group, which typically met at AIP or ASPO conventions, set out to broaden the mainstream land-use agenda of planning professionals and officials to include "race, poverty, and equal opportunity as well."[14] In particular, PEO wanted planners to take a stand against racist policies and acquire the skills for addressing the urban crisis. PEO's confrontational stance toward mainstream planning solidified at the 1966 AIP convention, when members passed a resolution stating unequivocally that planners should develop new skills to combat discrimination and achieve "equality for all groups including the poor, the disadvantaged, and ethnic minorities."[15]

This confrontational mode continued at a conference later that year in New York City when Columbia's Charles Abrams delivered a luncheon speech on urban problems. Abrams's expertise in international housing, housing discrimination, and global urbanization[16] combined with his biography as an immigrant Jew and night school alumnus to give moral authority to his speech. You will reencounter him later in the chapter leading the Division of Planning in getting a jump-start on the School of Architecture's experiment. At least one other extremely influential Columbia professor was at that gathering, PEO's incoming president Frances Fox Piven; though her tenure was in the School of Social Work, she, too, played a key role in the experiment—and in its undoing. But back to the story of PEO and the New York City conference. Overshadowing Abrams's speech was founding president Walter Thabit's fiery call to action. Thabit implored his audience in no uncertain terms to "think militant thoughts, present militant ideas, pass militant resolutions, and dedicate ourselves to militant actions . . . PEO must get tough on these issues, create coalitions with tenant organizations, civil rights and black power groups, and other professionals. We have to fight token, useless, and harmful local and federal programs."[17]

The confrontation between PEO and the AIP continued the next year at a convention in the nation's capital. While AIP's meeting featured a tour of the architecture of the all-white suburb of Reston, Virginia, PEO's meeting featured a tour of Washington, D.C.'s poor black neighborhoods and another call for planners to "speak out on the pressing issues of discrimination, the redistribution of economic and political power, and the impact of the war in Vietnam."[18] Shortly after the conference, Roger Starr, who had attacked Jane Jacobs's vision of human-scale neighborhoods, wrote a guest editorial in ASPO's newsletter. After belittling the media attention given to PEO's counter event, he derided the organization's support for advocacy planning, which called for planners to prepare the community's own plan, "as opposed to a plan imposed authoritatively from above,"[19] and then advocate the plan to officials.

Starr declared that advocacy planning was dangerous, that it hardened adversarial positions people might otherwise abandon, that it discouraged compromise, and that it deviated from the principle of basing planning decisions upon "an established body of law and precedent."[20] PEO's positions became so threatening to status quo planners like Starr that, unlike AIA, the organization was not allowed to testify at the Ribicoff hearings; in addition, planning agencies enjoined their staffs from participating in PEO and an AIP member even sent PEO materials to the FBI—and received in return a thank-you note from J. Edgar Hoover.[21] Nevertheless, with PEO's support some planners began to practice bottom-up, serving not as experts but as advocates for local agencies or community organizations, an approach that, as you will see, became quite popular among activist planners in New York City—and was key in Columbia's experiment.

Tensions in New York City

During the period you are traversing, Robert F. Wagner, Jr., brought to a close three terms as mayor of New York City. A Democrat who grew up in Manhattan as a prep school boy before going off to Yale University, Wagner led the city from 1954, when national legislation ushered in the civil rights struggle, until the end of 1965, when that struggle had boiled over with anger, especially in New York City's rat-infested ghettos. In his valedictory speech, he acknowledged the magnitude of the city's crisis, boasting that New York's problem-solving innovations provided a model to the nation, among them the mammoth urban renewal project in the Harlem/Morningside neighborhoods[22] that you already know about. Commenting upon "the worldwide revolution of the colored masses," Wagner summed up the mood of the city as he left office: "Clearly, there has been and is going on a basic upheaval, a violent casting off of restraints, a revolution against injustice and discrimination, a volcanic demand for equal justice and even for reparation and retribution for the injustices of the past."[23] During Wagner's mayoral term, parades of Negro and Puerto Rican protesters from the Harlem/Morningside neighborhood had appeared regularly at city hall, declaring that, as bad as their rat-infested housing was, they wanted to keep it; parades of institutions from the Acropolis also appeared, staunchly defending their ninety-two-block, four-phase bulldozing plan. These warring groups pleaded their case "under the crystal chandeliers of the Board of Estimate chamber, before the mayor, the borough presidents,"[24] and others. Meanwhile angry residents from the Lower East Side traveled to Washington, D.C., to picket the federal agency responsible for funding urban renewal projects. Protesting the city's "inhuman plans" to remove 2,500 residents from the neighborhood, they claimed that the city only paid "lip service" to federal guidelines requiring that citizens participate in developing renewal plans.[25] Wagner declared his support for citizen participation in democratic decision making but asserted that community groups had gone too far in trying to take over government functions.[26]

Another prep school boy/Yale alumnus inherited Wagner's volcano of colored masses. John Vliet Lindsay, a liberal Republican who had been a U.S. congressman and would later briefly seek the Democratic presidential nomination, became mayor in January 1966. Within days, some of his new commissioners toured East Harlem, promising residents a rapid response to the area's numerous building violations and pledging to create vest-pocket parks in garbage-strewn vacant lots.[27] Impatient with "cold apartments, leaking roofs, rat bites, and broken promises from city officials,"[28] a procession of mostly Negroes and Puerto Ricans—men, women, and children—arrived at Lindsay's office within two weeks of his inauguration. Simultaneously, another group descended upon the new building commissioner with a long list of complaints. The mayor's staff handled the situation well, telephoning landlords on the spot and directing complainants to an emergency repair trailer the city had already set up in the neighborhood.[29] But this first run-in was only a prelude to Lindsay's rocky encounter with the city's race/urban development drama.

Lindsay began one down, saddled with Wagner's urban renewal plan, which targeted fringe areas that were not blighted enough to scare developers away, but that were "gray" enough so improvements could yield quick profits.[30] With site selection being driven by developer greed, the social goals of expanding the city's supply of low- and middle-income housing and ending its bulldozer approach to urban development took a backseat.[31] However, Lindsay was able to revisit Wagner's plan because the feds were reducing New York's share of the nation's urban renewal allocation from 10 percent to less than 7 percent, with funding for housing reduced a whopping $47 million to just $20 million.[32] Wagner's plan certainly needed reconsideration, but the surgery that would be required in the wake of these gargantuan federal cutbacks heightened the ongoing tug of war between those who favored urban renewal, including the developers who would get choice real estate at a discount and the prospective recipients of new middle-income housing, and the mostly colored masses who would be displaced.[33]

To develop an informed attack on the city's slums, Lindsay engaged as an adviser Yale alumnus Edward J. Logue, an avid advocate of large-scale urban renewal who was equally committed to social transformation and to a sensitive blending of new and old architecture.[34] He also hired as parks commissioner Princeton alumnus Thomas P. F. Hoving, whose youthful staff quickly announced a revolutionary approach to the city's parks, including running design competitions, involving architecture students and freelance architects as park designers, and using new materials and cost-cutting construction techniques to expand the number of vest-pocket parks.[35] Still, Lindsay was dealing with bulldozer-type renewal projects that had been on the books for years as targeted neighborhoods slid into increasing decline. These projects relentlessly moved forward as the colored masses complained of being displaced by middle-income projects, being excluded from public housing built in neighborhoods where they were not welcome, and having their large old apartments replaced by too-small, too-expensive new ones.[36] So their parades to City Hall hearings continued, with police removing (but not arresting) shouting protesters—hearings that often ended in a standoff as crowds filed out still protesting.[37]

New York's Empowerment Response

As anger boiled over in New York City, two community organizations took the lead in advocating on behalf of the colored masses: the Architects Renewal Committee in Harlem (ARCH) and the Real Great Society (RGS/Uptown), which primarily served East Harlem. You will encounter both of these advocacy planning groups as key players in the experiment, so an introduction is in order.

ARCH was founded in 1963 as one of the country's first CDCs; its mission was to provide black communities with a voice in redeveloping neighborhoods that had been ravaged by suburbanization, deindustrialization, and urban renewal.[38] With support from federal and foundation grants, this nonprofit organization applied "the skills of urban and physical planning and architecture [to] the Harlem poor."[39] ARCH was often held up as a model for addressing the urban crisis by the media, PEO, and AIA, among others. Though it began with an all-white staff, in 1967 a predominantly African American staff of architects, community organizers, and other professionals took the lead. Consulting with community groups like the Committee for a Harlem High School, staff members raised their clients' awareness about the deleterious effects of proposed projects, coauthored alternative proposals with them, and then advocated for these alternatives in city government. For example, ARCH recommended that the city fund a multisite high school in Harlem rather than a single-site one. It served as community advocate in such heated neighborhood development disputes as those related to the gymnasium proposed for Morningside Park, light industry and a sewage plant proposed for residential areas, demolition of buildings on a main thoroughfare,[40] and the lack of ethnic minority representation on the City Planning Commission.[41]

ARCH also ran a program for precollege ethnic minority students called Architecture in the Neighborhoods. Expanding a national AIA grant with local contributions from the Rockefeller Brothers Fund, the New York Foundation, and the AIA New York Chapter, ARCH provided preprofessional training through summer courses and placements in architecture firms, and it awarded successful trainees five-year full tuition scholarships to attend professional programs in architecture.[42] At Columbia, ARCH worked with the Division of Planning to create community-based programs in architecture and construction, and attempted to broker a joint venture with Columbia and several Ivy League schools to increase ethnic minority enrollment.

In contrast to ARCH's genesis as a federal- and foundation-supported nonprofit that built capacity within Harlem, RGS was created the same year by former gang leaders on the Lower East Side of Manhattan, with a branch forming in East Harlem in 1967 called RGS/Uptown. This organization was more revolutionary in its tactics than was ARCH, and it went beyond black power tenets in seeking "to transfer total environmental development and total environmental control of East Harlem to the people of East Harlem."[43] Like its Lower East Side parent organization, RGS/Uptown combined traditional planning skills with gang-style street tactics, so that "the uptown group . . . was far more revolutionary, more conscious of race and Puerto Rican nationalism, and much more attuned to the militancy of current minority revolt."[44]

As you will see, this stance somewhat limited this organizations' involvement in the experiment. Nevertheless, a relationship developed between RGS/Uptown and the Division of Planning after a three-day rebellion broke out in East Harlem in July 1967, triggered when the police killed a Puerto Rican youth. An East Harlem leader, eager to calm the uprising, sought assistance from Columbia. Barely a month after the rebellion, the Division of Planning sponsored a two-day conference at Columbia for scores of East Harlem teenagers, providing them with room and board in university dormitories. With academics as well as government and industry officials in attendance, the conference was a virtual "who's who in New York City";[45] it amplified the voices of the young RGS/Uptown revolutionaries and began an ongoing relationship with Columbia. In effect, the Division of Planning had established relationships with ARCH and RGS/Uptown by 1967, both centered around bringing ethnic minority youth into the fields of architecture and planning.

Mounting Tensions at Columbia

As you can see, New York City's cauldron of discontent was nudging the School of Architecture ever closer to its experiment, but the fire had also gathered on the campus itself due to the university's involvement in the Harlem/Morningside urban renewal project. By 1965, Columbia was proceeding with an eviction process so vigorous that it caught the attention of the City Commission on Human Rights, the Faculty Civil Rights Group, and even the student-run newspaper, the *Columbia Daily Spectator*. By 1966, Columbia's expansion plan had mushroomed to $150 million for fourteen major academic and residential buildings, including the evermore-controversial gymnasium, now estimated at $9 million. By 1967, Columbia was well on its way to amassing almost $12 million in Harlem properties, reducing the area's apartments by about 12 percent, and eliminating 70 percent of SROs "in order to erase pockets of decay and disorderliness."[46] Racial tensions were inflamed by university administrators who declared that the nation's future leaders and their faculty could not be subjected to "the perpetual qui vive of a paratrooper in enemy country."[47] Using typical urban renewal tactics, they maligned the area as "uninviting, abnormal, sinister, and dangerous," and stereotyped its residents as a "dirty group."[48]

Ultimately, Columbia's tenant removal activities displaced 7,500 people, approximately 85 percent of whom were black or Puerto Rican, fueling antagonism between residents and the university during a period when racial tensions had reached a high pitch.[49] As you can see, Columbia University was deeply implicated in New York City's boiling-over volcano of colored masses. Then, without warning, a deep-pocketed philanthropist ambushed the university's stance on the race/urban development problem and, for a brief moment, cracked open an entrance into the ivory tower for the experiment—and for the ethnic minority recruits.

Response by the Ford Foundation

In 1966 as frictions mounted between the university and the surrounding community, the Ford Foundation's new president, McGeorge Bundy, entered the picture, stirring up a complex racial tidal wave. A former Harvard dean, national security adviser, and proponent of the Vietnam War (and another prep school boy/Yale alumnus), Bundy was "determined to use Ford's $3.7 billion in assets to leverage change in America."[50] Accordingly, he established racism—which he considered a threat to national security—as one of the foundation's two main areas of concern, the other being public television. Soon after taking office, Bundy provided a $35 million grant to Columbia, "the largest single-institution grant ever made by that organization."[51] The grant was to improve, among other things, the university's facilities, likely accomplished by expanding into the substandard, crime-ridden community that surrounded the campus.[52] In line with his commitment to support civil rights groups as well as black power activists, Bundy also identified that same community as an opportunity for Columbia to pave the way in developing solutions to the national urban crisis. So at the same time the university received Ford support for its expansion efforts, including $4 million toward construction of the Morningside Park gymnasium—now costing $11.6 million—it also received an apparently unsolicited $10 million to support research and experimental action in ghetto communities, especially Harlem.[53] Demonstrating an upper-crust, white liberal unfamiliarity with ghetto dynamics, Bundy proclaimed that "the great university on Morningside Heights is neighbor to one of the greatest problems and opportunities in American life . . . the problem and the opportunity of Harlem."[54] Through research, teaching, and action, Bundy was confident Columbia would help "open a wider future to New York and to all cities, to Harlem and to all who have disadvantages in our urban life."[55]

You can just imagine the astonishingly paradoxical relationship Bundy set in motion between Columbia University and the Harlem/Morningside neighborhoods when he funded the university's attempts to eliminate a sinister, dirty group while simultaneously opening a wider future to it. To make matters worse, foundation and university officials had opposite interpretations of the purpose of the grant. Ford officials indicated that the monies were for a combination of community-based action projects and university-based research and training activities, both to result in an improved understanding of urban and minority problems. They emphasized community participation and *new* activities rather than merely improving upon what the university was already doing. University officials, instead, indicated that they would pursue research and training activities over direct action projects and would use the money to coordinate *current* university programs related to urban affairs.

Bizarre as the situation was, grant planning proceeded with the university president convening a committee of five white males to advise him on how to dispense the monies. Claiming to "have consulted many university departments, several governmental officials, and over 200 representatives of the Harlem community,"[56] the committee specified the disposition of $2.7 million of the Ford grant. Lacking any brick and mortar projects, large-scale operations, or service to sizable numbers of Harlem residents, the committee advocated establishing a new center for urban-minority affairs to oversee an assortment of projects.[57] The foundation had already designated $1.8 million for endowed chairs in urban economics, sociology, and history, so almost half of the Ford grant was earmarked before the program ever got underway. The first director of the Center for Urban-Minority Affairs, Franklin H. Williams (an abrasive former U.S. ambassador to Ghana), immediately shortened its name to the Urban Center to underscore his intention to investigate urban, and not only minority, affairs.

As the Urban Center took shape, Columbia's paradoxical relationship with the Harlem/Morningside neighborhoods and its plan for constructing a ten-story gymnasium in Morningside Park came into ever-sharper focus. In April 1960, when Governor Nelson Rockefeller signed enabling legislation for the project, little or no opposition existed; nor did it exist the next year when Mayor Wagner signed a hundred-year lease with Columbia University for 2.1 acres of parkland between 113th and 114th Streets for a token annual rent of $3,000. However, with the passing of time, awareness of the uniqueness of the park grew. Codesigned between 1873 and 1887 by the famed landscape architects Frederick Law Olmsted and Calvert Vaux, also codesigners of Central Park, Morningside Park was sited on a cliff between 110th and 123rd Streets that was too steep for continuing the street grid, its spectacular geography exaggerating the separation of Harlem from Morningside Heights.

As Columbia's budgetary problems delayed the start of construction, not only did Hoving's crew of young turks take a stand against the project, but the mood and political sophistication of Harlem residents also heightened,[58] especially as a result of the hand-to-hand tenant removal battles that had attracted widespread public scrutiny. Though opinions varied, over time significant opposition mounted both within the community and on campus. This opposition focused upon the university's taking of public land for private use, the lack of community involvement in the decision-making process, and the design itself, which segregated university and community uses. Ultimately, the project acquired the label "Gym Crow."[59]

In their oral histories, some ethnic minority recruits recalled the ongoing conflicts between Columbia and its Harlem/Morningside neighbors:

> Basically Columbia University and the Church of England owned
> a large portion of New York City. Much of the housing around

Columbia University was all owned by Columbia. It was primarily faculty and student housing. It was a huge social issue because here Columbia was, sitting in the middle of this amazing place called Harlem, where all this great music and culture was spawned, but also a great deal of poverty exists as well. And here Columbia sits, with all these resources, and down the hill you have all this poverty. . . . One of the main issues surrounding the strike was that this wealthy landowner was here in the middle of Harlem, and what was it giving back to the community?

Kirk Bowles

Another cohort member's commentary on the gymnasium emphasized Harlem's position "down in the valley" from the university, as ethnic minority communities are typically in low-lying areas:[60]

There was also a huge controversy and citywide protests at the time about the fact that the university wanted to build a gymnasium in a public park adjacent to the campus. The park stood between the university campus and the Harlem community, which was down in the valley and the university was up on the heights—Morningside Heights. It was only through these protests that the university decided to provide some access for the Harlem community to the proposed gymnasium, but it was kind of like a backdoor "separate but unequal" entrance—you know, they put a little door down at the bottom of the park that they thought would suffice as far as providing some community access. But they really didn't want the community mingling with the university students and faculty. There were so many protests in the city at the time that the university eventually just abandoned the project and it never happened. But the point was that they were set to go ahead and they were going to do it in a city park—it was a public park—and they were going to do it with the city's blessing.

Craig Shelton

The controversy over the park had personal significance for Derrick Burrows:

I grew up right across the street from Morningside Park, so I had a particular, personal sentiment towards what was happening. That's the park I played in as a kid.

Derrick Burrows

But for Bruce Fenderson, the park controversy raised serious questions about the quality of the education he was receiving:

> It's just hard to explain this—but, you know, it took me nine years to get my degree. And I was supposed to be learning from one of the best schools in the country about how to do urban planning and design. And the way in which the university handled this gymnasium thing, it was just awful. . . . I mean it's hard to even imagine how, explain how, crude it was. To have them begin this project with no consultation with the community and to take a part of their park away from the community and they had this little concession that they were gonna make a little back door in the gymnasium for the people of Harlem to come into. It was just like such a low level of response. It was hard to believe after all the intelligent talk that it would come down to this.

> Bruce Fenderson

The School of Architecture

Before exploring the School of Architecture's response to the urban crisis, you should know a bit about the structure of the school, probably the most confusing part of this complicated story, and meet the school's administrators. As you recall, Kenneth A. Smith was dean during this period, the sole official administrator, his staff consisting of twenty-eight statutory faculty members, sixty-five instructors and teaching staff, and seventeen administrative staff. Smith had a degree in civil engineering from Massachusetts Institute of Technology and got his start teaching mathematics in City College of New York's night school. His break at Columbia came when he was hired in the School of Architecture as an associate (1935) and subsequently advanced to assistant professor (1937), associate professor (1946), professor (1953), assistant dean (1957), associate dean (1962), acting dean (1963), and then dean (1965). Along the way, Smith acquired some experience as a licensed professional engineer, but his résumé was notably lacking in academic or professional distinction.

The school had three divisions, each with an unofficial administrator. Romaldo Giurgola (*Columbia* 1951) was chairman of the twenty-member Division of Architecture. Born and educated in Rome, Giurgola was principal of an award-winning architecture firm with offices in New York and Philadelphia. Charles Abrams, whom you have already met, was chairman of the five-member Division of Planning, which served as the home base for an applied research center, the Institute of Urban Environment. Chester A. Rapkin directed the institute, his claim to fame being that he thwarted from demolition the neighborhood south of New York's Houston Street, which he ingeniously dubbed "SoHo." Harold K. Bell and his associate, Vernon (Ben) Robinson, in turn, directed the Urban Action and Experimentation Program (UAEP), an outreach program spawned by the institute. Outside the academy, the Bell/Robinson team were business partners in a construction firm specializing in prefabrication. Mario Salvadori—also born and educated in Rome—served as chairman of the three-member Division of Architectural Technology. A principal in the engineering firm Weidlinger Associates, he was known for designing architecturally expressive thin-shell concrete structures. Together these seven men—a dean, three chairmen, and three directors—provided the managerial and intellectual leadership of the School of Architecture, with the large Division of Architecture being less nimble in responding to New York City's race/urban development rage and the tiny Division of Architectural Technology not participating at all. Now that you have the big picture, a look at the differing responses by the Division of Architecture and the Division of Planning is in order.

Division of Architecture's Response

If you look at the Division of Architecture's modeling of Colbert's real-life pedagogy, you will see that faculty—like the architecture profession—were steeped in elitist practices and not yet ready to begin the experiment. For example, in one project, architecture faculty engaged a large group of graduate design students in conducting a six-month study for a Harlem-area planning board.[61] The well-publicized report that Smith delivered to the board naïvely proposed—for this "chronically afflicted" community—"a substantially integrated Harlem, based on excellence by 1975."[62] In another such project, faculty engaged students in developing proposals for transforming 125th Street, Harlem's main thoroughfare and most distinctive black space, into a "prominent commercial area."[63] Topping these instances of siding with mainstream powerbrokers was an architecture studio that asked students to investigate Governor Nelson Rockefeller's proposal for a $28 million twenty-story building with state offices and a cultural center. The building was to be located on 125th Street, towering over the thoroughfare's existing four- and five-story tenements; sadly, its massiveness would eventually come into being (see Figure 6).[64]

Figure 6. This photo shows the monumental scale of the twenty-story SOB towering over the more human-scaled four- and five-story tenement buildings that formed the fabric of the Harlem neighborhood circa 1978. (Photo courtesy of Sharon Egretta Sutton.)

   This proposal had evoked even more community opposition than the planning board's intention to integrate Harlem—or Columbia's intention to build the infamous gymnasium. As was typical, the governor had failed to seek residents' input into his proposal, which they indignantly dubbed the "SOB," using the acronym for State Office Building to convey their attitude about this bulky intrusion into the neighborhood. As the spirit of self-determination grew in this era of black power, many black activists went even further, characterizing the project as "a white takeover of Harlem."[65] Nevertheless, some architecture faculty waded into the controversy seemingly unaware of the racial dynamics but drawn by the SOB's complex program of offices, retail, and cultural activities, its location on a busy urban street, and its technical challenges as a high-rise structure. Their involvement of students once again gave credence to mainstream powerbrokers. Bruce Fenderson was one of the three ethnic minority students who were at the school prior to the student rebellion. For him, the SOB studio was his most disturbing educational experience:

> Our teachers . . . had decided that they were gonna make the design problem for the third-year class the design for the State Office Building that was located on 125th Street and Seventh Avenue . . . Wyatt T. Walker, a minister from the South who I did not know, he had convinced Governor Rockefeller—Governor Rockefeller was planning to build a state office building in downtown Manhattan, which eventually became the World Trade Towers. He was starting to panic about that and Wyatt T. Walker and African American leaders convinced him to take a portion of that construction money and build a state office building in Harlem.
>
> So that week, that project had made its way through the administration, and they had gotten most of the approvals that were necessary, and they had cleared the land to get ready for construction, and they went and found an African American architect who was behind it—the people of Harlem had not been apprised of any of this. And by the time they cleared the land, there was a lot of unrest and protest in Harlem about building this tall building that would bring all these white people into Harlem. So there were many people in Harlem who were against the construction of this building.
>
> So this was given to us as a class assignment . . . and I actually refused to do it—I went and found another site in the Bronx—because the feeling of conflict around this was so deep—and there was actually no place you could discuss it in the school—nobody in the school you could discuss it with. . . . The intervention by these African American leaders to get this building put there, the opposition within the community—sort of—with no intelligence in the design studio about any of this. I mean, it was mostly just design

a tall building and get the elevators in the right place, and get the number of people who could fit in the lobby and get up and down in the building. There wasn't anybody there who could actually help anybody understand what was the real story with this building.

Bruce Fenderson

By providing mainstream powerbrokers with blueprints for upgrading Harlem, these student projects essentially put a community face on Columbia's tenant removal process. With such insensitivity to ghetto politics as a starting point, perhaps you will agree that the School of Architecture was not yet ready to undertake its bold experiment in affirmative action. However, the Division of Planning was out front, laying the foundations for the experiment's recruitment effort and curricular reform.

Division of Planning's Response

Upon being appointed founding chairman of the Division of Planning, Abrams set about creating an institutional framework that could engage students, faculty, and planning practitioners in taking a multipronged approach to the urban crisis—both in New York and around the world. He secured university funding to expand the division's instructional budget (though far less than anticipated); he also secured a $400,000 Ford grant to launch the institute's international research agenda (also far less than anticipated) and sought funding from the Urban Center and Mellon Foundation to support domestic activities; and he courted Bell for a $50,000 contribution to launch UAEP's community outreach agenda. Abrams completely entwined the agendas of these teaching, applied research, and community outreach operations, blurring the line between education and practice, and between university and community.

For example, the institute funded faculty and student research, which then became master's theses and doctoral dissertations. It also sponsored urban planning seminars that constituents outside the university attended for a fee and matriculated students took for credit. With dual appointments in both entities, many staff conducted funded research and offered for-fee continuing education, while also teaching for-credit seminars and studios and serving as advisers in the degree programs. The institute was so closely linked with planning's degree-granting programs that its annual reports not only described the institute's research and continuing education activities, but they also described the Division of Planning, its students and faculty, curriculum, fellowship support, and study-abroad opportunities. As you will see, such blurring of boundaries became a defining characteristic of the experiment.

An early proponent of interdisciplinary education, Abrams believed that planners could not address complex urban problems within the rigid disciplinary silos of academia and lamented that students' prior education had narrowed their view of the interconnectedness of problems. He envisioned "an interplay between sociology, law and government, anthropology, economics, art and architecture, public health, and virtually everything that [was] being taught."[66] To address the challenge posed by the increasing complexity and interconnectedness of knowledge, Abrams maintained that planning education not only needed to encompass a wide range of subjects but that it also needed to offer opportunities for testing knowledge in the field. Further, he understood planning's new breed of students—older, smarter, more idealistic, more diverse—who were increasingly attracted to urban studies as they recognized urbanization as an inescapable fact of the human condition.[67] To enrich the makeup of the student body as well as the international component of the curriculum, Abrams solicited applications from around the world.

Whether focused upon domestic or international issues, Abrams injected the division with his infectious energy, personality, and commitment to equality. In the first two years of his tenure, a unit the dean had characterized as not very highly rated—one that university administrators only half-heartedly supported—witnessed a fivefold increase in applications and a 65 percent increase in enrollment, with particular success in attracting geographically diverse students. Abrams established an applied research agenda for the institute that centered upon housing and planning in the United States and in less developed countries. This agenda linked to the division's course offerings in both these areas, especially housing in less developed countries, and to students' real-life assignments locally and abroad. Abrams brought in distinguished practitioners as teachers and guest lecturers, connecting students, faculty, and practitioners to social idealism tempered by pragmatism. These successes—in community-engaged teaching and applied research, as well as in fundraising—positioned the Division of Planning, the institute, and UAEP to take the lead in the experiment. Now all that is needed is the final push toward insurgency—the explosions of 1968.

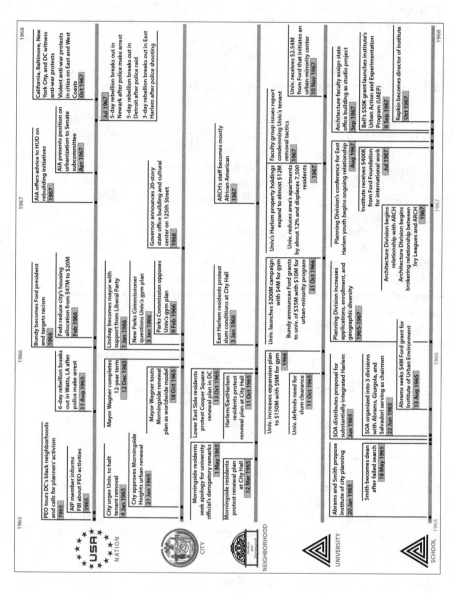

Figure 7. This timeline schematizes the events occurring between 1965 and 1967 in the five contexts that are the subject of this story. (For a larger version of this image, download the file at http://fordhampress.com/media/mconnect_uploadfiles/s/u/sutton_art_1.zip.)

3
1968 Insurgency

Perhaps you are old enough to remember the explosions of 1968; perhaps not. Either way, you will need to summon up their shattering force to receive the experiment in all its passionate potency. You see, the dramas of that single year pierced the national psyche in a way that "only the Depression, Pearl Harbor, and the Holocaust have."[1] Violence was omnipresent, with young people assuming lead roles in various mind-warping dramas. The country's record-breaking six million draft-age undergraduate students filled roles in some of the dramas, the masses of disaffected black ghetto youth starred in others, the horrifying casualties of military operations in Vietnam filled roles in still others, but the superstar of all the dramas was television, which night by night seared each explosion into the nation's collective memory.[2]

The National Dramas

Among the many national dramas, the Vietnam War stood out as the prime-time show. An antiwar/draft-resistance spectacle had begun heating up in the fall of 1967 as bloody protests raged in California, Baltimore, New York City, and Washington, D.C.[3] By January 1968, distinguished gray-haired antiwar activists had organized to support draft-age young men, including literary critic Dwight Macdonald, author Paul Goodman, author and pediatrician Dr. Benjamin Spock, and Yale University chaplain Rev. William Sloane Coffin, Jr.[4] To restore order, the government charged Spock, Coffin, and three others with conspiracy to encourage

55

draft evasion, "a felony punishable by up to five years in prison."[5] But the antiwar/draft-resistance drama persisted and, since young people's futures were at stake, college campuses, including Columbia's, became boiling cauldrons of protest.[6]

The spectacle of the war itself took center stage on January 31 when some seventy thousand North Vietnamese and Vietcong forces launched surprise attacks on the Vietnamese lunar holiday Tet, which had typically been an unofficial ceasefire. Though U.S. and South Vietnamese forces ultimately held off the attacks, the Tet Offensive, as it was called, marked a turning point in public opinion[7] after numerous television crews documented its horrific scenes of carnage. Realizing that the government had duped them into thinking victory was in sight, most Americans promptly withdrew their support—for the war, for its battlefield commander William Westmoreland, and for its commander in chief President Lyndon Baines Johnson.[8] Two brutal months later, on March 31, President Johnson made the stunning announcement that he was not only limiting the bombing in Vietnam and calling for peace negotiations,[9] but also that he was withdrawing from the presidential race.[10]

With the nation's nerve endings raw, the Dr. Martin Luther King, Jr., drama began at the beginning of April. Persisting in nonviolence though "denounced from both ends of the political spectrum," Dr. King had planned a massive Poor People's Campaign in Washington, D.C., that would seek "nothing less than a redistribution of the nation's wealth."[11] Buoyed by the news that President Johnson had backed down from the war, he would first go through with his original plan to lead a march of sanitation workers in Memphis—a plan that had been hijacked when violent demonstrators in an earlier march had to be subdued by the National Guard. On April 3, before an audience of two thousand in the Memphis Mason Temple, Dr. King delivered his last speech—a prophetic recounting of all the threats upon his life, beginning with a Harlem stabbing incident a decade earlier.[12] After his assassination the next day at the Lorraine Motel, the spectacle of ghetto violence quickly unfolded:

> In Memphis, the police chief was on television a few hours later. "Looting is rampant," he said. "The National Guard is coming back." In New York, John Lindsay went to Harlem, where he was astonished by the size of the crowds. He walked the streets for a while, until the scene became unruly and his bodyguards pushed him into a limousine that belonged to Percy Sutton, the black Manhattan borough president. . . . All night long there were scattered

reports of violence. . . . The stories coming out of Washington sounded especially ominous. There, in the black section near 14th and U Streets NW, Stokely Carmichael addressed four hundred people in the street. "Go home and get a gun!" he shouted.[13]

The King assassination riots resulted in widespread military mobilization, dozens of deaths, thousands of injuries, and untold damage to property in black neighborhoods, blurring the war in Vietnam with the war in the ghetto. Nevertheless, Dr. King appeared on stage from the grave for one final bow in this spectacle; on April 11, he would realize his goal of having President Johnson sign into law the Fair Housing Act. At last Negros were to have equal access to housing opportunities, but the ghetto war raged on.

Oddly enough, all this war/ghetto violence was almost perfectly matched by a freewheeling counterculture, as musicians, poets, filmmakers, and other creative types used their imaginations to critique a world caught on fire. From Stanley Kubrick's and Arthur C. Clarke's *2001: A Space Odyssey*, to the Beatles' "Hey Jude," to Abbie Hoffman's *Revolution for the Hell of It*, to Arlo Guthrie's "Alice's Restaurant Massacree," to "Aquarius/Let the Sunshine In" in the Broadway musical *Hair*, the counterculture used humor, pathos, satire, and pure shock to put back together what so many tragedies had torn asunder. Even black militants were tamed by counterculture, especially its music, from the invitation to chill out in Hugh Masekela's "Grazing in the Grass," to the plea of Diana Ross and the Supremes to avoid another "Love Child" by waiting just a little bit longer, to James Brown's and Nina Simone's inspirational calming of audiences in the volatile wake of Dr. King's murder.

The Local Dramas

The local dramas pretty much mirrored the national ones. Young people's antiwar/draft-resistance sentiments were amplified by Mayor John Lindsay, who brashly linked the U.S. urban crisis to the "insane military escalation in Vietnam."[14] In speeches to attentive high school and college students, including Columbia law students, Mayor Lindsay unequivocally declared "that what happens in the ghettos is deeply related to America's performance and behavior all over the world."[15] Columbia's conservative president, Dr. Grayson Kirk, also called for an exit from Vietnam, but not on moral grounds. For him the war impeded resolution of perilous social, political, and economic problems at home, among them fiscal instability,

the generation gap, inequality, and—prescient of the shattering explosion
that would soon greet Dr. Kirk at Columbia—racial strife and rebellious
young people with no respect for the law or authority.[16]

Columbia's rebellious antiwar students were especially irked by the
university's participation in a secretive think tank known as the Institute
of Defense Analysis (IDA), which they claimed involved them indirectly
in the war and tended "to compromise academic freedom by involving
academicians in secret scientific projects."[17] As you will see, the specter of
the IDA provided fuel for the coming explosion. But the students were
not alone; some faculty joined in the rebelliousness, in particular the seventy members of the Faculty Civil Rights Group, who had been dog-
ging Columbia's expansion into Harlem. In March—a little more than a
month before the explosion blew apart the university—the group issued a
twenty-eight-page report condemning the university's "oil slick" expansion plans, which it claimed would create an isolated "garrison enclave."
Instead, the group called for "the revival of an ethnically and economically integrated and balanced community."[18]

Unmoved, Columbia administrators plowed ahead, preparing to hire
the university's first master planner in seventy years. The distinguished
architecture firm of I. M. Pei and Associates would oversee a $150–
$200 million expansion into the surrounding neighborhood that was to
occur over two to three decades.[19] So you see, though the antiwar/IDA
drama loomed large in New York City and on Columbia's campus, the
Harlem drama offered an immediate link between the insanity of a distant
war and the admixture of racial strife and cultural inspiration occurring
right next door. Some members of the oral history cohort had grown up
in New York's cauldron of racial and cultural revolution. For example,
Kirk Bowles described with great passion what it felt like to be at the
center of social change:

> This was an extraordinary time, and anyone who lived through that
> period, particularly in New York, it was like being at the center of
> the universe. When you talk about being in Mecca, there was no
> place on the planet that had all these things happening all in one
> place as you had there. . . . It was truly an amazing time to be alive
> and in New York City. Being very much involved with protest
> rallies, going to concerts, surrounded by culture and excitement.
> You also had this developing dialogue between Martin Luther King
> and Malcolm X, whose previously differing points of view were
> also beginning to converge.
>
> Kirk Bowles

As Bowles noted, the drama of protest was enriched by an especially vibrant local culture, with Harlem hosting a paradoxical blend of strife and soul. In a city that "welcomed the immigrant and the outcast—the avant-garde, the radical, the disadvantaged, the adventurer, the artist, the author, the beat, and the hip,"[20] New York City—and Harlem—were arguably the locus of all that was tragic and triumphant in the 1968 spectacle.

The Drama on 125th Street

Harlem's main thoroughfare is 125th Street, which runs east–west in a valley formed by one of the city's three ancient fault lines, a valley that is especially deep at its western edge near Columbia. In this area of the city, 125th Street forms a literal "line in the sand" that separates Harlem from the Upper West Side of Manhattan—a valley so deep that north–south transportation arteries must bridge over it with viaducts. The tallest viaduct carries Riverside Drive across 125th Street at its westernmost edge; two others carry railroad tracks at Park Avenue and the Harlem River Drive at its easternmost edge, these being lower as the land levels out. Arguably the most spectacular viaduct carries the IRT subway across 125th Street at Broadway, the avenue where Columbia's main entrance is located. The graceful cast iron arc of this viaduct can be seen in the distance from other storied 125th Street landmarks like the Apollo Theater and the Hotel Theresa, exaggerating Harlem's down-in-the-valley location.

In 1966, when Governor Rockefeller announced his intention to construct a state office building on 125th Street, he put Harlem's main thoroughfare in the bull's eye of developer greed and political ambition. Envisioning a quick win from revitalizing this deteriorated but famed black space, power brokers responded with a flurry of construction proposals. Among them were a state-funded arts and cultural center, a privately funded city office building, a seven-block expansion of Knickerbocker Hospital, an opera house (seriously!), at least three proposals for using the air rights over the railroad tracks, and—characteristic of Columbia's banal architecture and urban design—a multi-block university-sponsored residential development with "a series of slabs on a podium base, all of unmitigated monotony and soulless scale."[21] The proposals were dizzying, ranging from office buildings to sports palaces to low-cost housing to a new department store to small shops to municipal garages, all envisioned as a white middle-class fix for a sordid black community. With a ten-person staff and no funds for feasibility studies, the City Planning

Commission was hard-pressed to make sense of them. "What to condemn, what to build, how to deal with the railroad tracks, where to put housing, how to relate community facilities; . . . admittedly none of this [was] within the realm or responsibility of the speculative builder. Nor [were] other real Harlem needs: coordination of zoning, the provision of low-rent housing, and cheap commercial space."[22]

An elected committee of citizens was equally hard-pressed to generate a plan for an irregular area roughly between Lenox and Park Avenues from 125th to 107th Streets—where students interning with the Real Great Society/Uptown would soon be working. Referred to as the Milbank-Frawley Circle, this neighborhood had received $1 million in federal funding, having demonstrated that 99 percent of its buildings had at least one violation and that at least 50 percent were deteriorated. Money in hand, a struggle between the black and Puerto Rican factions of the committee ensued and all but halted progress on the renewal plan.[23] Thus Columbia University's strategic location overlooked the many racial and political dramas that were unfolding down in the valley (see Figure 8).

Meanwhile, the city announced its intention to close the historic African American Sydenham Hospital, the only place where, according to Percy Sutton, "a black doctor [could] be free to practice medicine."[24] And to add to the fury that had built, the city applied for federal and state funding to construct a $70 million plant along the Hudson River just north of 125th Street that would treat 220 million gallons of sewage a day. Mr. Sutton denounced the sewage treatment plan as one of "the indignities that make people feel they are not equal."[25] You see, in this explosive year, the indignities of disagreement and discontent had become a way of life. At the same time, music, theater, poetry, and other cultural expressions gave that life aesthetic form and a sense of idealism that found its way into the experiment.

Prelude to the Insurgency

The anger that finally built into a collective expression of defiance among Columbia's students was catalyzed by three particular sticks of dynamite: the university's plans for the Morningside Park gymnasium, the draft for the Vietnam War, and the university's membership in the IDA. You might be correct in thinking that the gymnasium provided the most potent spark because it was a tangible manifestation of the race/urban development/higher education collision, driven by Columbia's Society for Afro-American Students (SAS) and their black community partners.

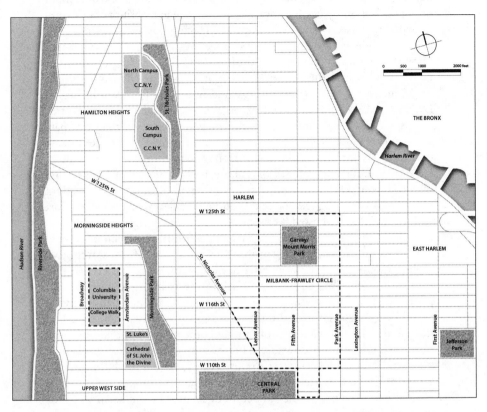

Figure 8. This map shows Columbia's location in Morningside Heights, which stretches from 110th and 125th Streets between the Hudson River and Morningside Park, and overlooks Harlem to the northeast and, further east, East Harlem and the Harlem River. It also shows the Milbank-Frawley Circle renewal area, which linked the black community of Harlem with the Puerto Rican community of East Harlem. Students undertook community-service learning projects in Morningside Heights, Harlem, and East Harlem.

Founded in 1964, SAS had attracted few members as most black students participated independently in extracurricular activities on campus
or in political activities off campus. However, the gymnasium controversy
provided the SAS with a catalyzing issue. Having learned about the controversy while attending community meetings in Harlem, SAS teamed
up with community members and New York's leading black activists to
take a stand against the park. The wick of this stick of dynamite was lit
on Monday, February 19, when excavation for the foundations began.
By Wednesday, construction activity—"chain saws chewing through tree
trunks, jack hammers uprooting park benches and parts of the stone par-
apet, and the bulldozer gouging out hunks of earth"[26]—attracted demonstrators trying to halt the desecration. Among them was the wife of
George R. Collins, a professor of art history at the School of Architecture
who had been collecting signatures in Harlem to block the construction.
Mrs. Collins complained about the outrage of destroying a work of art
by Frederick Law Olmsted,[27] but she left before the police arrested twelve
demonstrators. A week later, when 150 demonstrators again attempted
to halt the desecration, thirteen more arrests resulted.[28] In March, two
hundred demonstrators stormed a daylong Columbia conference that
featured Sargent Shriver, the nation's antipoverty chief, denouncing the
gymnasium and the Vietnam War.[29] The wick of the gymnasium dynamite burned especially bright after the assassination of Dr. King when
fear increased that militant groups might come up the hill one night and
"burn the whole place down."[30] Then twenty of the twenty-seven voting members of the Faculty of Architecture "passed a resolution urging
the president and trustees of Columbia to reconsider the controversial
plan,"[31] coming almost a month before one issued by the Faculty of Columbia College.[32]

The wick of the second stick was lit around the same time on February 16 when the Johnson administration abolished draft deferments for
most male graduate students and even men in vital occupations like engineering. A month later, a twenty-member student committee called a
daylong moratorium on classes that resulted in 75 percent of the day sessions being canceled as more than 3,500 students and one hundred faculty
members refused to attend classes. Jon Kotch, a twenty-year-old senior
who headed the committee, explained that instead of going to classes,
students could meet in assembly halls and attend cultural programs or
hear talks on how to avoid the draft. "We are opposed to the war," Kotch
explained, "and we are opposed to the draft that takes men for the war.
We are here to determine the alternatives—jail, expatriation, or what-

ever steps there are." The moratorium was broad based with students and faculty representing Columbia and Barnard Colleges, and the Schools of Architecture, Law, International Affairs, and General Studies. Though the cultural programs were undersubscribed, the antiwar/draft-resistance sessions were jammed, with several attracting standees ten deep at the sides and rear of auditoriums.[33]

During the moratorium, heavy leafleting of the campus with antiwar literature helped burn the wick on this stick of dynamite, but the third one had an immediacy that heightened the conflagration. This stick involved the future of six students and cut to the heart of their deep sense of disempowerment; its wick was lit on March 26 when 150 students participated in a raucous demonstration in Low Memorial Library demanding Columbia's withdrawal from the IDA. The demonstration violated a 1967 presidential ban on indoor demonstrations and resulted in the university administration singling out six of the protesters—all leaders in the local chapter of Students for a Democratic Society (SDS)—and placing them on disciplinary probation. Known as the IDA Six, their amnesty became a central demand of the insurgency.[34]

Now that you understand the full potency of passion and protest that was about to erupt on Columbia's campus, you can proceed to the event that will get you inside the School of Architecture—to receive the experiment.

The Insurgency

The insurgency exploded with shattering force when SAS president Cicero Wilson and SDS chairman Mark Rudd jointly endorsed a campus rally that became a point of no return. Scheduled for noon on April 23, the rally took place at the heart of the campus—a sundial located at the intersection of Campus Walk, the east–west axis that connects the university externally to the city, and the north–south axis between Butler and Low Memorial Libraries that connects the university internally. After Wilson and Rudd both made speeches, a crowd of about three hundred demonstrators tried to deliver a list of demands to the president's office in Low Memorial Library. Not surprisingly, the building was locked, and demonstrators' way was blocked by about two hundred counterdemonstrators.[35]

Undeterred, the demonstrators proceeded to the gym construction site. An architecture student, Alan Feigenberg, explained his anger at seeing the desecration that was in progress:

A few hundred of us made this great trek of four blocks over to Morningside Park, and here we saw this abomination, right in the middle of a public park, two acres cut off by this cyclone fence and guarded by three cops. . . . The people who are laying the foundations for this gymnasium have just gouged out one of the most beautiful parts of the park; the surface features, the trees, and the rocks which made up the cliff, are already gone after only about two months of excavation. Well, it looked so disgusting that everyone was angry, and about five guys started to attack the fence.[36]

In a burst of unrestrained physicality, men and a few women ripped apart the cyclone fence with their bare hands, their numbers and fierceness apparently scaring off the three policemen. Though many people had been arrested in prior demonstrations simply for refusing to leave the site, this willful destruction of property resulted in just one arrest.

The Occupation

Emboldened by their success at the gym site, the SAS/SDS leaders marched the insurgents back to Hamilton Hall on campus, home to Columbia College's administrative offices. There they took the affable Dean Henry Simmons Coleman hostage, drew up a list of six demands, and began recruiting others to "join the hundreds of students, faculty, news media, rock bands. Plus . . . a captive Dean Coleman."[37] Their demands were that disciplinary action be lifted against the IDA Six and anyone involved in the demonstration, that the Harlem gym construction be stopped, that the charges against anyone protesting at the gym site be dropped, that all relations with the IDA be severed, that the president's prohibition on indoor demonstrations be dropped, and that all judicial decisions be made in open hearings with due process. The insurgents declared that they would not leave until these demands were met.

Despite concurrence with the demands, the SAS and the SDS soon went their separate ways, their parting provoked by black power leader H. Rap Brown, who arrived late that night. Accompanied by about twenty-five Harlem residents, Brown informed the white protestors "that the Harlem community is now here and we want to thank you for taking the first steps in this struggle. . . . [Now] the black community is taking over."[38]

With that speech setting the tone, the eighty-six black students in Hamilton Hall (55 percent of whom were working class) evicted the white students (70 percent of whom were upper middle class) early

Wednesday morning. The evicted white students immediately seized Low Memorial Library. Then that evening, when Dean Smith announced that Avery Hall "would close early . . . because of the unusual events on campus," the architecture students refused to leave,[39] making Avery the third occupied building. On Thursday, graduate social science students took over Fayerweather Hall, home of the History and Sociology Departments. Finally, on Friday, a radical contingent of occupiers from Low Memorial Library and Fayerweather Hall took over Mathematics Hall, home of the Mathematics Department. Thus, over a period of four days, the insurgents gained control of five university buildings.

The Players

The players gave the insurgency its defiant but well-organized nature. You have already met SAS and SDS, and you briefly met an essential SAS ally, which gave it power no other player had—the black community. The role Harlem residents and black power activists played made the insurgency "no longer simply a student building takeover, but a *black* student and community protest."[40] As a black philosophy major explained, SAS "is in liaison with the community and not with white leftist radicals. . . . This is why, although the demonstration against the gym was organized by SDS, we threw them out."[41] Still, black community partners provided a shield for all the protesters and changed the course of the insurgency. More than likely, university administrators delayed calling in the police for a week because they feared that taking action against the black students would bring the militants up the hill to "burn the whole place down."[42]

You should meet the representatives of the striking students in the five buildings, the Strike Coordinating Committee (SCC). This group, dominated by the SDS, "facilitated communication between the buildings, the faculty, the administration, and the press,"[43] using their Ivy League skills to structure a well-oiled operation. And of course, you should meet those who opposed the insurgency, the Majority Coalition, which consisted primarily of undergraduate students, including many athletes—"the jocks," as the insurgents called them—and some faculty. They held counter demonstrations, recruited others to their cause, and formed a human barricade to prevent sympathizers from delivering food and supplies to the insurgents.[44]

You should also meet the Ad Hoc Faculty Group (AHFG), which served as a third-force mediator among university administrators, the insurgents, and the Majority Coalition. AHFG "labored and cajoled over resolutions, harangued and persuaded students, argued bitterly with lagging colleagues, made human shields of themselves between warring student factions and between the students and the police, donated pocket money for food, stood midnight-to-dawn watches at the university's gates, and pleaded with both sides to keep the talk going and the violence down."[45]

Finally, you should meet the superstar of the insurgency—the media. In particular, the *New York Times* praised Columbia's student-run radio station, WKCR, for doing "a remarkably alert and responsible job."[46] Fifty to sixty students worked in shifts to cover the disturbance, posting correspondents in the occupied buildings for live coverage. Early Friday morning, the university administration ordered WKCR to suspend its operations but immediately backed down—a wise decision since reporters were not only behaving with restraint, they were also actively trying to de-escalate the conflict, advising students to stay in their dormitories, noting that final examinations were approaching, and providing telephone numbers for faculty members to call if they wanted to volunteer for security assignments.[47] In addition to WKCR, the student-run newspaper, the *Columbia Daily Spectator*, provided in-depth coverage between April 24 and May 8. So noteworthy were these publications that they were eventually compiled and reproduced as a set.[48]

The five to six hundred insurgents occupying captured buildings and as many supporters on the outside displayed a combination of Ivy League excellence and passionate commitment to democratic ideals. Despite the university's curtailment of services and the insurgents' exhaustion, the buildings were kept remarkably clean and well organized. Each building had a steering committee, which held mass meetings (where policy positions were reached by consensus) and communicated meeting decisions to SCC via walkie-talkies, telephones, and runners. With the help of AHFG, supporters on the outside circumvented the Majority Coalition to toss food and medical supplies above the massive plinths and into the monumental windows of the occupied classical-style buildings.[49] These insurgents demonstrated the very capacities they wanted to be allowed to use as students—ones students at the School of Architecture would bring to bear in cooking up the experiment.

The Players in Avery Hall

Since this story is about the School of Architecture, you should have a special introduction to Avery Hall's insurgents. In a student body numbering about 275, thirty or so students—primarily architecture students but also at least two planning students—occupied Avery Hall, along with varying numbers of students from other parts of the campus.[50] They made up less than 11 percent of the student population (notably only about 6 percent of the student population participated university-wide). Yet they acted defiantly, emboldened by the resistance to authority that was occurring around them, thus opening the floodgates of transformation at the School of Architecture. Avery's insurgents dared to confront the debilitating discord that existed not only between the university and the surrounding community but also within the school itself—a discord Colbert had unsuccessfully attempted to unmask five years earlier but which had continued to fester.

Infamous for being isolated from university life and the larger society, this small group of architecture and planning students—which incidentally did not include any of the school's few black students (though perhaps they were in Hamilton Hall)—was drawn into disrupting Columbia's campus in solidarity with SAS that, along with Harlem residents, led the most forceful protest against the gymnasium. As two architecture students, Tony Schuman and Rolf Busch, explained, the project touched the core of their ethics as aspiring professionals:

> That gym bothered me almost more than the war. It was something I could see and touch, a visible gouging of one side of the park and the whole project violated almost every architectural principle which my friends and I said we believed in, and which the few good teachers we had, like Prangnell, had taught us.[51]

> I didn't care about Dean Smith telling us to leave, and I didn't care about SDS, which I knew very little about, and I didn't care about IDA, which I knew nothing about, but I cared about the gym. I had spent a large part of this year studying the whole project, and I knew a great deal about it, so much that I felt a responsibility to help the demonstration succeed. It was partly an architectural problem and, as an architect, I knew the gym was wrong.[52]

Beyond their professional concerns about the gymnasium, Avery's insurgents held greatly varied worldviews from more conservative to more revolutionary, but they eventually united behind the six SAS/SDS demands. According to Alan Feigenberg, "After a few days I felt that everyone who was still in the building had proved their commitment, and I was also much more aware of how people could agree on supporting the six demands while disagreeing greatly both on what the demands meant and on the tactics to win them."[53]

This agreement grew out of hours of intense debate about the issues that were percolating across campus, with top-down governance uppermost on their list of grievances. You see, some of Avery's insurgents objected to the School of Architecture's marginalization by and from the larger university; the university's lack of consultation with faculty, students, and the community; and the trustees' management of the university as a private corporation rather than as a public-spirited institution. These insurgents focused internally upon the university administration. Some objected to the university's expansionist and racist policies, their anger provoked not just by the gymnasium but also by the displacement of thousands of black and Puerto Rican tenants "to make a nice, clean, residential community for the nice, white, middle-class faculty."[54] These insurgents focused externally upon the school's lack of engagement with its poor neighbors and their housing needs, and relatedly to the dearth of black and Puerto Rican students in the school.

Others were dissatisfied with the nature of professional practice, having been radicalized by Peter Prangnell, a studio instructor who had promoted a revolutionary spirit before he left Columbia to accept a better-paying position at the University of Toronto. According to architecture student Ken Greenberg, "Even in the short time he taught here, Prangnell served as the catalyst for almost every student who was open to new ideas and was willing to be shaken up. . . . We owed a lot to Peter. He made us aware that architects were doing hollow, shabby things, and he convinced us, perhaps more than he wanted to, of the present irrelevance of our profession. . . . We'd been politicized as architects, and we felt like declaring, stating openly . . . that we didn't like what our professional colleagues were building."[55]

These insurgents were frustrated by their profession's focus upon corporate practice, having themselves decided "to ignore the money and the status of the big professional firms and to choose instead some form of advocacy architecture."[56] Still others were radicalized by the unwillingness of a conservative tenured faculty to mediate with them. Thus, while some of their concerns reflected those of the larger insurgent group, others were specific to the School of Architecture's poor status within the university and to the school's and their profession's irrelevance in society. Initially, Avery's insurgents wanted to add three demands to those put forth by SAS/SDS, including that it should recruit more black and Puerto

Rican students, but SDS leaders convinced them that adding demands would only "confuse the demonstrators and perhaps weaken solidarity."[57]

During the occupation, Avery's insurgents began conceiving an alternative education. With the guidance of faculty who dropped in on the occupation, they delved into the school's significant internal problems, including lack of student engagement and diversity, poor teaching, and an outmoded curriculum that lacked social relevance.[58] They also focused externally, scrutinizing the university's expansion policies and developing alternative proposals for the gymnasium site and for Morningside Park. With this understanding of internal and external challenges, Avery's insurgents began to conceive a new educational structure that would merge "the need for curriculum reform with the concern for social issues."[59]

The Bust

As you can well imagine, the New York City Police Department—a force combining uniformed officers with plainclothes men dressed up like students—was more than ready to put down the insurgency. The force had no doubt undergone mob training to prepare for the dreaded racial Armageddon, and they had also gained hands-on experience during countless antiwar/draft-resistance and housing/urban renewal demonstrations. On Friday, in order to prevent any more building seizures, this well-prepared force "moved masses of men onto the campus of Columbia University and occupied every open building that had not been taken over by student demonstrators."[60] Following a strategy worked out with university administrators, they sealed off the campus to everyone except students, faculty, and reporters, establishing barricaded checkpoints at either end of College Walk so teams of policemen, university security, and faculty could check identification.[61]

With the black community thus sealed out, policemen moved off campus to set up a communications vehicle with a giant antenna and parked vans and cars to accommodate mass arrests. In a small garage on 114th Street, "about twenty policemen stood by to guard the construction site for the gymnasium, a key cause of the demonstration."[62] Most important, they established a heavily guarded command post in the basement of Low Memorial Library under the student-occupied administrative offices. You see, Columbia's garrison enclave for scholars was militarized (see Figure 9).

On Sunday, AHFG offered its "Bitter Pill Resolutions": students

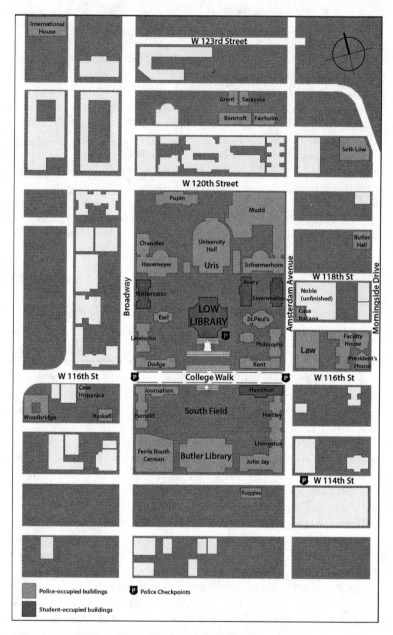

Figure 9. This map shows the militarization of Columbia's campus by the New York City Police Department with a large, well-prepared force occupying every building, except for the five that student insurgents had taken over. Additionally, it shows barricades at either end of Campus Walk that sealed off the area from outsiders and two command posts, one on 114th Street to guard the park and another in the basement of Low Memorial Library under the student-occupied administrative offices.

would vacate the buildings and in exchange Columbia would withdraw from IDA, abandon the gym construction, and impose uniform disciplinary procedures to be determined collectively by students, faculty, and administrators. University administrators and insurgents both flatly rejected the bitter pill.[63] With AHFG mediations at a standstill, the New York City Police Department, including hundreds of plainclothes men, swung into action. At 2:00 a.m. on April 30, the eighth day after the first occupation, the force entered buildings, sometimes through underground tunnels, sometimes through the main doors. You are correct in guessing that the policemen went first to Hamilton Hall where, some say, an advance warning had been sent. There they arrested all eighty-six insurgents, who chose to leave peacefully. The white students were not so lucky; those occupying the four other buildings—and especially those who were demonstrating outside—were viciously beaten.[64] Reportedly, "students were pummeled, dragged along concrete steps, kicked, punched, and struck with police saps."[65] The worst abuses came from the plainclothes men who were not wearing identification (and might have included some of the jocks). The most significant violence occurred on Low Plaza when the policemen charged spectators, creating a stampede of bloodied bodies. Within two terrifying hours, the force had cleared all five buildings, secured the campus, and made 712 arrests, including 111 women.[66] Almost two hundred students, faculty, reporters, and policemen were injured, while "countless more had been traumatized by the violence."[67]

The Bust at Avery Hall

You need to know more about what went on in Avery Hall so you will understand the frame of mind students brought to the experiment. You see, whatever beliefs led the Avery insurgents to occupy the building, whether more conservative or more revolutionary, the bust radicalized them—as it did the faculty who knew the police were on the way and had come to support them.[68] Several architecture students described the trauma they experienced:

> I saw a couple of cops break through the line in front of me. Kouzmanoff was kind of to my left and I was way over to the right side and I saw him bend over and double up, and then I saw that the cops were smashing through the faculty line. The faculty were

holding their arms wrapped around each other, but the cops broke through like they were going through butter. Then I saw Lifchez doubled over holding his side after some cop hit him on the back (and I found out later that three ribs were broken).[69]

I saw [some cop] was wearing his badge upside down and that he had black tape over the number, so I asked him "why are you hiding your badge?" And then he hit me. Then he pushed me toward the stairs, and I saw more people being beaten. I felt at this moment the same way I felt the time I was raped, when there was a gun at my head, when two men were threatening to kill me if I didn't cooperate. The bust felt like that.[70]

We saw these people we've been living with, and it was like seeing your brother—I felt they were like my brothers and my sisters— and it was so unbelievable.[71]

I served in Vietnam and Korea, but somehow this looked worse— you know, like the movie where the Nazis mowed down the unarmed civilians. There were about one thousand kids standing on the south field, since the north part of the campus had been mostly cleared by this time. About two hundred cops were standing on College Walk facing the kids, and there was this great confrontation of massed ranks. Then the cops suddenly charged, swinging their clubs like nothing mattered—people, nothing. And then I just closed my eyes, and I felt very sick, not physically but emotionally.[72]

If they wanted to take our power from us, meaning the buildings, then the more people in the buildings the better, and the bloodier the scene the better . . . It wasn't all failure. There was a certain success and degree of radicalization, with lots of people becoming aware, for the first time in their lives, of certain power realities in this country.[73]

Though both showed press passes, policemen repeatedly struck a *New York Times* reporter on the head using handcuffs as brass knuckles, finally throwing him down Avery's curving marble staircase, while another policeman punched a *Life* photographer in the eye and smashed one of his

Figure 10. This photo shows injured students, faculty, and reporters receiving medical attention after police broke through a faculty line and brutally cleared Avery in the early-morning hours of April 30, 1968. Their injuries included many scalp wounds and an assortment of concussions, broken ribs, broken noses, broken teeth, and groin injuries. (Photo by David Finck, courtesy of the Protest and Activism Series XIV, Columbia University Archives.)

cameras.[74] You can just imagine how life changing this early morning bust was for the insurgents (see Figure 10). With screams still echoing through the high-ceiling Beaux-Arts building and blood not yet cleaned off its curving marble staircase, you are at last inside Avery Hall, ready to receive the experiment in all its passionate potency.

4
1968–1971 Experimentation

Now that you understand the intensity of this era's struggle for social transformation, you are ready to enter Avery Hall. You will approach an elegantly proportioned 1912 Italian Renaissance building from the west, proceeding dead center to a two-story-high portico supported by the familiar Ionic columns. If it is windy, you will need two hands to pull open the massive twelve-foot-high oak doors, which are framed by another set of never-closed decorative iron gates. Before walking through these doors, take a moment to absorb the transformative context that surrounds you. Violence interspersed with a freewheeling counterculture have not only jolted the nation and the city, they have jolted Columbia University and the School of Architecture. Given that the fault lines of these quakes run straight through the nation's urban ghettos, they have particularly jolted the city-making professions of architecture and planning. Most significantly, the quakes are about to open up unimagined opportunities in the crust of racism for the ethnic minority recruits who will soon walk through these massive oak doors.

A Context of Insurgency

For the most part, the key players in the arc of insurgency—the ethnic minority recruits—arrived on Columbia's campus after the bust, but they were even more jolted by the era's quakes than were their Avery peers-to-be. Though cohort members had not experienced the trauma of the bust, they recalled experiencing the civil rights struggle, primarily in New York City but also in other parts of the country, including in the South. Thus they shared with the Avery insurgents a commitment to change a racist society and the Eurocentric education offered at Columbia. But the two groups differed on an important dimension: while the insurgents had, for the most part, acquired their political awareness and skills as a result of the occupation, most of cohort members had honed theirs out of necessity over a lifetime. As John Little put it, "I would say I was socially conscious from the standpoint of—I didn't have a choice. I mean, being African American and the civil rights movement." Many cohort members attributed their political and community engagement to being inspired by activist parents or teachers, as was true for Kirk Bowles. He cited his family's involvement in the nation's early civil rights activism beginning in the early 1930s and continuing into 1940s and early 1950s:[1]

> I come from a family that was always very socially conscious. My father's grandfather, who helped raise him, was one of the main lieutenants in the Marcus Garvey organization back in the thirties or forties. There was always a sense of social consciousness and awareness in my home. My parents . . . were an amazing couple in that, for people who didn't grow up in New York or a big town, they were very socially aware of local and world events.
>
> Kirk Bowles

Other cohort members attributed their engagement to other young people's activism. For example, Laura Marie Swain was captivated by the students who tried to integrate Central High School in Little Rock, Arkansas, in September 1957 because they were her same grade level:

> I was kind of hearing all those things in the background when I was going to high school and these other kids were trying to integrate their high schools in the South. I recall my intrigue with news stories of the Little Rock Nine who were exactly my grade level—high school juniors they were when they attempted to integrate Central High School in Little Rock, Arkansas, with crowds of white people jeering at them.
>
> Laura Marie Swain

First-person encounters with civil rights leaders, often due to family relationships, also exposed cohort members to the struggle, as occurred with James Hamlin, who grew up in a deeply segregated Kansas City. He recalled that his father, a civil rights attorney and the first black person elected to the Kansas State Legislature, had connections to movement leaders, including "Thurgood Marshall, [who] stayed at our house once in Kansas City." Similarly, Mark Hamilton, who grew up in the heart of the civil rights movement, recalled that "Dr. Martin Luther King, Jr., was a friend of my family, and because of how I grew up in Atlanta I knew him personally." Bruce Fenderson did not have family connections but rather sought out civil rights leaders and, like Laura Marie Swain, was also influenced by other young people. He remembered:

> I had come in contact with the young people of my generation that started the sit-ins and they really affected me very much. Because they were making history . . . I had the opportunity to meet Malcolm X and a number of different people, Stokely Carmichael . . . I also pretty much was influenced by James Baldwin, who actually came to stay with me in California for a month.

Bruce Fenderson

You see, the members of the oral history cohort had honed their social consciousness and political savvy by growing up at the epicenter of the quakes that pierced the crust of racism. In time, they joined with the insurgents and a larger group of activist students and faculty to steer the School of Architecture toward America's promise of democracy.

Insurgency on Columbia's Campus

The New York City Police Department cleared out the occupied buildings but, as you might imagine, that action did little to quell the insurgency. Quite the opposite, the display of brute force ignited a counterforce of incredible creativity. Following the bust, an expanded Strike Coordinating Committee (SCC), now consisting of seventy-six elected representatives of about one-third of the student body, called for the ouster of the top administrators and for a total boycott of classes—which the Ad Hoc Faculty Group (AHFG), reconstituted as the Independent Faculty Group, supported.[2] SAS marched from 125th Street with its Harlem partners, also demanding the administration's ouster but focusing upon cessation of the gym construction.[3] Providing his community constituents with feedback about their effectiveness in the campus-wide demonstration, Cicero Wilson declared that "the political pressure, the presence of State Senator Basil Paterson and Assemblyman Charles Rangel, for example, and the presence of the black community outside the campus gates, kept the cops off all the students."[4]

SCC's boycott brought Columbia to a standstill for the remainder of the school year, setting into motion a "liberated" campus that involved thousands of students. As you stand in front of Avery's doors, just imagine the seamless blend of rebellion and release that surrounds you: an enormous strike banner still hanging high above Avery's doors, students blocking its entrance, some holding neatly lettered signs, an array of teach-ins filling the campus lawns due to the SCC's stipulation of no indoor classes (see Figure 11), a performance by the Grateful Dead echoing off the classical-style buildings, a counter commencement that ends with a frolic on the gymnasium site, a white student at a Harlem rally being greeted with the hand gesture that indicates victory, a tenant group teaming up with SDS members to seize a Columbia apartment building. Then Wilson explains at a Harlem rally that Columbia has "a new thing," which will allow him to seek increased admissions, financial aid, and campus space for black students; a black studies program; and an increase in black

Figure 11. This photo shows an outdoor class during the he SCC boycott when one professor and his teaching assistant set up a blackboard to teach students seated on the grass. (Photo courtesy of the Office of Public Affairs Photograph Collection, Columbia University Archives.)

faculty.[5] Despite the air of liberation, the insurgents soon clashed with the police again as university administrators held steadfast to their policies.

Insurgency in the Columbia/Harlem Relationship

Being an immigrant Jew with a night school education, Abrams was just the man to take on Columbia's elitist administrators. His family had been among the more than one million Jews entering the United States via New York Harbor during the first decade of the twentieth century.[6] Not unlike blacks who experienced racial hostility even in New York City, immigrant Jews were considered an "ignorant and brutalized peasantry [who might diminish the] quality of American citizenship."[7] Not unlike blacks who lived in the housing others had abandoned, Jews occupied the most decrepit and overcrowded housing in ethnic ghettos.[8] Abrams's first-person perspective on race, poverty, and inequity undoubtedly helped him identify with Harlem residents in ways that even the most liberal white Anglo–Saxon faculty at Columbia may not have. Surely, it must have helped him make the acquaintance of Bayard Rustin, Harlem's openly gay civil rights activist who believed that Jewish and black communities faced similar discrimination. Abrams would draw upon their relationship in taking on university administrators.

During the strike, Abrams had been a one-man peacemaker, attempting to broker a deal between the insurgents and the university, even though he did not support their building takeover. After the bust, he again confronted university administrators, using his legal skills to argue leniency for the insurgents. As they had in the past, administrators simply ignored Avery's peacemaker.[9] Having struck out twice, Abrams decided to go for broke: he would negotiate a deal between the university and Harlem. On May 8, he contacted Rustin and proposed a list of eleven things the university could do for Harlem, using the work of the Urban Action and Experimentation Program (UAEP) as a template for community engagement.

Abrams's list called upon Columbia to survey its departments "to determine how best to bring the university's talents and resources to bear on Harlem's needs,"[10] suggesting collaborative community-based studios and laboratory courses. It stipulated that the university should provide housing, job and language training, and education that would qualify Harlem's "drop-outs . . . for entry into Columbia." It specified that the university should get the city's business community to invest in Harlem, stipulating that both Columbia and the business community should deposit money in Harlem banks. It specified a joint university/community advisory group to determine the use of the Ford monies. It called for a modification to the gym plan to have "a common entrance and the allocation of special days" for shared university/community use of the facility. And, unsurprisingly, it called for the creation of a separate School of Urban Affairs not only to teach planning and conduct planning research, but also to serve "the Harlem community through actual projects."[11]

By the next day, Avery's peacemaker was busy trying to arrange a meeting between Rustin and university administrators, who sent him on a wild goose chase to someone who had no authority to arrange such a meeting. The persistent Abrams followed up with a letter explaining the importance of meeting "to identify the possible areas of cooperation between the community and the university so that the long-standing underlying misunderstandings can be settled."[12] Though arranging the meeting took over two months—and though by then Abrams had requested a leave of absence from Columbia to accept a professorship at Harvard—the meeting did occur at the end of July. Abrams was not at the meeting, but his fingerprints were definitely in evidence. Just imagine this meeting. It took place not in the administration's majestic Low Library offices, but rather in a three-story walk-up at 217 West 125th Street—in the heart of Harlem. A. Phillip Randolph had an office there above a store. Just imagine two white men getting out of a taxi and heading into the building around noon, with lots of black people no doubt milling about on this bustling street. Just imagine the transformation in Columbia's community relations that was surely in the making.

Once inside, the two administrators were greeted by Randolph and Rustin, who had more ambitious ideas for what Columbia could do for Harlem than those on Abrams's list. Early on, Rustin launched into the oddity of having white leaders come into Harlem to negotiate with black leaders, saying that Columbia needed "to have a black spokesman speaking with authority from a high position in the administration." In other words, Rustin's list included the appointment of a black trustee at Columbia.[13] After declaring that Dr. Kirk should "lend his name and prestige" to getting a health center built in Harlem, Rustin rattled off a list of complaints about Columbia being a slumlord, having millions invested in South Africa, and not admitting blacks to its medical school. He then urged that "Columbia make some dramatic moves to convince the Harlem community that it is acting in good faith," like renting some of its faculty apartments to Harlem residents. When university administrators produced a report outlining the many things Columbia had already done for Harlem, Rustin retorted that the report needed to be shorter and clearer "so that it would be read by more of the general public."[14] Rustin ended the meeting by reading Abrams's list. With no commitments being made, the two administrators made their way back down the stairs, hopefully finding a taxi to ferry them back to Columbia's campus.

Soon after the meeting, university administrators obliged Abrams with a confidential copy of the notes summarizing their encounter on West 125th Street, and Abrams continued badgering them to adopt the ever-growing list of things Columbia could do for Harlem. Now imagine the scene that unfolded in August: Dr. Kirk finally resigned and Acting President Andrew W. Cordier took over. Cordier convinced the trustees to abandon the gym site and then began revising Columbia's colonial-era governance policies to be more inclusive of the university community. In time, he established a university senate and a tripartite disciplinary committee as envisioned by the AHFG and Abrams headed off for Harvard, having hit a home run. Now you need to back up and find out what the rest of the School of Architecture faculty were doing while its peacemaker was brokering the Harlem deal.

Insurgency in the School of Architecture

The School of Architecture faculty were not so inclined as Avery's revolutionaries to reject their colleagues' "Bitter Pill Resolutions." Instead, they met off campus on April 28, at the offices of the Institute of Urban Environment and voted (eleven in favor, nine opposed, no abstentions) to accept the resolutions, though they would align with the insurgents in insisting upon amnesty for all striking students.[15] On Sunday following the bust, the faculty met again, this time at the request of the provost who expected that classes would resume the next day. However, students and staff had already preempted this possibility by adopting the SCC boycott and blocking Avery's entrance (see Figure 12): faculty would only enter Avery Hall to hold classes when—in the opinion of the students and staff—"normal conditions will have been restored." At that meeting, the faculty also voted to support the boycott, empowering the dean to appoint a committee of faculty, staff, and students to get the school up and running.[16] You see, with those acts of defiance of university authority, the School of Architecture would soon be governed democratically.

Designing an Experimental Operation

If you keep in mind the teach-ins and political and cultural activities taking place outside on Columbia's trampled lawns, you will have a

Figure 12. This photo shows SOA students blocking Avery's entrance and recruiting passersby to join the SCC boycott in the days following the bust. (Photo courtesy of the Office of Public Affairs Photograph Collection, Columbia University Archives.)

sense of the no-holds-barred planning that went on inside Avery Hall. During the first two and a half weeks of the university-wide boycott, students and staff worked frantically to write a resolution articulating a post-insurgency agenda for the school, which Dean Smith agreed to present on their behalf at a faculty meeting scheduled for May 17. A few of the authors attended the meeting, observing as faculty discussed their resolution. After the usual tedium of wordsmithery, the faculty adopted the resolution (with nineteen in favor, one opposed, no abstentions). The document became known as the "May 17th Resolution," and it specified interim rules that allowed everyone to have a say in the school's "experimental operation."[17] Reflecting the spirit of liberation that was no doubt wafting into Avery's large, classical-style windows (see Figure 13), the student/staff scribes concocted interim rules that refashioned the school's hierarchical governance structure as a democratic one, thereby violating a breathtaking number of university statutes.

For example in absolute contradiction to the required unilateral faculty governance, the interim rules ordained shared student, staff, and faculty governance. They established three divisional councils charged with determining each division's curriculum, staffing, and operating procedures;

Figure 13. This photo suggests that the sound of teach-ins and political and cultural activities wafting into Avery's large, classical-style windows may have inspired the audacity SOA faculty members demonstrated in adopting the "May 17th Resolution." (Photo courtesy of the Office of Public Affairs Photograph Collection, Columbia University Archives.)

they created an executive council charged with determining school-wide issues;[18] they replaced the Committee on Instruction (typical throughout the university) and limited the dean's absolute authority over staffing decisions; and—most blasphemous of all—they established a Committee on the Budget that would develop a budget in consultation with the councils.[19]

University administrators (and some faculty) repeatedly pointed to the outrageous conflicts between the interim rules and university statutes, noting that they decentralized authority and weakened faculty governance.[20] Critics declared that the rules would assure "continual and everlasting mediocrity,"[21] and that no competent dean would ever accept the role they outlined. Objecting in particular to the excessive powers given the chairmen and the unequal representation of the Division of Planning due to inclusion of the Institute of Urban Environment, Dean Smith vowed his staunch opposition "to serve at the beck and call of so many" or "to chair any meeting at which the powers of the deanship were thus eviscerated."[22]

But a majority of the faculty and the chairmen stood their ground, declaring they would be destroyed and would resign en masse if the "May 17th Resolution" was not honored. After much debate and many amendments, the faculty adopted the interim rules almost a year later on April 25, 1969 (twelve in favor, six opposed, no abstentions),[23] placing school governance at the center of an intense power struggle between factions of the faculty and university administrators that lasted for two more years until the school's experimental operation came to a close.

Jump-Starting the Experiment

After the faculty adopted the "May 17th Resolution," a spirit of experimentation, like everything during that time period, literally caught on fire. An unstoppable intensity was let loose when "a series of meetings of the entire School of Architecture—all divisions, all faculties, and all students—began to take place in a very dramatic if not revolutionary atmosphere. Between all the yelling, emotional outbursts, attempts to co-opt the entire movement, and the usual ego trips, several motions did get passed. Passed by all those present voting."[24] An all-school meeting began directly after the faculty meeting, with a remarkable one-third of the school community attending. Immediately following, a third meeting occurred in the Division of Planning, convened to establish its divisional council. Five days later, the Division of Architecture convened and then reconvened two days after that to establish its divisional council. In other words, in the week immediately following the faculty's adoption of the "May 17th Resolution," a significant portion of the school community met in a dramatic spirit of liberation to hammer out the experimental operation of the school. Planning would continue throughout the summer until classes commenced in the fall.

Deepening the Experiment

University administrators planned that the spring of insurgency would end on June 4 with commencement ceremonies. To avoid associations with the militarized campus, they would be held in the safety of the Cathedral of St. John the Divine a few blocks away, where a professor would give the commencement speech instead of the much-maligned university president. But some of the graduates disrupted the plan. Sporting their light blue academic gowns, they silently walked out and strolled up Amsterdam Avenue where a crowd had been awaiting them (see Figure 14).

Figure 14. This photo shows a crowd of students, faculty, and parents on Amsterdam Avenue awaiting a procession of graduates who will leave planned commencement ceremonies a few blocks south at the Cathedral of St. John the Divine to attend counter-commencement ceremonies in Low Plaza. (Photo courtesy of the Office of Public Affairs Photograph Collection, Columbia University Archives.)

The processional arrived in Low Plaza, exorcising April's violence with a joyous counter-commencement ceremony in which the former president of Sarah Lawrence College lightheartedly conferred upon graduates the "B.A. degree: Beautification of the Arts." Then about five hundred students, faculty, and parents headed off for a romp in Morningside Park.[25]

Just one week later, council members in the Architecture Division hunkered down to take charge of their education. Declaring that "the twelve men who had been elected to this highly responsible post [had] indeed taken upon themselves an impossible task,"[26] they laid out their definitive vision of architecture education: it would be open-ended, offer choices, and connect students outward to the university and beyond. Two position papers unequivocally specified a student-centered, problem-based, interdisciplinary approach to learning and—reflecting a stereotypic view of ethnic minority qualification—urged "that *capable* Negros and Puerto Ricans be sought after as possible members of the design staff"[27] (emphasis added). In short, the members of the Architecture Division Council did, bottom-up, what no dean had been able to do top-down: they finally banished the Beaux-Arts hold on the architecture curriculum.

In July, the Planning Division Council began meeting off campus in the apartment building where the Institute of Urban Environment had its offices. Their revolutionary spirit may have been dampened by tenants more interested in cooling off from the sweltering heat at open fire hydrants than in protesting Columbia's expansion. Or it may have been dampened by their dynamic leader Abrams's announcement that he would abandon them and head off to greener pastures at Harvard. You can only guess council members' frame of mind as they settled into a humongous task: unraveling the dynamic state of their rapidly expanding profession with its proliferation of information and increasingly demanding students. What you can judge is their tenaciousness in deciding what planning was, how it should be taught and evaluated, and how the division should govern itself. As in architecture, these council members took on what Abrams had been unable to resolve, namely, how the planning division fit into a school and university in which it had no statutory existence. Expansive though it was, the council's charge involved planning expertise—and the group valiantly rose to the occasion.

The Executive Council did not form until later in July, when most New Yorkers with any sense begin to evacuate the city before summer's dog days make life unbearable. Meeting weekly, these troupers worked into the night hammering out nine resolutions and then holding a school-wide referendum at the beginning of the year so the entire school community could ratify them. Some of their resolutions were specific to Avery Hall, others presaged larger professional education dilemmas apropos to demonstrating competency and achieving cultural diversity. Those resolutions specific to Avery related to suspending disciplinary proceedings against the insurgents, converting the Division of Planning into a department, providing students with 24/7 access to the building, and codifying governance procedures. Those that presaged professional education dilemmas related to adopting pass-fail grades accompanied by qualitative faculty evaluations, discontinuing attendance requirements, permitting alternate means of demonstrating proficiency, and recruiting ethnic minority students—a bold resolution that made this extraordinary story possible.

The Executive Council proposed that three ethnic minority students be admitted and funded each year, that a percentage of scholarship money be set aside for them, that some openings be reserved for "dropout" students who were committed to receiving remedial education, and that a high school outreach program be expanded. It also proposed what the university should do to increase ethnic minority enrollment, including adjusting "its admissions procedures in the undergraduate schools to accommodate ethnic minority students requiring remedial programs."[28] Though seemingly progressive, the resolution reflected what proved to be an unfounded stereotype of ethnic minority students as low achievers who would need remediation. Despite this flaw, you get a sense of the thoughtfulness with which these well-educated Ivy League students and their faculty supporters proceeded from the raw passion of insurgency to a plan for taking charge of their education. If what had gone before had been about disagreement and discontent, the summer of 1968 at Avery Hall (and in the Institute for Environment) was about dogged determination—and part of that determination was to bring more ethnic minority students into the school.

Restructuring the Curriculum

The summer's intense spirit of experimentation resulted in a completely transformed curriculum at the School of Architecture in terms of content as well as instructional methods. For sure, its framework had been set in place long before the liberation, beginning with Dean Colbert's interdisciplinary real-life learning initiatives. The framework was further advanced by divisional chairmen who undertook a more open-ended, community-centered curriculum during the preceding year.[29] That is when Abrams launched UAEP and began securing funding to undertake community work,[30] but the chutzpah of the student-led councils upped the level of ingenuity and commitment to revolutionary change.

    Though the transformed curriculum involved lectures, seminars, and studios, you will primarily explore the studios because it was through this part of the curriculum that students engaged with the surrounding community, which is the primary focus of this story. The councils adopted two overlapping approaches to studio instruction: the Architecture Division adopted *student-centered learning* (for-credit hypothetical and community service studios offered in Avery Hall), while the Planning Division adopted *community-service learning* (for-credit studios offered in Avery Hall as well as paid internships offered in "storefront studios" in Harlem/East Harlem community). A diagram (see Figure 15) can perhaps clarify this rather complicated curriculum, but the most important thing for you to keep in mind is not the details but rather the sense of a constantly evolving, opportunistic approach to education that was enormously labor-intensive.

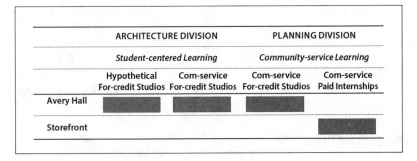

Figure 15. This diagram of the transformed curriculum shows that the Architecture Division adopted for-credit studios in Avery Hall (which featured student-centered learning), while the Planning Division offered both for-credit studios in Avery Hall and paid internships in "storefront studios" in Harlem/East Harlem (which featured community-service learning).

STUDENT-CENTERED LEARNING

The dream of democratic governance that propelled bloodied insurgents and striking students and staff onward was the freedom to shape their own education. The twelve revolutionaries who took on the impossible task of restructuring the Division of Architecture turned this dream into what became known as the *platform system*. According to Laura Marie Swain, "It was this whole new way of doing studio. It was called the platform system. Students from any year could be together and decide on the projects they wanted to do."

The revolutionaries envisioned platforms as voluntary associations of students engaged in research or action projects of their own choosing, with a diverse cadre of faculty, staff, and visiting experts providing guidance.[31] Platforms would emphasize student initiative, be open to all grade levels, and last for as long as a particular project required. Because students would chose which platforms to join and because advisers would help them chart individualized learning plans, the revolutionaries believed that student motivation, student-faculty dialogue, and project diversity and relevance would improve.[32] They further resolved that "there shall be no future tenure"[33] for faculty in this open-ended, student-centered approach to learning.

In practice, some platforms dealt with typical professional concerns such as adaptive reuse and housing, but the system also provided an "avenue through which faculty and students could offer their services to the community."[34] For example, C. Richard Hatch, founding director of the Architects Renewal Committee in Harlem (ARCH), offered a community-service platform in the fall of 1968 that engaged students with the organization's advocacy against university expansion, while Bond sponsored various community-service platforms for both ARCH and the Real Great Society (RGS/Uptown).[35] As ingenious as it was, the platform system posed huge challenges both for students (who needed to possess an array of sophisticated skills) and for faculty (who needed to invent anew the syllabus for each platform). Most problematic, platforms developed widely divergent skills, defying architecture education's requirement that all students demonstrate equivalent skills.[36] Accordingly over time, the system became successively more constrained. Participation was eventually limited to upper-level students, and community-service platforms were eventually limited to one semester, two at the most, with increased requirements for integrating community and academic work.[37]

Despite these challenges, remnants of this revolutionary approach to student-centered learning survive in architecture education even today, albeit in a more constrained form.

COMMUNITY-SERVICE LEARNING
Whereas the bust triggered the Architecture Division's experimental student-centered learning, a full year earlier, in July 1967, the Division of Planning's conference to calm rioting among East Harlem youth triggered its experimental community-service learning. Whereas twelve revolutionaries on the Architecture Division Council conceived the platform system, the concept for community-service learning evolved from post-conference conversations among Smith, Abrams, Bell, and two young turks who were on the teaching staff, Albert Mayer, a member of Planners for Equal Opportunity, and doctoral student Robert L. Kolodny (*Columbia* 1973). In synthesizing the conversations, Mayer wrote that a new studio could "make a significant contribution to East Harlem and possibly to the national urban crisis by . . . including in a major way working with the East Harlem youth group and other local people."[38]

That is, whereas the Architecture Division's platform system responded to students' need for a more flexible, democratic education, the Planning Division's community-service learning responded to advocate planners' need to "help local people accomplish faster and more effectively what they would like to do."[39] Whereas student-centered learning engaged all students in acquiring the skills to plan and design an array of environments,[40] community-service learning, instead, primarily engaged justice-oriented students in acquiring the skills to help Harlem/

East Harlem residents redress such place-based inequities as substandard housing, schools, and recreational facilities "on their own terms."[41] Finally, whereas student-centered learning did not typically require external funding, community-service learning did because students were providing tangible professional services to community clients. Philanthropic support combined with student credit hours allowed those services to be provided gratis to communities that could not otherwise afford them. As Bruce Fenderson explained, "Poor communities ought to have access to planning and design expertise . . . under kind of the model that poor people have in legal proceedings and . . . they should have access to resources to develop their own plans and designs." Avery's revolutionaries established such a model—one that is widely practiced in schools of architecture and planning today.

Restructuring the University

During that first heady year, members of the Executive Council grappled with reconceiving Avery's operations. However, their tour de force was an audacious proposal for restructuring the university's relationship to the Harlem community, which they directed to the president of the university. You may find their behavior a bit over the top, but perhaps they recognized the gravity of the Columbia/Harlem conflict. Perhaps they recognized that Columbia was but one example of an institution at war with its surrounding community, others being Yale University, the University of Pennsylvania, the University of Pittsburgh, the University of Chicago, the University of Southern California, Trinity University, and even Howard University, just to name a few.[42] Perhaps they recognized that the urban crisis was fueled, in part, by these institutions' callous expansion activities. Perhaps they recognized the growing pressure upon urban universities to collaborate with the oppositional forces germinating in university-dominated communities. At any rate, under the leadership of Caroline Moore, a second-year planning student,[43] council members penned an elaborate proposal for restructuring university-community relations.

Moore's cover letter for the proposal proclaimed, in unwavering prose, that the Executive Council was the central policy-making body of the School of Architecture, equally representing the school's students and faculty. The proposal itself laid out a much riskier restructuring scheme than either Abrams or Bayard had imagined.[44] For starters, it recommended that all university departments be assessed for their relevance to society, relationship with other departments, and projected spatial needs. To carry out this assessment, it recommended hiring an academic planner from outside the university, to be selected by a student/faculty/community search committee. Until the assessment was complete, the proposal stipulated a moratorium on all construction, on and off campus, and especially on the removal of tenants from university-owned properties. When expansion did proceed, it called for a public review of alternative plans.[45]

The proposal then specified a collaborative university/community structure. In what seemed an unrelenting critique of the alienating modus operandi of Urban Center director Franklin H. Williams, it recommended that the university hire a top-ranking community relations officer, to be identified by another student/faculty/community search committee. Unlike Williams, an appropriate candidate would have "considerable credibility in the eyes of the community and students," be accessible to the community, and be able "to influence university policy and action in response to community sentiment."[46] The proposal then stipulated how the university's chief planner, the distinguished I. M. Pei, would work. In addition to interfacing with another of those student/faculty/community advisory committees and other stakeholders, the proposal specified that Mr. Pei "operate from a field office on Broadway [so] he can establish legitimate contact with all segments of the Morningside community."[47]

The proposal went on to outline an institutional framework for implementing community improvements, unequivocally recommending that the university get out of the real estate business. Instead, it directed the university to underwrite a joint enterprise of local institutions and residents (with majority control by residents) to undertake community redevelopment. It calculated that, through the sale of institution-backed bonds, the enterprise could finance market-rate and subsidized housing for students, faculty, and community residents. And it specified that this resident-controlled entity go beyond housing construction to encourage individual home ownership, prevent land speculation, advance new materials and methods, and undertake job training.

The council proposal did not for a moment consider improving upon the gym plan, as Abrams and Bayard had, but rather fundamentally rejected the facility's presence in the park. Accusing the university of biding its time to renew construction activities, the proposal insisted that the university adopt ARCH's master plan, which included an "educational park," to be used by school children and their families. Finally, to realize a vision of university/community collaboration, it pledged the School of

Architecture's leadership in helping students obtain course credit for assisting in community redevelopment work. It also recommended that the Urban Center fund a student- and resident-operated information center to disseminate information and evaluate community improvement proposals so as to "accelerate community awareness . . . and participation in a total planning process."[48]

In short, the Executive Council's proposal recommended assessing the social relevance of the university's academic agenda, insinuating that the process would call into question the need for expansion. Further, it specified that all aspects of academic planning be carried out with student and community input, and it recommended that Columbia underwrite a resident-controlled nonprofit housing corporation. Most audaciously, it put the tiny School of Architecture into a leadership role in university/community relations. As far-fetched as the proposal was—as disconnected as it was from the realities of Columbia's power structure—it was extremely well informed and well argued. The proposal exhibited superior knowledge of participatory planning principles, community redevelopment processes, and university/community conflict resolution strategies. Some of its recommendations did seep into the school's experimental curriculum, and some Urban Center funding did come to pass. Most remarkably, the proposal offered a forward-looking and provocative vision of community engagement that many urban universities are pursuing today.

With the experimental operation in place, you are now ready to accompany the ethnic minority recruits as they walk through Avery Hall's massive oak doors.

Ethnic Minority Recruitment

With the urban crisis running at full tilt, the late 1960s were an incredible time to be an ethnic minority student in the city-making professions of architecture and planning, especially in New York City and at Columbia University.[49] In architecture, a fierce speech by the civil rights leader Whitney M. Young, Jr., at AIA's 1968 national convention blasted the organization's lack of social responsibility, inspiring immediate action. Following the convention, AIA secured a $500,000 matching grant from the Ford Foundation and initiated a national minority/disadvantaged scholarship program.[50] In New York City, local contributions augmented these funds to create ARCH's Architecture in the Neighborhoods program, which offered preprofessional and professional education to the city's aspiring ethnic minority architects.

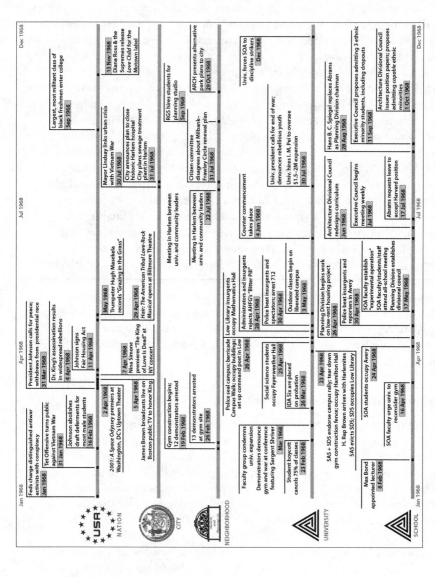

Figure 16. This timeline schematizes the tumultuous events of 1968, which led to what was arguably the nation's boldest recruitment effort in the city-making professions. (For a larger version of this image, download the file at http://fordhampress.com/media/mconnect_upload files/s/u/sutton_art_1.zip).

In planning, model cities and urban renewal projects created a demand for ethnic minority planners, heightening awareness of the need to prepare socially responsible city-making professionals who could "improve the complex condition of people of African descent."[51] Advocacy proponents were well aware that a realistic effort to plan with ghetto communities would require increasing the minuscule number of ethnic minority planners. Under Abrams's leadership, most faculty bought into the notion that ethnic minority students would enrich the Division of Planning through their superior understanding of ghetto conditions, which would optimize "an educational opportunity for *all* our students and faculty."[52]

Supporting this commitment to training ethnic minority students for the city-making professions was an infusion of both private and public monies. In addition to support from the Ford Foundation and the professional organizations, the Carnegie Mellon Charitable Trusts, the Rockefeller Brothers Fund, the Vincent Astor Foundation, the U.S. Office of Equal Opportunity, and the U.S. Department of Housing and Urban Development targeted fellowships, scholarships, and work-study support to ethnic minority students in architecture and planning. Locally, Dr. Kenneth Bancroft Clark's Metropolitan Applied Research Center, which advocated for the urban poor, provided a source of tuition support, and Columbia's architect trustee Vincent George Kling (*Columbia* 1940) also provided support, though objecting to the intermingling of social and political issues with architecture.[53]

Recruitment to the Experiment

If you have been paying attention, you might have realized that the fervor and funding for educating city-making professionals would hardly be sufficient to pry open Avery's Italian Renaissance doors and permit so many ethnic minority recruits to enter. Getting inside would require a sea change in attitudes about the capabilities of a group that had, up until this time, been a rarity at the School of Architecture. James A. Jackson, a high-achieving pre-med student who entered the school back in 1962, told a story that reveals just how big a change would be required:

> When I applied to Columbia and I went for my interview with Dean Smith, he said to me—he was a big, Texas sorta cowboy type—he said, "Oh, I think we had a colored guy here once before and he did pretty well, so I think you probably would do okay."

So that shows you where the school was in 1961 or 1962. Because there was one before. In any case, [Smith] turned out to be okay.

James A. Jackson

Despite those who demonized Smith as both racist and sexist, likely due to the occasional disparaging remarks he made to ethnic minority and women students, Bruce Fenderson agreed with Jackson's assessment:

The man who was the dean of the school, who was a very nice man—was always nice to me . . . [—gave me] money to go on a trip to recruit students from the South . . . plus Howard, Tuskegee Institute, Jackson University, and maybe one or two others to re-cruit African American students.

Bruce Fenderson

Nor were these the only reports of Dean Smith's support for the recruitment effort. On campus, he became "one of the first deans to recognize the need for more minority recruiting when Franklin Williams approached him on the subject."[54] And according to cohort members Philip Bertoli-Pearson and Carlos Méndez, Dean Smith supported recruitment travel by Harry J. Quintana (*Columbia* 1971), who became director of RGS/Uptown, to universities on the East Coast and in Puerto Rico.

The Recruitment Snowball

You will find the story of the School of Architecture's recruitment drama, as relayed by cohort members, to be one of pure Ivy League bravado—a little smoke and mirrors and a lot of deep-pocketed tenaciousness. Unfailingly, members described being recruited to Columbia as a memorable moment. Together they painted a picture of an all-out search for ethnic minority students that began right after the insurgency with just a handful of headhunters and snowballed as rumors spread about the school's quest for ethnic minority students, which in turn attracted more ethnic minority students who themselves became headhunters. Three black students were enrolled in the school at the time of the insurgency, one of whom originated this snowball process with a little help from white students who put their lettering skills and the school's blueprint copying machine to good use. As Bruce Fenderson explained:

I designed the initial effort to get black students to the school. . . . Two of my colleagues . . . actually made a poster that said—that looked like an official publication of the university—that said, "Columbia University needs African American and Puerto Rican architecture students." They made this poster and put it up everywhere, as if it were an official publication of the university, but it was actually done by the students.

Bruce Fenderson

Then, while the Executive Council was debating its resolution on recruiting "dropout" ethnic minority students, two of the black students teamed up with Max Bond and created their own enterprise. With funding from the dean, they made recruiting trips to ten cities and established a summer training program for disadvantaged youth.[55] The following spring, armed with a letter authored on behalf of the school's admissions committee, they fanned out to six historically black colleges and universities in search of black students who would be at or above the achievement level of the school's existing Caucasian population. As the national headhunting proceeded, the quest ensued locally in the city's other schools where faculty began encouraging their ethnic minority students to apply to Columbia. As these recruits were admitted to the school, they, too, became talent scouts, searching their network of friends for potential applicants. For example, John Little described how he was attending Pratt Institute when a Columbia recruit approached him about applying to the school:

When I was in undergraduate school, [a close friend] asked me, "Didn't you want to be an architect?" . . . And I said, "Yeah, I did," and he said, "Listen, I want you to actually consider applying to Columbia." So I did. And he was actually a student in the school. His name was Richard Thomas.

John Little

However, the school's recruitment theatrics did not rely solely upon grassroots initiative. At the same time cohort members recalled how the quest for ethnic minority applicants spread via the grapevine, they also described administrators' active engagement in conducting interviews, helping with applications, and convincing people to apply, sometimes over an extended period of time. What is truly remarkable is the degree to which administrators—and faculty—were able to shift gears and wholeheartedly join the thrust toward educational equity. For example, Philip Bertoli-Pearson explained how "Harry [Quintana] recruited us and then I got interviewed at that time by the chair at that time, which was Romaldo Giurgola . . . a very nice man, and he looked at my portfolio, blah, blah, blah, and I got in." Carlos Méndez described a comparable experience as did Laura Marie Swain, who said she was referred by one of Giurgola's employees:

> I was actually housesitting for one of my interior design professors in Croton-on-the-Hudson when I got a call from someone at Columbia, I don't remember who, asking whether I would come for an interview. And the way they got my name was that another one of my professors at Parsons, Lou Goodman, an architect, worked for the chair of the department, Romaldo Giurgola.
>
> Laura Marie Swain

Like Bertoli-Pearson and Méndez, Swain described showing her portfolio to Giurgola during a very congenial interview and deciding, on the spot, that she wanted to transfer into the school. However, some recruits took more convincing. For example, Derrick Burrows said that, over the course of the summer in 1968, Abrams had "chatted" with him and "interested me in Columbia and in studying city planning." During the following year, while he was completing his undergraduate architecture studies at Howard University, Burrows applied to Columbia and another school that was his first choice. Then he recalled receiving "a number of calls from Columbia University, and that kind of enticed me. And after some thought and weighing fellowship and scholarship opportunities, I decided to attend Columbia." Similarly James Hamlin needed a period of persuading before he decided to resign his full-time academic position in the Midwest and move to New York City. He recalled:

> I was teaching at the University of Kansas. I went to a teacher's conference in San Francisco and . . . that's where I met Garrison McNeil and a couple of other people, like Frances Piven, from Columbia. So they recruited me to come to Columbia. They kind of worked on me for a year and a half. So I did, finally.
>
> James Hamlin

However, as might be expected, not all the cohort members provided glowing reports about the recruitment effort. Derrick Burrows, for instance, complained that "many of the whites at Columbia weren't very friendly or enthusiastic about these minority students and minority teachers who were there." And a remarkable number of ethnic minority candidates were not recruited but applied on their own, Sylvia K. Atkinson being one who did just that. Atkinson described being stuck in an architect's office "designing toilets for three months," saying she had applied to Columbia in search of credentials that would fast-track her career out of the toilet department:

> I applied, and I was accepted, and then I wrote back and said, "Can I have money?" And they said, "Yes." Well, now, but little did I know that there had been an insurrection. I didn't know. I was like, you know, in the South. I didn't really hear a lot about what was happening in New York at the time. So I didn't know that someone selected me because I was black, you know, that I got a chance to go—I really didn't.
>
> Sylvia K. Atkinson

Atkinson did not say when she realized that she was part of a recruitment effort, but lacking financial aid she undoubtedly would not have been able to realize her "chance to go." These and other stories related by the oral history cohort not only illustrate the wide net cast by the School of Architecture in its search for ethnic minority applicants, but they also illustrate the sense of drama—the almost breathless excitement—surrounding the one-by-one tracking down and enrolling of nonwhite students in the school. A jewel among these breathless descriptions is Calvin Page's detailed account of his initial visit to Avery Hall, which occurred in 1970 after a significant group of ethnic minority students, faculty, and staff were present:

> When Jim Doman took me up there, like I said, Stan Britt was already there . . . as was Sharon and all those. But Stan was the so-called head of the black students' group there, which was something to say because there were enough black students to actually have a little group there at the time. And Jim Doman introduced me to him, because at the time you almost had to be screened by the black student group. And so Stan and I hit it off very quickly. But he introduced me to all of the other principals there, that one day.
>
> And I mean, this was like unannounced. There was no appointments or anything, I just went up there with Jim Doman, and he was sort of my . . . godfather in that sense of my mentor, leading me around and introduced me to Ken Smith—I'll never forget that Ken Smith was the dean of the school—introduced me to

Romaldo Giurgola who was the director of the architecture program, introduced me to Hiram Jackson who was sort of the black on the faculty administration related to the recruiting of blacks, introduced me to Max Bond who was the most prominent of all the black faculty. And when I say "introduce" I mean we had sit-downs from anywhere between fifteen minutes with some, to up to an hour with others. The most impressive of the interviews was with Romaldo Giurgola, who really was gonna make the decision as to who got in and who didn't . . .

I told him that I had . . . worked at 101 Park Avenue, so he was impressed with that. Of course I had worked with Jim Doman; he was impressed with that. And then I mentioned that, you know, I had seen some works of architecture around the world. And you know, he asked me where, and I knew that he was an Italian, and I told him, well, you know, I had been to the Coliseum, I had been to St. Peter's, I had been here and there and also mentioned I had been to the Pyramids. . . . And I remember him saying, "Well, we look forward to you coming." So in that sense, what he was saying was, you know, "You're admitted, as of now."

Calvin Page

Graciously welcomed by a snowballing talent search, members of the oral history cohort were motivated to succeed by their significant presence within a mostly white middle- and upper-middle-class student body. As you will see, their route was enabled by the resources of an Ivy League university, the support of the school and community, and the extraordinary collegiality of their peers.

5
1969–1971 Transgression

You are about to ascend the steepest part of the School of Architecture's arc of insurgency. The revolutionaries who were dragged out of Avery Hall in the wee hours of that bloody Tuesday morning got you part way up the arc when their screams exorcised the ghosts of the school's poor leadership and Beaux-Arts curriculum. The students, staff, and faculty who adopted the Strike Coordinating Committee boycott of classes propelled you a little further along, taking you to a steeper part of the climb when they set in place an experimental operation at the school. They used the brilliance of interim rules to conceive the school's "transformational role, including that of securing equality and social justice" in the surrounding community.[1] Then they restructured the curriculum to underpin that transformational role. Now you are going to ascend even higher, beyond experimentation, to the steepest, most slippery part of the arc where the safety of higher education and the Ivy League has vanished—the part where an unparalleled crop of ethnic minority recruits will walk through Avery Hall's oak doors, ascend its curving marble stairs, and occupy its glorious studios.

Your guides along this part of the journey will be the school's most fearless revolutionaries—the planning students and the ethnic minority recruits. Some of your most animated guides will be the more militant recruits. They will insist—demand—that you peer over the edge of the arc onto a new world where school learning advances change in poor communities and where blacks are in charge of that change. You see, these recruits have been invigorated by the Black Student Movement, which began in 1965 but surged forward during that explosive year of 1968. They know that the rash of protests that had besieged campuses nationwide multiplied after Dr. Martin Luther King's assassination. They know that, in the fall of 1968, "the largest and most radical incoming class of black students in history walked into the academy."[2] They know that many of those students had taken over offices, halls, and even entire campuses, sneaking into buildings in the early morning hours, forcing out workers (sometimes with bare fists, sometimes with weapons), barricading doors, and refusing to "leave until their demands were met."[3]

Your most animated guides know that insurgents' demands—often framed as nonnegotiable—were for recruiting black students and faculty; for establishing scholarships and black studies programs, diversity offices and race committees; and for ending white supremacy. They know that the Black Student Movement soared to record levels on February 13, 1969, when black students and their allies "disrupted higher education in almost every area of the nation." Your most animated guides know about this movement because they have been part of it. For example, remember that August André Baker and William Manning both participated in take-overs at majority private schools and that Craig Shelton participated in a push to hire a black faculty member at the City College of New York. Remember that Sylvia K. Atkinson was also part of such efforts. She attended a historically black university where students "rebelled to protest administrative fetters" and elected a homecoming queen "with a gleaming Afro."[4] Recalling how she sought to disrupt her Eurocentric, bourgeoisie education, Atkinson said:

> You know, I came from Howard where . . . I was part of a demonstration that took over the administration. It was kind of a "black is beautiful," "the revolution will not be televised." It was like, "Black Panthers where are you?"
>
> Sylvia K. Atkinson

Your black power guides know what happened at Cornell University on April 19, 1969, when Cornell's Afro-American Society (AAS) seized Willard Straight Hall after someone burned a cross on the lawn of a university residence hall housing black women. They know about the Pulitzer Prize–winning photo of AAS insurgents exiting Willard Straight Hall to walk across campus to their headquarters—an image now seared into their hearts and minds. Your black power guides know that "one by one . . . black students, brandishing their rifles, shotguns, knives, clubs, spears, and expressions of seriousness, victory, fear, and wonder, trotted out of the dark Gothic structure into a sea of bright cameras that latched onto their seventeen rifles and shotguns like leeches."[5]

They know that not only were these armed insurgents not punished, their demands were fully met. They know that university administrators nationwide have scrambled to meet the nonnegotiable demands of yet another unparalleled crop of black freshmen who arrived in the fall of 1969—the very year Avery's experiment was getting fully underway with its own significant crop of black students in attendance. They know that black student insurgents, while often suffering tremendous repression and opposition, were changing the course of higher education,[6] and they are giddy with the idea of being part of that change. They know that by participating in change, they will be shedding centuries of presumed black inferiority. And they know for sure that they will come away invigorated by a new sense of self—a black self who has an unalienable right to be militant and make demands.[7]

So your black power guides will explain their impatience with Eurocentric brainwashing and express their fierce desire for a *relevant* education that will equip them with the skills to enable "ghetto dwellers to achieve black power and to transform their neighborhoods."[8] They will demand that you peer over the edge of the arc and absorb "the revolutionary idea that black people are able to do things themselves."[9] Frankly, you may get confused at this point in the journey. You see, your fearless guides have accomplished an amazing feat; they have dissolved the thick Italian Renaissance walls that by tradition enclosed Avery Hall with its large windows, Ionic portico, and heavy oak doors. Like Cornell's black riflemen, they have fearlessly transgressed institutional norms, and in the process they have blurred all the dichotomous relationships that sustain higher education's elitism. Boundaries dissolved, what is outside in the community has come inside into the school, and vice versa; what is teaching has become learning, which has become working to serve others; what is research has become the practice of community engagement.

To make your journey worthwhile, your guides will introduce you to the huge group of ethnic minority recruits who will successfully graduate, thanks to the "adoption of a broader spectrum of evaluations in admissions and initiation of new programs,"[10] along with robust financial support. Like the hundreds of onlookers who watched the spectacle of Cornell's black riflemen parade across campus, you may feel intoxicated, shocked, and even angry that so much tradition has turned upside down, but not to worry; you will not be at this heady height for long.

Ethnic Minority Recruits in the Ivory Tower

Ivy League institutions tend to have "more resources, better facilities, more generous financial aid, and more faculty members who have strong reputations in their fields. In addition, students are surrounded by class-mates of exceptional ability, who set high standards of intellectual excel-lence and offer challenging examples to emulate."[11]

Surrounded by cream-of-the-crop faculty, students, and alumni, lower-income ethnic minority students are offered a glimpse into the world of privilege, which can heighten their motivation to succeed.[12] After gradua-tion, these institutions pave the way to employment opportunities, higher salaries, prestige, and power. For ethnic minority graduates, an Ivy League degree may be essential in helping them "overcome any negative stereo-types that may still be held by some employers, and create opportunities not otherwise available."[13] For the recruits, the architecture of Columbia's campus, which is modeled after the ancient Athenian agora, offered a tan-gible symbol—a daily reminder—of the privileges they would inherit. Each day, the ritual of entering College Walk through the iconic iron gates that armed New York City policemen had once barricaded reaf-firmed their status. Now they freely entered an expansive plaza, ascend-ing a broad flight of stairs past the majestic Low Library, invincible in its Roman classical style, ascending once more to the east toward Avery Hall (see Figure 17).[14] As Laura Marie Swain recalled:

> The architecture [of the campus] was not lost on me. I was really uplifted by being on this campus . . . I would ride my bicycle onto campus, and I felt like I owned the whole world. I was part of this really powerful institution. It was quite an impressive and life-changing experience.
>
>   Laura Marie Swain

Walking through Avery Hall's oak doors during that brief moment of opportunity conferred upon the ethnic minority recruits untold re-sources—and they were quite prepared to receive them. Unlike the drop-out ethnic minority students that white faculty and students imagined recruiting, cohort members reported arriving at Columbia having al-ready risen above whatever disadvantages of social class they may have had. They claimed that they were not only prepared academically to en-ter the Ivy League, but that they had the leadership skills to contribute to advancing excellence in the school. For example, Vassar alumna August

Figure 17. This photo of Avery Hall suggests how its Italian Renaissance architecture, which is associated with the major achievements in art and architecture of a
revered civilization, can communicate a sense of privilege to its occupants. (Photo
courtesy of White Studio, Historical Photograph Collection, Columbia University
Archives.)

André Baker reported being well prepared for Columbia, though she had
a momentary lapse of self-esteem:

> I was accustomed to a pretty rigorous curriculum, and I started
> out wondering whether or not this curriculum here was going to
> overwhelm me or not. I'll always have that concern, you know?
> And I guess it's because growing up black, there's a fear that you
> may not measure up. Never mind the fact that I graduated from
> Western High School in Baltimore, which is the academic high
> school in Baltimore, and then Vassar College, which was a very
> strong academic institution.
>
> August André Baker

In contrast, Calvin Page reported that voracious reading habits allowed
him to overcome growing up in Brooklyn as a ward of the state and enter
Columbia well prepared. He recalled, "I was good at what I did and . . .

I loved it too. I loved history, you know, loved obviously architecture, design, drafting." On the other hand, John Little attributed his preparedness to the leadership skills he developed in his church as a choir director and as a member of various civic groups:

> I actually trained choirs from a very early age, but . . . I was also involved with things like Knights of Columbus and Kiwanis and other civic groups that were outside of the church . . . improving the civic organization in my neighborhood. And I was even the president of the Civic Association at one point.
>
> John Little

So, you see, as your ethnic minority guides approach the steepest, most slippery part of the arc, they are absolutely ready to receive the experiment and appropriate all the Ivy League privileges it had to offer.

Appropriating Ivy League Resources

Among the most treasured resources that Columbia bestowed upon the recruits were travel fellowships. In 1953, a gift from the estate of Elizabeth Steel Fellows set up the William Kinne Fellows Memorial Fund in honor of William Kinne Fellows (*Columbia* 1894). Typically referred to as the Kinne Award, the fund came to be used for a combination of summer scholarships and graduate fellowships, both supporting travel and study primarily in European countries and in Greece. Over time, the rules relaxed to allow Kinne Awards to support foreign students, domestic travel, and group travel. For example, James A. Jackson explained that in 1965 Alexander Kouzmanoff "found out that I had been chosen to go on this program called the Experiment of International Living, going to India. Once they found out that I had been chosen to go on this trip to India, they gave me money from that fellowship to cover the cost of my participation in the Experiment of International Living. . . . So even though I didn't qualify to go to Europe, they said 'Well, hey, we have this money here to put toward that trip.'"

The experimental operation brought about further elaborations in how the Kinne monies were used. In particular, Bond convinced the faculty to allow him to use the Kinne funds to take nine architecture and planning students to Ghana (see Figure 18) during an extended spring vacation in 1971. This not only entailed missing two weeks of normal course work, it also meant making those awards in advance of the other

Figure 18. This photo, taken in front of the Kwame Nkrumah University of Science and Technology (KNUST) Department of Architecture in Kumasi, shows some of the Kinne Award recipients during the Ghana trip. In addition to KNUST, the group toured the city of Accra, a slave castle, and various projects Max Bond had designed for the government, most notably the Bolgatanga Regional Library. *Left to right*: Lloyd deSuze, Ghanaian professor, School of Architecture student, David Kirkwood, Sharon Egretta Sutton, and Marva Britt. (Photo courtesy of Stanford R. Britt.)

twenty-two awards that would be given later that year. With this precedent established, many cohort members reported traveling independently in Africa to make connections, as Sylvia K. Atkinson put it, "between black folks here and in Africa." These study-abroad fellowships, according to William Tate, "just made the whole learning experience both in and outside of the classroom have a very significant impact on my life." Some cohort members even received two travel fellowships, as occurred with John LePoi, who went on the Ghana trip and then received a second fellowship after graduation:

> With three other of the students who had some fellowships as well, I went to East Africa and did a very extensive three-month tour of East Africa: three countries, Kenya and Tanzania, but I went on my own after to Uganda. So those were opportunities which I never

would have gotten in my life had it not been for the fellowship program at Columbia.

John LePoi

Another resource the ethnic minority recruits obtained once inside the oak doors was access to the Avery Architectural Library, not only during their time as students but throughout their entire lives. The Avery Collection is "one of the two largest architectural collections in the United States and perhaps the finest anywhere in the specialized field of architectural history . . . a unique and specialized asset of international significance."[15] As Craig Shelton put it, Avery Library was "one of the premier architecture and planning libraries in the world," and across campus Butler Library was "one of the largest collections of books of any university in the country." In addition to the university libraries, students had access to the New York Public Library's famous reference collection, including a large collection of photographs that could be copied or even borrowed.[16] Interestingly, several cohort members spoke of the Avery Library as a "discovery"—perhaps due to a general perception that the noncirculating collection was a hidden treasure—and Kevin Alexander Kersey was foremost among the treasure hunters:

> When I discovered the Avery Library I felt like I had discovered gold. I spent hours in the library. The library was one of the richest things there was . . . The school itself was a gold mine.

Kevin Alexander Kersey

However, arguably the most significant resource the ethnic minority recruits obtained once inside the oak doors was a coveted career path. Although you will learn later on about the difficulties they encountered upon exiting Avery's gold mine, walking in through its doors opened other unimagined doors, helping them overcome the discrimination they would inevitably face as second-generation trailblazers within their disciplines.

Appropriating Ivy League Faculty

Scholars concerned with making architecture more inclusive have documented the off-putting pedagogies that discourage women and ethnic minority students from pursuing the field, among them a directive teaching style, an aesthetic rather than social emphasis, a narrowness of content,[17] and—for ethnic minority students—a Eurocentric outlook that "channels students into becoming custodians of the status quo."[18] Though some cohort members described being discouraged by just such pedagogies, most conveyed fond memories of top-tier, demanding faculty who were also accessible and influenced them in profound ways. Particular favorites among the studio critics with uplifting teaching styles were Kouzmanoff, Giurgola, and Bond, as noted by William Tate:

> The highlight of being at Columbia was the design studio. The interface with professors like Kouzmanoff and Giurgola and Max Bond—it shaped me into the kind of architect I am today.
>
> William Tate

Cohort members also revered studio critics David Evan Glasser, Ada Karmi-Melamede, Richard A. Plunz, Charles J. Rieger, and Robert A. M. Stern. Others were drawn to Victor F. Christ-Janer, who replaced reviews with roundtables when, according to James Hamlin, "the students were able to express their opinion about the others' work." Beyond the studio, cohort members expressed fond memories for structures professors like David H. Geiger and Charles W. Thurston who, according to Calvin Page, "had everyone in a state of fear." John Little recalled:

> I really appreciated some of the technical teachers, like . . . David Geiger I appreciate. And even, I still remember Charles Thurston, in terms of mathematics, and I really appreciate what he did in terms of the thoroughness from math right back through calculus and the engineering mechanics. And there was another structural teacher, I just can't recall his name, but . . . I still use his conceptual approach to understanding the structure of a building.
>
> John Little

Henry Louis Poindexter recalled his first structures class with the legendary Mario Salvadori, a gifted lecturer whose class took place in one of Columbia's fabulous rotundas:

> The first structural class I went to . . . the teacher's name was Mario Salvadori . . . one of the most renowned structural experts in the world, and the particular—and it was a huge—it wasn't a classroom, it was like a big rotunda—and there were people from every school—medical—everybody was there—law. And the first—the most gratifying thing, he brought out the Tacoma Narrows Bridge

that was called "Galloping Gertie," the bridge that fell down, that swayed. And that was to me, that was—the model was there, he spoke, and it was so enjoyable. And it was gratifying because there were so many students there . . . and you could hear a pin drop.

Henry Louis Poindexter

Likewise, August André Baker remembered Chester A. Rapkin as a captivating lecturer in the Planning Division:

[My most memorable course] was the Economics of Income-Producing Properties. It was taught by Chester Rapkin, who's on the Planning Commission for the city of New York. And it stood out in my mind because he was a great storyteller. He had stories about the physical development processes in the city of New York, which just kept you glued to his face. I mean, you know, you just sat with your mouth open. I found that fascinating. He had his own perspective, as it turns out. But it was a good . . . I learned a lot about New York City. And I needed to learn a lot about it, because New York City frightened me.

August André Baker

The informal relationships cohort members enjoyed with faculty were extremely important. For example, Craig Shelton recalled the accessibility of the planning faculty, especially David Seader, the school's second black faculty member:

We had total access to the faculty. It was a team effort on the part of the faculty. [David Seader], who was coordinator of programs in the Urban Planning Division at the time, was . . . a really cool guy who could relate to us because he was just as radical, I guess, as we were. They had other young faculty in the Urban Planning Division, so it was a good experience interacting with them. And they were always very accessible. We were in and out of their offices all the time . . . I can recall . . . the closeness of the students and the interest the faculty took in the students . . . We would work on projects together, go on field trips together . . . It was just gratifying to be able to work with the faculty and go on these various trips together.

Craig Shelton

James Hamlin also recalled the motivational aspects of informal relationships not only with faculty but also with distinguished guests who visited the school. For example, here Hamlin described an opportunity to socialize with Robert Venturi, one of America's leading architects, following a lecture:

> Sometimes Christ-Janer would take the whole class out to dinner at a Chinese restaurant or something and we could kind of, on an informal basis, go over the different projects and things we were doing. I guess that was my assignment. With just everyday I just wanted to be in class and doing my projects and talking to . . . the other students in class—just a great desire to get into everything that was going on. I'd go to all the lectures that would come through and I guess having beer across the street at that beer hall place across on Broadway. Meeting some of the lecturers on an informal basis across the street over there was great, too, like Venturi.
>
> James Hamlin

Not all informal relationships were social, though; sometimes faculty did after-hours teaching, as William Tate relayed in a story about an unnamed professor who responded to a late-night telephone call for help:

> I remember we had one instructor, he literally gave us his home number and said, "Call me anytime," and we took him up on that. One evening I remember . . . we were all studying to prepare for a course, and we couldn't figure something out, and we called him at ten o'clock at night at home, and he stayed on the phone with us for maybe an hour, seemed like an hour, trying to help us see if we could work through it.
>
> William Tate

Though most study participants had fond memories of both formal and informal relationships with the faculty, they also remembered getting into heated exchanges with them, resisting lectures on the ancient Roman architect Vitruvius, challenging an expert in Caribbean anthropology who did not speak Spanish, challenging a famous architecture historian about the identity of a building he had never seen in person, and objecting to assignments that served the elite or critiques that suggested a naïve understanding of the needs of poor people. Cohort members like William Tate remembered that these challenges to authority "were very beneficial, really helped you to focus your argument for what it was you wanted to do . . . beyond the hyperbole."

Appropriating Ivy League Mentors and Staff

Though faculty members of color were scarce on campus, Columbia became a magnet for the city's emergent network of ethnic minority city-making mentors. For example, AIA estimated that, in the late sixties and early seventies, the nation had just six hundred black architects (likely an overly generous estimate), but its New York City chapter claimed thirty of those,[19] some of whom organized at AIA's 1967 annual convention in Detroit to found the National Organization of Minority Architects.[20] An association with Columbia not only benefited the recruits, it also burnished the reputation of individual mentors and the network as a whole. Columbia additionally attracted support from the local chapters of the professional associations as well as from state agencies and numerous community development organizations, which connected the recruits to a nascent and tight-knit community of ethnic minority professionals and also provided them with both formal and informal instructional resources.

Max Bond, considered "the dean" of African American architects, had gained superior credentials by leaving the United States, where racism limited his opportunities, to work in Ghana. This experience made him a respected mentor of the more junior ethnic minority teaching staff and of students throughout the school. Laura Marie Swain explained:

> Bond was a very beloved person and architect from a very distinguished family. I think his cousin was Julian Bond, and his dad was president of a university in Liberia. So he was from a very distinguished family. So to have this young man who had studied in France, was one of the most beloved faculty in the school—everybody loved Max, no matter what color they were. But he was our special mentor.

> Laura Marie Swain

In addition, the dean's office hired administrative staff to support the recruits, in particular Hiram E. Jackson III, who became the assistant dean for minority affairs. Abigail Abruña characterized the value of this position to the professional development of nonwhite students "in terms of creating some kind of post-academic and practical vision of what, you know, what those studies could lead to for the black and minority students." Cohort members also credited ethnic minority staff members Alverna Adams and Ghislaine Hermanuz with being "instrumental in sort

of pulling us together as a group." But the staff member most acknowledged as being committed to the success of the recruits was Loes Schiller, a social worker from the Netherlands who was employed early on
at St. Luke's, a Columbia-affiliated hospital that served its share of low-
income Harlem residents, doubly qualifying her to shepherd the recruits
through the school—"an 'angel of mercy' and a true human being," in
Kirk Bowles's view. John LePoi summarized her pivotal role:

> Schiller . . . was quite helpful because there were several things that
> we had to abide by in terms of rules, regulations, forms for every
> year or every two. And she was quite helpful and she reminded
> us of what we had to do, assisted us in how to do it if we had
> difficulty. And she got us through the financial side of things and
> the administrative side of the school—the requirements. So I think
> they had somebody in place to attend to that particular group. So
> while I would have to say that . . . they satisfied the pressures of
> affirmative action and bringing in a minority group, we were not
> left there alone to fail.
>
> John LePoi

Appropriating Ivy League Peers

Cohort members consistently described their peer relationships as highly
collegial both during classes and after hours. Many characterized their
classmates as collaborators and mentors—"just cut buddies," as Calvin
Page called them using black slang for "friends"—who helped one another, thereby contributing to one another's individual progress and to
the group's collective success. Lacking teaching assistants to help with
assignments—and in some cases lacking adequate instruction from the
faculty—cohort members reported that students who were strong in a
particular subject would assist others who were having difficulty. Jimmie
Lee Jacobs remembered:

> I would get pointers from other students . . . Some of them kind
> of kept to themselves, but if you asked them a question or they
> came over and looked at what you were working on in the design
> studio, you could get help. If you're taking structures, or some of
> the more formal lecture courses, you could . . . teach each other if
> you chose to.
>
> Jimmie Lee Jacobs

Quite a few cohort members also described late-night study groups, as did Kevin Alexander Kersey:

> There was a group of us, Sharon Sutton was one of them, who would spend the night at the school and we would critique each other's work. It was a mixed group, racially. And we would spend the night, have our sleeping bags at school. And we would interact quite a bit and help one another . . . My first term, Sharon stood up with me until four in the morning helping me work on my project and I never forgot that.
>
> Kevin Alexander Kersey

The open studio environment in which students worked on assignments, helped one another, and socialized 24/7 contributed to the school's supportive climate, as did its shared governance structure. As more recruits arrived, the Black and Puerto Rican Student-Faculty-Administrators Organization (BPRSFAO)[21] became a formal support mechanism, conducting orientation sessions for incoming recruits and hosting colloquia with ethnic minority speakers.[22]

Appropriating an Ivy League Education

Columbia prides itself on offering its students a distinctive learning environment, located within a great metropolis but also connected globally to many other cities and regions. Cohort members relished this environment; they recalled their exposure to other cultures and ways of working, pointing to the cultural and intellectual diversity that stemmed from a national and international student body. According to Jimmie Lee Jacobs, "It was kind of nice that the students were from all over the country and the world," and James Hamlin agreed that "it was just great to meet all the people and learn about their cultures and their approach to architecture." Carlos Méndez felt that having "people from very different nationalities and countries and foreigners" invigorated the planning program, noting that "there was about eight of us . . . in the group, and everybody was from a different country." Philip Bertoli-Pearson was especially delighted with the cultural mix:

> I met . . . all kinds of people coming from the Island [of Puerto Rico], coming from the U.S., coming from the community. I became part of a very, very unique team of people from different

backgrounds, mostly Puerto Rican, but there were black and Cuban, more Cubans.

Philip Bertoli-Pearson

Several cohort members relished the interracial relationships they were able to forge—a rarity at this point in history. For example, John LePoi noted that "the minority students mixed well with white students," and Jimmie Lee Jacobs bragged that he "had students across ethnic lines to be [his] support." For Mark Hamilton, born and raised in the segregated South, having relationships across racial and socioeconomic lines was a novel experience:

> We all developed a closeness . . . we became like family. We did a lot of studying together—my first encounter where we had a good bond and friendships with some of the white classmates, who later went back to their parents' firms, went to other places, and we all kinda stayed in touch.

Mark Hamilton

Other cohort members relished the opportunities they had within the School of Architecture to specialize in such areas as international development, prefabricated housing, and health facilities design. Abigail Abruña was particularly taken by a planning studio that dealt with the Dominican Republic:

> The particular time I was there in the studio—the planning studio—was of interest to me because it focused on development actually in the Dominican Republic. And so, it was an opportunity to actually look at how to intervene in development of a sort of more world situation.

Abigail Abruña

Transforming the Status Quo

The ethnic minority did not just passively consume the benefits of the ivory tower; they actively sought to transform the status quo. To do so, they did not join in the council structure of the School of Architecture but rather focused their attention within the BPRSFAO. As was true for black student organizations nationally, BPRSFAO was concerned, in particular, with issues that affected the school's everyday learning environment. Cohort members reported pushing for activist professors, encouraging community participation in design reviews, advocating for community-based planning, and nudging other students to be involved in community design work. Many recounted being involved in recruitment and convincing the administration to bring in more ethnic minority students, faculty, and staff; serving on the admissions committee and screening applications; and raising the awareness of the ethnic minority recruits who were in the school but, as Bruce Fenderson complained, did not have "any idea how they got there." Cohort members also assumed responsibility for developing new Afrocentric curricula and assigning recruits to internships.[23]

While the elected councils held meetings to generate policies for transformation, BPRSFAO took its ideas directly to the dean. Kirk Bowles recalled continually meeting with Dean Smith:

> The whole culture of Columbia had changed after the strike of 1968; that first year, things were in disarray. Students were trying to move forward and do what they had to do, while the administration was trying to keep the accreditation. The school wasn't quite sure how to manage the transition.
>
> Kirk Bowles

According to Bowles, the recruits were helpful in the transition because they "were used to having a different experience where real projects were produced," making them experts in the restructured curriculum's community-service studios. However, as was true with many white students, not all the ethnic minority recruits wanted to spend time trying to transform the school's elitist culture. Several cohort members, like William Manning, said that though they had been politically active during their undergraduate years, they felt it more appropriate to focus solely upon their professional studies at Columbia. In Craig Shelton's words, "My focus was on completing the urban planning program and getting the degree."

Ethnic Minority Recruits in the Studio

The base of Avery Hall is an impenetrable plinth that anchors the building firmly onto New York City's bedrock. The middle portion, where you enter the oak doors—which houses the library and administrative offices—is less solid with a soaring portico, oversized columns, and tall arching windows. The top portion, which is set back and has much larger windows that make it appear lighter still, houses the studios and class-rooms. The crown is an attic space underneath a sloping copper roof. The high-ceilinged north and south studios on the two top floors are magical, each filled with light from nine floor-to-ceiling windows that ring the building's perimeter. Though the structure has since been altered, when the ethnic minority recruits were in residence the sixth-floor studios were especially magical because part of the space reached up into the attic, a height of about thirty feet. Some athletic student invariably climbed up onto a ledge in the North Studio to adorn, in some amusing way, the bust of Julius Caesar that sat there.

Sheltered Inside in Avery's Studios

Every year during the first week of classes, a flurry of activity would turn Avery's vast studios into a warren of self-built cubicles. Students framed their gigantic oak drafting tables with whatever scraps of lumber, gypsum board, and other discarded materials they could scavenge to create personalized workspaces. In time, they added cardboard models, coffee cups, tools, books, and reams of tracing paper, lining the walls with photographs, maps, and drawings. Soon the studio became a veritable shantytown within an Italian Renaissance palace (see Figure 19). Here you are in the heart and soul of Avery's experiment, the studio "where students spend ceaseless hours crocheting incongruous facts into highly personal visions; an inner sanctum where devotees invent dreams to solve the problems of humankind; a Brigadoon where they draw, build models, ride skateboards, prepare late-night meals, sleep, discuss projects, work one-on-one with student and faculty mentors, and boast of all-night marathons."[24]

The studio is both a type of course and a physical space. In architecture programs, studio courses typically demand the most credit hours and occupy the most physical space,[25] and this was true at Columbia. In planning programs with a physical design focus, as Columbia's had, studios are also required, but they account for many fewer credit hours than in architecture. Over the years, studio pedagogy in both fields has remained a relatively constant reflection of the competitive, high-stakes methods employed at L'École des Beaux-Arts, an atelier-style architecture school established in nineteenth-century Paris. For example, student work is typically reviewed in public by a jury of other faculty, local practitioners,

Figure 19. This photo shows David Hughes reading in his commodious, personalized studio space atop Avery Hall, which he could utilize 24/7 to work on design assignments, study alone or with peers, socialize, and on occasion even sleep. (Photo courtesy of David Hughes.)

and, in elite schools like Columbia, famous practitioners who are flown in for the occasion, making them highly theoretical, insider debates. Studio juries do not normally include community members or professionals from other disciplines who might engage in a broader, more practical discussion of the work.[26] Numerous researchers who have studied studio culture have documented students' frustration with these outdated traditions, with women and students of color reporting the greatest discontent.[27]

The twelve men on the Architecture Division Council sought to disrupt these off-putting traditions through their concept of student-centered learning, which would feature teamwork, informal peer critiques, and formal reviews with many different players. In the Planning Division, the young turks' community-service learning concept completely banished the Beaux-Arts Eurocentric brainwashing by featuring technical assistance to community groups. Then, too, shared governance meant that students were helping determine policies related to grading and awards, and a growing body of ethnic minority recruits became a strong force for opening up the studios to Columbia's "new thing."

Despite the transformation of studio pedagogy, cohort members described the unremitting demands of their studio assignments, which took all their time, caused them to choose between studio work and other classes, and isolated them from campus life. Many described practically "living in the studio," especially those who resided nearby. Carlos Méndez said he "only left the studio to go to classes," Jimmie Lee Jacobs said school was "like an endurance race," and Sylvia K. Atkinson (who did not even have a studio course) said she "did architecture all day long and into the night." Nevertheless, such comments seemed not to be complaints but rather expressions of pride at being sheltered within Avery's inner sanctum. For example, Jimmie Lee Jacobs gave an impression of delight in having his own studio space where he could work at all hours of the day and night:

> We all had our own separate desks and we'd leave our work there and work . . . 24/7, you know, and my dorm was just a fifteen-minute walk from there, so you know, I really lived there. You just went back to your dorm to go to sleep . . . When it got down to the crunch hour, the last minute, people slept there.
>
> Jimmie Lee Jacobs

Absorbed in the idea that they could shape their learning agendas and connect with the gritty world of their reality just a few blocks down the hill, some cohort members reported that the school's speculative quality gave them the sense that an elitist learning environment had become more inclusive, more accepting of the demands of the movement, more responsive to students, and more progressive in its city-making practices. According to Laura Marie Swain, the intensity of the studio was made all the more motivating by the aura of possibility that existed in the school and the larger professional community at that time. She recalled the free-wheeling counterculture of experimentation caught on fire:

> There was this tremendous emotional thing that was going on. Everything was just running at full tilt. The war was in progress. There was a lot of emotional engagement at the time. And there was this total freedom in what you could do. You could really make up anything you wanted to make up . . . And so that was all very exciting, and it gave you a real sense of possibility. In the whole world, there were people who were thinking of new ways to build things, which really didn't happen again until recently with global warming . . . There was somebody out there, Paolo Soleri, who

had this idea for a building that would be an entire city. There were
all of these crazy ideas! We were going to have the revolution in
architecture. That was all quite wonderful, being part of that sense
of possibility that you wanted to learn, not just what everybody had
already learned how to do, and that you were just learning a set of
skills. You had the possibility to invent. That made the education
very, very dynamic.

Laura Marie Swain

Just imagine your fearless ethnic minority guides inhabiting Avery
Hall's light-filled inner sanctum, shedding centuries of presumed black
inferiority, having total freedom to make demands and invent dreams
of a just world. Now observe what happens when the thick Italian Renaissance walls that traditionally separated Avery's students from the rat-
infested ghetto around them dissolve, allowing them to take what is inside
the school outside into the community.

Exposed Outside in Storefront Studios

The storefront experiments you will observe as you ascend beyond the
safety of the ivory tower took place roughly between 1967 and 1971 and
occurred primarily in the Division of Planning. They took students out
of Avery to test their abilities in the real world, which required external
support. Through dogged fund-raising, the division captured $465,000
in Urban Center funding plus numerous other foundation and industry
grants, while gaining additional resources through its principal partners in
transgression: the Urban Action and Experimentation Program (UAEP),
the Architects Renewal Committee in Harlem (ARCH), and the Real
Great Society (RGS/Uptown).

The division's first studio, the East Harlem Planning Studio, was team
taught by Albert Mayer and Robert L. Kolodny and offered only to planning students.[28] "Getting into the dirt and grime and human contacts and
understanding" of the local community,[29] faculty and students worked to
overcome the paternalism that had compromised the school's earlier real-
life studios. Its client base drew upon UAEP's network, including the Association of United Contractors of America and an array of community
development corporations, citizen groups, and block associations. By the
end of the first year, the East Harlem Planning Studio had completed fifteen impressive projects.

This first endeavor morphed into the Community Development and
Planning Studio, which was offered to planning, architecture, law, busi-

ness, social work, and education students, with their home schools providing faculty liaisons. This interdisciplinary studio modeled how the university could meet its moral obligation "to make professional skills available to those who need them most but can least afford them."[30] With funding from the Mellon Charitable Trusts, the Astor Foundation, and the Urban Center, the studio produced plans for a community-owned minibus system, storefront community center, shopping facilities, real estate management institute, and job training center, along with a how-to booklet for turning vacant properties into community assets.[31] In recognition of these results, the studio received renewed funding the following year.

Though the studio projects did not entirely align with UAEP's community development projects, Mayer and Kolodny looked for ways to collaborate, especially on housing and job training projects. One of their cleverest collaborations produced a course in cost estimating that the university offered two nights a week to contractors affiliated with UAEP. Their students designed and administered the course, a UAEP cost estimator and volunteer subcontractors provided instruction, the Business School provided space, and the Urban Center provided funding. The course attracted mostly small Harlem contractors who wanted to compete more effectively with majority firms. In addition to funded collaborations such as this one, UAEP also supported unfunded ones, becoming the principal client for community-service studios in the Division of Planning.

Though some cohort members said they were seeking a general professional education, many felt that developing the skills to serve marginalized communities was the driving force of their professional education. Some believed that they could best contribute to the movement by designing better office and school environments or by planning more sustainable development in third world countries, but many others wanted to improve housing for low-income peoples, whether through design or through public policy. An overarching theme among this group was the affirmation they felt in being able to apply their skills purposefully in the local community, as was true for Mark Hamilton:

> We also had what we called an urban design studio, where we went out into the community and took what services we knew and provided services to the community. I got involved with providing information to renters about the possibilities of tenant ownership, creating a park in the city—we got involved in the community.
>
> Mark Hamilton

For many cohort members, the experimental operation's emphasis upon using school learning to advance community change naturally put them into leadership roles, as Craig Shelton explained:

> Being that I was somewhat familiar with Harlem, I guess I ended up being a guide to some of the students. I think it was their first introduction to . . . being in the middle of an African American community. So, I guess, there was some trepidation or fear . . . I tried to ease whatever reservations they had about going into the community.

Craig Shelton

STUDENT INTERNSHIPS

Whereas service-learning studios provided academic credit for community work, internships provided much-needed employment for the ethnic minority recruits, who were hired as researchers, trainees, and liaisons between community groups and the school. Many of these internships occurred through UAEP, which by 1969 had grown into an impressive agency overseeing dozens of projects. It was not only the Urban Center's clearinghouse for all the proposals from community organizations that required planning and design services, it "had developed a number of clients for whom it served as consultant, thereby financially contributing to its own support."[32] UAEP was involved in such large-scale efforts as planning a city block for renovated owner-occupied housing and drafting legislation to establish a public-private land bank. However, its primary achievement was a six-story public housing project developed in partnership with two large corporations (American Standard and Celanese) to demonstrate the economic feasibility of using prefabricated construction techniques. Bell and Robinson overcame considerable university and city bureaucracy to secure a city-owned site, the New York City Housing Authority's commitment to purchase the completed building, and the university's permission to participate in the joint venture. The partnership resulted in a $1.2 million turnkey project that housed about seventy families in the Harlem area—the first of its kind—and brought substantial media attention to the Division of Planning.[33] Projects such as this one created numerous internship opportunities, especially for the school's ethnic minority recruits.

ARCH and RGS/Uptown also offered student internships, with ARCH hiring individual students to staff its community consultation projects. As Kirk Bowles explained, "ARCH was created by a grant to work with local community groups to provide better housing and other related services." Students were hired to work on those projects, and they also served as mentors in ARCH's precollege program, as William Tate did:

> I worked closely with ARCH for about at least two years, my first year being an employee at ARCH—running an outreach program, monitoring the high school students who were interested in the profession of architecture, and working with them both with their studies, and giving them some idea of what kinds of things we were doing as students in the School of Architecture.
>
> William Tate

Calvin Page mistakenly thought that Bond had founded ARCH, not realizing that whites staffed the organization for its first three years with C. Richard Hatch as executive director and that Bond only remained for one year before opening his own practice. Details aside, Page perceived a completely fluid relationship between ARCH and the school:

> I knew ARCH and I knew what it was, and I knew all the people there. And at best, ARCH was used as a recruiting ground, you know, because Max Bond had started it. Plus Max Bond could bring anybody up from up there, and from down at ARCH up to Columbia, and so on.
>
> Calvin Page

Unlike ARCH's hiring of individual students, RGS/Uptown hired students to participate as a group in its storefront studios, often taking advantage of UAEP's funding stream. The first of those studios, the Urban Planning Studio (UPS), began during the 1968–69 academic year and was a third iteration of the Mayer/Kolodny service-learning studios. RGS/Uptown staff member, Harry J. Quintana, conceived UPS in reaction to the faculty-run studio, which he criticized as not sufficiently responsive to community input. This iteration undertook a yearlong study of East Harlem and completed a substantial number of projects. However, UPS "was hindered by severe staff shortages" and by the blurring of internship and academic work, "as well as by the time-consuming administration of the Columbia program."[34]

Undaunted, Quintana, created a fourth iteration of the studio, RGS/UPS, to reinforce the idea of community control. He then screened students to make sure they understood that he was "the boss" and that they were being hired to provide technical expertise to the community. The ultimate in institutional transgression, this iteration ambitiously brought city makers together across disciplinary, social class, gender, and ideological lines to collaborate with former gang members. According to Philip Bertoli-Pearson, RGS/UPS "was a wild, crazy place," and like ARCH, it had a fluid relationship with the school because Quintana also taught an urban design studio in Avery.

During its first year, RGS/UPS renovated a townhouse as its headquarters and completed numerous community projects. During its second year, it produced even more impressive outcomes, most notably three built vest-pocket parks and several housing feasibility studies; it also consulted with the Board of Education on an alternative high school.[35] Nevertheless, the results of RGS/UPS were mixed with "some notable successes and some serious (though predicted) problems."[36]

Completing Magical Projects

The projects cohort members recalled were wide ranging and frequently practical in nature. They reported working on every building type from a penthouse apartment to a subway station, an office building with a financial prospectus, a huge landfill project, and a neighborhood redevelopment plan. However, their projects primarily dealt with low-income multifamily housing and secondarily with schools in low-income neighborhoods. William Tate explained the pressure the ethnic minority recruits put on faculty to assign projects that would be relevant to what they expected would be community-oriented careers:

> We were primarily focusing on the kinds of projects and assignments that . . . would be more relevant to urban issues, social issues. So we felt that would better prepare us for practicing architecture in an urban environment.
>
> William Tate

Several cohort members' projects grew out of the work of ARCH, particularly its alternatives to the controversial proposal for the State Office Building (SOB) on 125th Street, which intersected with residents' outrage over the area's lack of a high school. Harlem had more than 250,000 residents and about seventeen thousand potential high school students, but no high school. The city had appropriated funds for three new high schools near Lincoln Center and one for the northernmost tip of Manhattan, and then in its 1969–70 budget it recommended three more high schools, none in Harlem due to the Board of Education's policy of ending de facto segregation (and its assumption that white students would not, or should not, travel to Harlem).[37]

A community coalition that had organized to block the SOB engaged ARCH to explore the feasibility of building a high school on the site,[38] which began a dialogue about what a Harlem high school should be. Coalition members concluded that "a high school for community participation would necessarily have to be a very different kind of facility from existing schools. Opportunities for multiple use, shared facilities, and scattered site development must be carefully considered. The development of a single site with all activities concentrated could be less beneficial to the community than a dispersed facility."[39]

The following school year, two cohort members recounted fleshing out the dispersed facility concept in separate projects. Philip Bertoli–Pearson recalled that he was part of a team at RGS/Uptown that developed the concept. They challenged the prevailing educational approach of building high schools for four thousand students, asking "can we design a high school that is to the scale of a community and can make students real instead of just one number of four thousand?" Bruce Fenderson also described developing the small schools concept, but in much greater detail for his senior thesis:

> What I had done in my thesis was suggest that rather than putting all three thousand students on one site, that they break the school up into small schools, which is now standard practice all over the country. And that they use the small schools as a catalyst for the reinvigoration of the community, and the idea behind it was breaking the schools up into something that's smaller, so that local contractors and local developers could actually participate in the building of the schools.
>
> Bruce Fenderson

Recall that the Architecture Division had reorganized studios into a platform system in which students could come together, elect projects, and determine their direction. Cohort members who organized to participate in Bond's West Harlem Platform decided to develop ARCH's educational park concept, proposing that Morningside Park be developed to serve three public elementary schools. The schools themselves would bring children and adults together to learn, obtain social services, engage in neighborhood problem solving, and socialize. This platform also adopted the small schools notion, specifying that the school facilities be scattered in smaller structures, with the northern part of the park serving as an outdoor environment linking the schools and the community.[40] Still, not all cohort members worked on projects for low-income communities. Laura Marie Swain, for example, chose to do a housing project on an enormous site in Lower Manhattan that would eventually become Battery Park City (see Figure 20):

> In my second year . . . we were developing a whole housing project—a landfill project—on the lower tip of Manhattan. It was a huge project . . . and my idea was, instead of building buildings that went straight up, massive buildings that covered blocks all over the place, that I was going to build spiral buildings, so the buildings would just sort of spiral up into the air. And there wouldn't be a clear line between the interior of the building and the outside of the building. I didn't want to make them quite as tall as the World Trade Center, which was being built at that time, so I thought I would make them ninety stories.

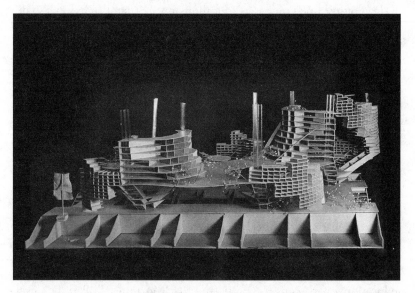

Figure 20. This photo shows a partial model of the tour de force spiral buildings Swain envisioned for an area in downtown Manhattan occupied by dilapidated shipping piers, which the mayor and private developers proposed to reclaim with landfill. (Photo courtesy of Sharon Egretta Sutton.)

Needless to say, it's not easy to design a spiral, because no matter where you try to make the plan, the building is always different. What would make it interesting about designing that kind of space is that that kind of building is almost impossible to design—at least without computers, which there weren't then. But I worked on it and I had a model that kind of showed the whole thing schematically . . . I didn't complete the model but I had enough of it to show what it would look like.

The main reviewer was a very famous person named James Sterling, a well-known British architect. I remember what I was wearing and that I hadn't slept for many days . . . I did my whole presentation sitting on the floor, explaining these spirals. He was a nice reviewer—I don't remember specifically what the feedback was. I do remember that the project was the entertainment of the day . . . That was the tour de force of my educational career, never to be repeated.

Laura Marie Swain

Ethnic Minority Recruits as Superstars

Driven by a revolutionary spirit, the ethnic minority guides who led you along the steepest, most slippery part of the School of Architecture's arc of insurgency dared to turn tradition upside down. Once inside Avery's heavy oak doors, they accessed the power to challenge "the boundaries that separate community and university"[41] and, in so doing, devised "a template for reinvigorating education for the public good."[42] For the cohort members, bringing studios into the community and vice versa made professional education more relevant to their life experiences and career aspirations. Importantly, their outreach activities in the surrounding communities allowed them to play a leadership role in assuring that any proposed interventions were by and for those communities. That Bond brought in architects from ARCH and took students "down there" to work, that Quintana was teaching an urban design studio in the school and was also "the boss" at RGS/Uptown, that academic studios and paid internships were interconnected—all these crossovers blurred the boundaries between a theory-based education and the community-based practice to which many cohort members aspired.

For the ethnic minority students who were recruited to the school but who remained outsiders-within, these blurry boundaries seemingly had advantages, allowing them to benefit from the school's unique location, be exposed to the "dirt and grime" of urban and community issues, and engage purposefully in collective, interdisciplinary problem solving. Cohort members took great delight in reporting their superstar role in the school. To paraphrase John LePoi, they were confident in what they could do and what their abilities were. They had the academic, professional, and political skills to assume leadership roles in helping steer the school through the unknown waters of a student-centered, community-engaged education. Some had professional or undergraduate degrees in architecture or related fields; others had teaching experience, including at Columbia; still others had worked in offices and agencies; and most had developed leadership skills as civil rights activists or in their churches and communities. On solid ground academically, many of your guides took an activist role in transforming the school, beginning right after the bust when two black students worked with Bond to spark an ingenious snowballing recruitment process.

Numerous cohort members described gratifying experiences as high-achieving students. To name a few, Kenneth Ashton boasted that he received "acceptance, or I want to say accolades," for the quality of work he was doing. Kirk Bowles boasted that he completed a unique housing design for his thesis that prompted a job offer from his adviser. William Tate boasted that his studio critic was so pleased with his thesis that she made a job referral to a distinguished Canadian architect. Calvin Page, who had extensive drafting experience, boasted that he brought into his class "whole new ways of presenting your project. In fact, I was the first one to present all of my drawings as a slide presentation." Mark Hamilton boasted that he had gained an aura of leadership "from the point of what I call thinking [on your feet]—the ability to own a space." And several cohort members boasted that they achieved the ultimate success—being the first in their family to earn a college degree. Further, the blurring of school and community made learning relevant to the recruits' real lives, as Carlos Méndez noted:

> You know, like I wasn't doing some work in the studio that was very foreign to what we were doing in [the community]—even what was happening in real life and what was happening in the studio sort of became, you know, tied in together and became one thing.
>
> Carlos Méndez

As you can see peering over the edge of the School of Architecture's arc of insurgency, the period between 1968 and 1971 was a magical, intoxicating time. With experiments in a constant state of flux, the school had a dynamic, though sometimes confusing, quality. The ethnic minority recruits who entered Avery during that brief moment of opportunity helped blur the dichotomous relationships that sustain higher education's elitism. They turned tradition upside down, thereby gaining a new and demanding sense of self—a self that could own a space and redress inequities in their community.

6
1969–1971 Unraveling

During your brief sojourn at the apex of the School of Architecture's arc of insurgency, your ethnic minority guides had truly amazing experiences. Across the country, virulent black student activism pushed colleges to expand affirmative action and the financial aid it required, which led "to a sharp jump in black college enrollment in the 1970s."[1] Columbia University reflected this national trend, but the School of Architecture sprinted ahead to take an unparalleled lead in educational equity. In 1970, the school had an astounding 14 percent ethnic minority enrollment, up from 2 percent in 1968, and then those numbers soared even higher in 1971 to 16 percent, a level "probably not equaled in any other architectural school in a predominantly white university."[2] As phenomenal as they may seem, the numbers were only one aspect of your guides' amazing experiences. Even more powerful was their sense of being part of an ethnic minority community that was advancing change in the city and university. Your guides' presence in the ivory tower was buttressed by that community's collective triumphs.

It was buttressed when the Architects Renewal Committee in Harlem (ARCH) took a stand for self-determination by creating alternatives for the proposed State Office Building that responded to community needs and values.[3] It was buttressed by ARCH's Ford-funded pipeline project, with its tutoring and internships in the city's best design firms and its scholarships in the nation's best architecture schools. It was buttressed when the American Institute of Architects (AIA) leadership declared that through such pipelines, architecture would become "a major professional opportunity for blacks."[4] It was buttressed when Vernon (Ben) Robinson of the Urban Action and Experimentation Program (UAEP) opened a factory in the Bronx where unskilled black and Puerto Rican workers learned to prefabricate walls and floors for a high-rise apartment building.[5] It was buttressed when the project won acclaim from U.S. Department of Housing and Urban Development secretary George Romney.[6] It was buttressed when the university promoted your guides' beloved mentor, Max Bond, to a professor position. It was buttressed when Ford Foundation evaluators applauded their contributions to social equity, especially their involvement with admissions and with UAEP and the Real Great Society (RGS/Uptown).[7]

Your guides' presence in the ivory tower was most assuredly buttressed when the respected Romaldo Giurgola unreservedly declared that "perhaps the single most positive fact of these past years has been the effort made by the school to offer [professional] education to minority students. Through the adoption of a broader spectrum of evaluations in admissions and initiation of new programs, new energies and ideas have come to the school, thus assuring it of continued vitality. We have probably the best students and instructors from minorities of any school of architecture, and their work and dedication is exemplary."[8]

Your ethnic minority guides had amazing experiences at the apex of the School of Architecture's arc of insurgency because they were part of a community that had propelled itself forward by leaps and bounds. But they had little chance to revel in their achievements as the arc began its downward descent almost immediately. The underpinnings of the descent began in the larger society and then seeped into the university and school. In the wink of an eye, widespread ambivalence toward upending racism and economic inequality took over and propelled the arc of insurgency downward. You see, just as multiple dynamics helped create the collective will to correct historical inequities, multiple dynamics helped smother it: the Vietnam War, urban unrest, white backlash, forced busing, escalating energy costs, and a newly affluent middle class unwilling to support social programs.[9] Facing downward middle-class mobility and the challenges of achieving a democratic society, many whites felt besieged, their 1960s vision of racial justice devolving into a "meaner, more selfish outlook, hostile to the aspirations of those less fortunate."[10]

Somewhere along this downward trajectory of waning resolve to achieve educational equity, affirmative action became equated with the loss of academic excellence. In the wink of an eye, the 1960s thrust toward equal rights shifted to a 1970s survival-of-the-fittest mentality. To squash the equal educational opportunity programs that were just beginning to gain traction, a group of racist academics materialized, spreading rumors of impending disaster from "violations of academic and intellectual meritocracy."[11] It pejoratively labeled goals for achieving diversity as "quotas," which acted like an oil slick as your guides tried to stop their descent.

Somewhere along the way, a fiscal crisis stoked the fires of social conservatism when federal spending for the Vietnam War increased but tax revenue to pay for those expenditures did not.[12] Short of funds, President Richard Nixon balanced the budget on the backs of the poor, slashing support for Kennedy- and Johnson-era social programs. Federal cuts filtered down to the states, with Governor Nelson Rockefeller's cuts filtering down to slash New York City's support for education, healthcare, and public assistance. Except for the police, the city froze hiring, which cut back services and job opportunities for its many ethnic minority workers. True to Mayor John Lindsay's prediction, federal disinvestment in cities fed their desertion by businesses and middle-income families, further depleting the tax base.[13]

Fuelling this downward trajectory was an all-out attack on social reform, which spread like a virus to everything it touched. To lead the attack, the Nixon administration instigated an investigation of tax-exempt organizations that had funded civil rights activism, aiming its arsenal squarely at the Ford Foundation.[14] Ford's venturesome policies had provoked the ire of House Ways and Means Committee chairman, Wilbur Mills, who set out to stifle the organization's activism. A Mills-led congressional hearing resulted in a 4 percent annual tax being levied against foundations' investment incomes, along with other legislation barring foundations from attempting to influence government policy. These punitive restrictions bolstered the conservative bent of Congress and signaled to many philanthropists that they should not follow Ford's lead as agents of social change. Closer to home, a U.S. Senate committee investigated RGS management practices, resulting in the abrupt termination of its funding even though the committee never filed any charges.[15] Lacking an economic lifeline, the arc of insurgency tumbled further downward.

Even before the clouds hanging over the national landscape darkened the city's landscape, Columbia entered its own fiscal crisis. The university's deficit had ballooned from just $3 million in 1964 to $16 million by 1970 as salaries and construction costs rose but tuition did not.[16] A tuition increase of about $200 per year in 1970 was woefully insufficient to address the mounting severity of this crisis. As you can imagine, disproportionate financial aid to ethnic minority students became the focus of white backlash as faculty who were never fully committed to educational equity began underscoring the high cost of supporting this needy group. You see, a virulent collective anger had built to launch Columbia's arc of insurgency, and an equally virulent collective anger built to push it downward. In both instances, race was front and center, forcefully intersecting with urban development on Columbia's campus and in the School of Architecture.

Unraveling of an Experimental Operation

Your descent from the heady heights of insurgency will take you past social and fiscal conservatism, past cities sinking into decline, past white backlash, past internecine warfare in the School of Architecture. Along the way, you will experience the slow but sure unraveling of the school's experimental operation.

As you learned earlier in this story, Columbia's statutes specified a top-down management structure, with high-ranking university administrators holding leadership positions in the School of Architecture. The experiment attempted to disrupt this structure by empowering faculty and students to manage their own affairs, which sparked numerous battles with university administrators. One of these battles related to amnesty, with the faculty insisting that all striking students be granted amnesty and administrators insisting that disciplinary procedures were essential to a bargain struck with the city for dismissing criminal charges against students. The faculty retorted that charging a few students with offenses would result in many other students and some faculty stepping forward to assume equal responsibility, which would disrupt the entire school.[17] Eventually, this go-round ended with a missive to the dean from central administration that directed him to begin disciplinary procedures but, at the same time, acknowledged the faculty's commitment to students.[18]

Another battle related to the school's illegal interim rules. This struggle was not so easily resolved, perhaps because some faculty truly believed that university statutes would change as a result of the insurrection and then the University Senate would adopt its disputed rules.[19] University administrators stood firm that the school could operate under its own rules as long as those rules did not conflict with university statutes, which mandated faculty governance.[20] They insisted that current statutes allowed consultation with students without assigning them statutory rights and offered their help in redrafting the rules to comply with the statutes. This battle persisted for two years until April 1971. With the insurgency fading from sight, the faculty relented and began a process of revising the school's rules in accordance with university statutes, which by then had been modified.

A third battle resulted from continual administrative mix-ups. A year into the experiment, perhaps due to the disarray all the changes caused, the dean began making numerous managerial blunders, such as failing to renew expiring faculty appointments,[21] making personnel changes without the provost's approval,[22] and submitting budgets filled with errors and omissions.[23] He even dispatched architecture's all-important strategic plan too late for the accrediting team to review prior to its visit, issuing the plan minus critical information on faculty workload assignments.[24] At the same time, the dean was forced to ask university administrators for additional monies to supplement his regular budget—to cover commitments made to incoming recruits;[25] to cover the salaries promised by the chairman of the Division of Architecture, who apparently had not been informed of his budget;[26] and to negotiate with the Urban Center on its support for the assistant to the dean for minority affairs.[27] These costs overruns were exacerbated by the school's habit of drawing down on gifts to cover operating costs, its inability to obtain external funding, and the university's ever-increasing budget deficit.

Capping these battles were untold complaints from faculty and students, who leapfrogged over the dean to bombard university administrators directly. As the experiment unraveled and the complaints escalated, administrators stepped in to manage what they referred to as the "crisis in Avery" by assigning a manager from outside the school. This external administrator, who characterized the crisis as "the agonies in Avery" and "a hair-raising tale," reported the school's day-to-day affairs directly to the president of the university. Explaining the extent of this supervision to the present, he said, "I receive blind carbons of almost all correspondence to the dean, meet with factions, review appointments, run 'smokers' [informal faculty meetings], jockey the school's committees, and undo problems that would otherwise be resolved in the courts, or via AAUP [American Association of University Professors] cases."[28]

As you can imagine, such scrutiny at a time of fiscal crisis put the School of Architecture at serious risk for elimination, and the planning division took the lead in moving the school toward extinction.

The Division of Planning's Descent

The downward trajectory of the Division of Planning began when Abrams left for Harvard. Imprudently, the faculty recommended as his replacement the untenured Hans B. C. Spiegel just as he came up for mandatory tenure review. Following Abrams's departure, Spiegel quickly became a key figure in administering both the division and the institute while also teaching, including a large university-wide elective course, and fund-raising for the ethnic minority recruits.[29] Yet, despite Rapkin's enthusiastic support, Dean Smith torpedoed Spiegel's tenure application, maintaining that his specialization in social planning "was of questionable academic durability."[30] Naturally, university administrators denied his tenure.

Then civil engineer Sigurd Grava (*Columbia* 1957) came up for review. Smith again torpedoed the application, this time endorsing Grava but then failing to secure appropriate external review letters. In this case, university administrators awarded tenure but informed the dean that Grava's promotion went through only because denying it would have created an intolerable teaching situation in the planning division.[31] In a nutshell, the founding chair of the division jumped ship, a second chair failed tenure review, and a third achieved tenure under a cloud. This sequence of events created "very serious staffing problems in the Division of Planning."[32]

Compounding the division's staffing problems was the disappearance of funding for the Institute of Urban Environment. From its inception in April 1966 until June 1971, the institute had an aggregate budget of roughly $800,000 or about $135,000 per year.[33] However, when its primary source of funding from Ford ran out, it began to subsist on just $15,000 per year from the general fund. After being denied tenure, Spiegel remained for a while as an institute research associate, but he soon accepted an offer as director of Hunter College's visionary urban affairs program. Lacking staff and inordinately burdened by teaching, Rapkin was distracted from his responsibility to administer the institute's old contracts and secure new sources of funding.[34] By the time Abrams died on February 22, 1970, his vision of the Division of Planning as a leader in transforming the urban crisis had also died.

DEFUNDING THE URBAN CENTER

When the Division of Planning launched a faculty search, university administrators intervened, arranging for Dean Smith to secure at no cost an assistant professor of law as the division's part-time chairman. What soon became clear is that the appointment was just the first step in central administration's redirection of both the planning division and the Urban Center. The center had just issued a report that disparaged university efforts to increase ethnic minority enrollment while applauding the School of Architecture as one of the few schools that had made significant progress on recruitment and retention. The report reinforced central administration's conflation of the center with the planning students' growing interest in ethnic minority communities and the division's "potentially explosive" involvement in urban minority affairs.[35]

To block both units in their reform efforts, university administrators articulated a plan for disengaging from Ford's urban and minority affairs agenda. To deflate efforts by center staff to push the university on the issue of educational equity, administrators announced their unqualified support for the report, promising to make "a substantial move in the desirable directions of the recommendations."[36] Having co-opted the report, they then framed the center's previous efforts as "a *consciously* planned 'phase one'"[37] that engaged a diversity of approaches to urban problems. In a new second phase, the center would become the "most useful point of contact with communities of urban dwellers and urban policy-makers."[38]

Expecting the expiration of center staff appointments, university administrators set about securing the remaining Ford funds of about $1 million by declaring an immediate moratorium on all center grants. They applauded the projects the center had undertaken over the preceding three years and, at the same time, undercut their educational significance.[39] University administrators also took a stance against a departmental approach to urban studies (i.e., against the Division of Planning), calling for a brand-new profession in social policy practice. They announced that they would use the remaining Ford funds to establish an interdisciplinary program in social policy that would link to political science, law, and business (but not to planning). The program's goals would be "tied to service in urban society—not to service in the city."[40] That is, its goals would link to social policy *theory* rather than "getting into the dirt and grime and human contacts and understanding" of a local community,[41] as the Division of Planning had been doing.

University administrators would discontinue the center's involvement in academic affairs, instead encouraging it "to engage in those community programs for which it is able to generate funds elsewhere, with perhaps a modest input of Columbia money."[42] In addition, the center would oversee extracurricular learning experiences and become a source of support for ethnic minority students and faculty. For this agenda, it would need new leadership capable of raising funds. To make the disconnect between urban studies and minority affairs complete, university administrators specified that "black studies . . . should be at the initiative of Columbia's black faculty and students . . . [and] will necessarily demonstrate a substantially different center of gravity from the program in social policy, since black studies must include course offerings in ethnic art, music, languages, and the like . . . [However] there is . . . no plan by either black faculty members or black students to undertake or design a 'black studies' program at this time."[43]

In sum, university administrators stripped the Urban Center of its funds and refashioned it as a resource center for ethnic minority students, faculty, and community members. This carefully devised strategy not only cut the Division of Planning off from a major source of support for its ethnic minority students and community-based work, it also shut the division out of the university's new urban affairs agenda.

The Division of Architecture's Descent

The arc's descent picked up speed when the school's centerpiece program, the professional degree in architecture, received only provisional accreditation in June 1970. During its visit, the accreditation team discerned many groundbreaking aspects of the program's experimental operation. Though being misled by a pre-accreditation report that comingled the Division of Planning's achievements with those of the Division of Architecture, the team lauded architecture's ethnic minority recruitment program and the curriculum it had produced in the aftermath of the insurrection, especially its balance of technical and theoretical issues and its issue-oriented platform system and service-learning studios.[44]

Nevertheless, the team also found serious malfunctions in the program, which it attributed to a byzantine administrative structure, inequitable faculty workloads, unacceptably low faculty salaries, and lack of intellectual rigor. The team deemed these malfunctions all the more serious because a previous team had identified similar problems five years earlier. Architecture's provisional re-accreditation caught the immediate attention of a university attorney, who alerted university administrators that, without full accreditation, the courts would not approve a *cy pres* application to allow use of bequests from two endowments for expanding Avery Hall and its library.[45] University administrators halted work on the *cy pres* proceedings, forestalled disclosing the accreditation report to the trustees, and instead set to work developing a plan for the School of Architecture's future.[46]

DESIGN STUDIO MELTDOWN

Despite its overall negative assessment, the accreditation team applauded the architecture program for having addressed problems the previous team found in the design studios. In particular, the team praised the high-quality studio work being done by students in the evening program, noting that it reflected their combined exposure to professional employment and education. Unbeknownst to the team, Avery's external administrator had an emergency meeting with the dean and the division chair just five months before the visit to resolve a meltdown in the design studio. The focus of the meltdown was the platform system, which showed signs of disintegration "after only two years of struggle to implement it."[47]

Though most of the faculty did not openly oppose the system, they also did not provide the leadership to make it work. For one, they did not coordinate the content of platforms to ensure that students acquired the entry-level technical skills that an architectural education was supposed to offer. As John Little noted, the curriculum "fell short from that standpoint in terms of training me as an architect that could at least hit the ground and do something" in an office. This shortcoming irked cohort members like Calvin Page who "had come to Columbia . . . trained as a draftsman to a degree in high school and then having worked with Doman," the godfather who, as you know, facilitated Page's recruitment visit. You also know that many of the recruits had come to Columbia with practical skills acquired while attending technical schools or working in offices. So you can see why the recruits with their early nuts-and-bolts exposure to the field became major opponents of the platform system's lack of structure. They recognized all too well the predicament of novice recruits who lacked the social connections to leapfrog ahead in their careers without entry-level skills. For example, Kirk Bowles raved about his education but felt the studio sequence left graduates ill prepared for the world of work:

> If I hadn't worked and gone to schools where they were teaching real skills—the skills that we got going to Columbia when we were there, could not land you a job in an office. You had a degree from Columbia University, and that is great. If you didn't have a job to go to already, like your father's office or family business, then you were in trouble.
>
>   Kirk Bowles

The meltdown over how design studio should be taught propelled the social class differences within the architecture program into high relief. For white students with family resources and social connections, the lack of exposure to practical skills was not problematic; for many ethnic minority recruits, it became a tremendous barrier to being successful in a field not known for its openness to nonwhite employees. As Kirk Bowles explained:

> While most of the black and Hispanic students were in the studio trying to make ends meet, get the course work done, and just survive, many of our white counterparts were trying to decide where to go skiing for their Christmas vacation, going to work in daddy's office downtown, and that was very much the "real deal" and we were all aware of it. . . . The difference is that we were trained to go out and function at a "worker bee" level, in contrast to the students traditionally attending Avery . . . [who] were receiving "executive" training, preparing them to take over the family business, or run their daddy's office. They were there to earn their credentials; we were just trying to survive in a profession that didn't know what to do with us.
>
> Kirk Bowles

The recruits' need to be employable worker bees highlighted the school's longtime problem of having a poor instructional staff.[48] As James A. Jackson explained, some professors were prima donnas who assumed that their job was to nurture genius "as if there was nothing they could teach you about the fundamentals of design." He remembered one teacher whose sole feedback was "What you have here is nothing, you have nothing! And criticism like that wasn't very helpful." John Little went further, accusing some studio instructors of being "vicious cretins" who felt like novice student work was beneath them to critique. But Kevin Alexander Kersey, himself now a teacher, was the most articulate in capturing the lack of pedagogical skills on the part of many practitioner faculty:

> I remember one review that I actually ended in tears because the teacher wouldn't focus on what I was concerned with. . . . We were designing a school, and I was trying to create an environment within the school. The teacher was talking about how the streets were dangerous and this, that, and the other. I didn't care. The

streets were not a big issue to me. We got into an argument and I was supposed to back down, and I didn't. And so it got very ugly because I just wouldn't give in. . . . One of the things I realize now, many of the teachers didn't have the skills to teach.

Kevin Alexander Kersey

Then, too, some cohort members found the assignments unrelated to what they expected to be doing as ethnic minority professionals. Even though many assignments were community-focused or dealt with the sort of building types that might be found in low-income communities, like subsidized housing or schools, many others dealt with building types for affluent clients, like luxurious homes or vacation retreats. To John Little, such assignments seemed irrelevant to his future prospects in the field:

I remember my first design project was for a penthouse, and I tried to tell my own design instructors that I doubt that I'm gonna have too many penthouses to design once I get out of here, and I just didn't think that was going to really help me in the long run, but we went through it so I understood something about it. But in reality, I thought it was, you know, like a waste of time.

John Little

So you see, the outstanding results the accreditation team observed in the design studios were due, at least in part, to the technical skills that many of the worker-bee ethnic minority recruits, like Kirk Bowles and Calvin Page, brought with them. Paradoxically, the design studio meltdown that Avery's external administrator sought to resolve was also due, at least in part, to the presence of these recruits, who were disgruntled with the school's freewheeling platform system—an approach that idealistic faculty and students had constructed through a prism of white privilege. The lower socioeconomic status of the ethnic minority recruits and their lack of family connections meant that they required structured studio instruction in the skills needed to gain access to an elitist white male-dominated profession. But the external administrator downplayed the racial undertones of the meltdown, explaining to university administrators that "design critics and design students (Division of Architecture) have agreed . . . to calm down while I 'supervise' the management of the School of Architecture. The details of the supervision are not important and are, in any event, too embarrassing to discuss. . . . There are some race undertones in this; standards need not be compromised because the particularities involved are outside the conventional academic pale and involve as many aesthetic as intellectual questions."[49] Perhaps you will agree that the external administrator's glib conflation of race with compromised standards masked the very real race and social class dimensions of the design studio meltdown.

PERSONNEL COMPLAINTS

Architecture teaching staff and faculty increased scrutiny of the school by registering numerous personnel complaints, which invariably came from favorites of the ethnic minority recruits. For example, one came from the noted architect and city planner Oscar Newman, who developed his classic theory of defensible space around this time. According to Newman, the architecture division chairman had contracted with him in fall 1970 to teach a theory course and related studio the following spring.[50] When the chairman later reduced the offer to just a theory course at half the original compensation, Newman registered a complaint with Dean Smith and the Columbia Chapter of the AAUP.[51] Smith countered that Newman had already left Columbia for New York University during the period in question. The school's external administrator negotiated a resolution, compensating Newman for just under the original amount of his contract for the two courses.[52]

Smith claimed that Newman never taught either of these courses,[53] but Carlos Méndez remembered the course as one of two that stood out in his education:

> The other [course] I remember is by the theory teacher, which was great—the one that wrote *Defensible Space*. . . . He was our theory teacher, which was another course which I really, you know, urban design theory, which was really great.
>
> Carlos Méndez

Another complaint came from nine part-time studio instructors who took the "extraordinary measure" of contacting university administrators about "the existing state of affairs at the School of Architecture."[54] These faculty members complained that they had no voice in decisions, were paid well below university rates, and consistently had their pay reduced by the dean from what the chairman promised. But, they pointed out, they taught the curriculum's core course for the greatest number of hours weekly, with tenured professors teaching only ancillary courses.[55]

This dispute was resolved, undoubtedly with the external administrator's assistance, by making a small increase in the salaries of three of the nine aggrieved part-time design staff and by changing Max Bond's title from lecturer to adjunct associate professor.

Personnel complaints also came from Charles Rieger and Albert O. Halse. Rieger and Halse had both achieved tenure when Leopold Arnaud was dean. After Arnaud stepped down, Rieger, who was a fellow in the Société des Architectes Diplômés in Paris and had been architecture's top design critic, was demoted to the evening program.[56] Halse, a registered architect with a doctoral degree in education who authored four books on rendering (one now in its third edition), likewise wound up in the evening program, his rendering course given over to a fine artist.[57] Both Rieger and Halse struggled to be recognized and integrated into the faculty. Rieger continually pressed for promotion to full professor and Halse repeatedly threatened to lodge a formal complaint with the University Senate for his lack of an appropriate teaching assignment. Despite their complaints, both remained decidedly on the periphery of the school. In the words of Avery's external administrator, Rieger was "a representative of the Beaux Arts tradition for which there [was] simply no place in 1971."[58]

Yet cohort members who were otherwise critical of the quality of their education praised Rieger and Halse. In particular, Kevin Alexander Kersey, who complained that "many of the teachers didn't have the skills to teach," remembered Rieger as one of the few good teachers. Through his aside about Rieger's French birthright, Kersey also seemed to imply that he lacked the racial biases of his American counterparts:

> The support I really had was from . . . a few of the professors there that I could talk to. One was Professor Charles J. Rieger . . . I befriended him and he invited me to his home and I would some- times sit and complain about the school and how things were run. But he was very instrumental in me getting through the school. He was French, by the way.
>
> Kevin Alexander Kersey

John Little criticized the school's excessive theoretical focus and com- plained that the architecture courses "were a little broad . . . good with the broad strokes, the general strokes, but short on detail." Despairing that he could not be more positive about his education, Little dug into his memory and finally recalled that both Rieger and Halse had taught him something useful:

I don't want to say it was all a waste of time. I had a lot of—you know what? I had an art teacher named Professor Rieger. And he actually taught me something that I still use today in terms of field measurement. We actually went out and field measured [a mansion] in New York City, and the tools and the methods and things like that that he actually—he was the same guy that just taught us to just sketch. . . . Also rendering, an appreciation for rendering from Albert Halse.

John Little

Interestingly, Little assumed that Rieger was an art teacher—someone on the periphery of the school—rather than a distinguished architecture professor.

Dean Smith's Resignation

The provisional accreditation report prompted the resignation of Dean Smith, who summed up the School of Architecture's deteriorated state of affairs at a faculty meeting in November 1970. According to Smith, the school was plagued by administrative difficulties arising from the interim rules and pass-fail grading system, by financial aid shortcomings due to a nationwide and university fiscal crisis, and by space and equipment needs that the hold on Avery's expansion exacerbated—a situation worsened by the time given over to architecture's accreditation visit. Noting the need for continuity in rectifying this state of affairs, his eight years of service, and his approaching mandatory retirement date, Smith announced that he had notified the president of his intention to retire,[59] which set in motion the search for a new dean. The external administrator upped the ante, threatening receivership should a new dean not be found immediately. As you can see, the school was hurtling down its arc of insurgency, but more blows were in the offing related to the racial dimensions of this drama.

Unraveling of Race Relations

Earlier in the story, you learned that administrators and faculty were remarkably able to shift gears and join the trust toward educational equity. However, not everyone shifted gears. After the students who had instigated the insurgency graduated and a national backlash against affirmative action took shape, the resistance to change became quite pronounced in the curriculum and in the interactions between the recruits and some white faculty and students.

Subjected to a Eurocentric Curriculum

Though some faculty were open to helping the ethnic minority recruits discover a black aesthetic, others persisted in indoctrinating them into a Eurocentric outlook that channeled them into "becoming custodians of the status quo."[60] The exclusionary focus upon Western culture as the genesis for architectural thinking was especially troubling to Bruce Fenderson:

> There was a lot of focus on Europe, on the achievements of Europe, and also the rebuilding of Europe after the Second World War . . . but there was absolutely no reference to the experiences of black people. In a decade in which there was so much public attention made to African Americans, as an African American I found myself completely without any frame of reference to understand how African Americans had contributed to this field.
>
> Bruce Fenderson

The lack of a frame of reference—either for understanding the contributions of African Americans to architecture or for understanding how to provide professional services for this population—put recruits who undertook Afrocentric issues at a disadvantage. For example, Sylvia K. Atkinson, who was earning a degree in hospital and health facility design, decided to write her master's thesis on the ecology of health in black communities. However, she soon realized that:

> Because it was off the beaten path in terms of the kinds of theses they had before . . . it was more difficult to find people to read it and evaluate it and know what I was talking about. But I wanted to write about that and so I did, but that was hard.
>
> Sylvia K. Atkinson

Writing a master's thesis on the economic redevelopment of 125th Street in Harlem proved even harder for Craig Shelton. To his great disappointment, the planning faculty, progressive through they were, could not accept his grassroots approach to revitalizing this ghetto street. Stymied, Shelton abandoned his studies for a while, but then he returned and wrote an epilogue that convinced his committee to sign off on his thesis. Similarly, Mark Hamilton described being criticized about his ideas for improving the quality of life in public housing. He had deep convictions about housing as a result of observing deplorable living conditions while working in Harlem and during a tour of duty in Vietnam.

Hamilton proposed commodious living spaces for families with safe outdoor spaces for children's play, a nursery and playground on the third floor of a public housing building, and naturalistic Afrocentric spatial concepts "as opposed to the squares and boxes that were built here in the states." Recalling that faculty rejected such ideas as impractical, Hamilton wryly observed that residential amenities were a given for well-to-do populations but were considered unrealistic for the occupants of public housing: "Public housing was like, 'people should be glad to get what they get.'" But Kevin Alexander Kersey said he actually felt duped by faculty who assigned public housing projects without providing the knowledge he needed to design for low-income residents:

> Some projects we were designing for low-income people. But I felt like we didn't know enough about low-income people. I felt it was just a façade—doing a housing project without focusing on lifestyle, discussing how people live in different income groups, different ethnic groups. That was not discussed. It was low-income housing. And I felt that we weren't qualified to do it correctly unless we discussed it . . . I felt deceived. I felt tricked.
>
> Kevin Alexander Kersey

Subjected to Backlash from the Ghana Trip

As you will recall, Max Bond was able to secure Kinne Awards for nine students (including one white student) to travel to Ghana during an extended spring break in advance of the awards twenty-two students received for summer travel. Bond was able to get faculty to agree with this plan by arguing that most of the recruits would not be able to take advantage of the Kinne Award during the summer due to their need to work. Some faculty advocates of affirmative action accepted his plan as a reasonable way "to compensate for generations of racist and sexist inequity."[61] However, other faculty condemned it as the premature awarding of fellowships based upon quotas rather than academic excellence—a manipulative distortion and abuse of the spirit of the Kinne Award that merited legal investigation.[62]

In response to the considerable backlash this trip caused, the Ghana awardees mounted an exhibit in the attic of Avery where the Black and Puerto Rican Student-Faculty-Administrators Organization (BPRS-

Figure 21. This photo shows the Ghana study tour exhibit that Kinne awardees mounted in Avery's attic, including a display of photographs, artifacts, and (in the foreground) a model and drawings of Swain's Vista project. (Photo courtesy of Sharon Egretta Sutton.)

FAO) typically held its meetings (see Figure 21). However, the exhibit only increased Laura Marie Swain's worries about the trip being accepted as relevant to architecture:

> There was an attic space in the building on the seventh floor . . . and we painted the space and we did a big exhibition of our trip to Ghana. I had worked on a little project with the Vista volunteers trying to figure out how to build the mud huts more efficiently. And I had done a drawing and model of that project. Other people had photographs and artifacts that they exhibited. I was worried that it'd look like some sort of an African trinket shop that oughta be up in Harlem, but . . . well Max helped us make it look architectural.
>
> Laura Marie Swain

The valiant efforts of the study tour group did little to halt the arc of insurgency's downward trajectory.

Subjected to Discrimination

The ethnic minority recruits experienced both subtle and overt discrimination in the School of Architecture. Some cohort members talked about having a sense of isolation within a privileged group. For example, both James Hamilton and John Little described being part of the school but still being segregated within it. James A. Jackson recalled that his privileged peers "came to school with exposure to many different life experiences" that he lacked, making it difficult for him to participate in their conversations. But Hamilton, Kenneth Ashton, Vernon Walker, William Manning, and Abigail Abruña all recalled overt resistance to their presence in the school. As Hamilton put it, "Quite frankly, I'm not sure that they were really that anxious to really get involved or even want us there."

Walker went further, remembering how the group was "given a very tough time early on" and even "ridiculed as minority students." Both Ashton and Manning remembered faculty "who were sometimes condescending . . . who were not supportive of black students." And Manning also recalled having the feeling of being "there to satisfy a quota." Many cohort members reported the sense of having to prove their worth or, as Abruña put it, of needing to demonstrate "that they were not just the kind of charity of the school, but they were people that had something to contribute to the profession." Ashton claimed that some white faculty and staff "just didn't think that . . . minorities should be participating or in the occupation at all—that architecture was not something that African Americans or Puerto Ricans had the ability to aspire to."

But Manning was the most outspoken in describing racial discrimination within the school. Having earned an undergraduate degree from Wesleyan University, he was the privileged son of elite African American professionals and was especially rankled at being stereotyped as inferior:

> I did not always feel . . . that either the white students or the professors there really took us seriously. I just didn't think that they felt that we were going to become architects and go into practice or do anything with the profession of architecture. These observations were apparent primarily in the design studios and the way that our design projects were evaluated, and the comments that were made. I often saw that the projects done by the minority students did not get the same reaction as a project that was done by a white student.
>
> William Manning

At 22 percent of the student body, female students had a greater presence than the ethnic minority recruits and were as economically privileged as the white male students. Yet Kirk Bowles reported that female students also experienced considerable discrimination, including harsh judgment from some studio critics. He recalled that "the then-dean of the school was not partial to having women in the classes or even in the school. He got himself into serious trouble by saying publicly that, in his view, women didn't belong in the school or in architecture at all." Bowles went on to say that the father of one of the female students was a major donor so, unfortunately for the dean, his remark had repercussions. Manning, who was equally outraged by racial and gender discrimination, described two comments by faculty that he considered offensive. One comment was to an ethnic minority student, and the other was to a female student:

> This professor commented to the female student—in the course of talking to her and evaluating her design project—that she ought to consider being a housewife, instead of an architect . . . I never saw a professor try and dissuade a male student or white student, but I saw them try and do that with the female students and minority students.

> William Manning

In addition to the general perception of being discriminated against, three cohort members related specific incidents of racial discrimination, which took on mythic proportions as other recruits retold the stories. One incident was reported by Derrick Burrows, who described attempting to strike up a relationship with a white student from the Midwest. After "a number of black and Hispanic students" socialized with this student at a bar near campus, Burrows said:

> He invited us one weekend to come for drinks . . . at his favorite bar. And we all agreed that we were going to go down there, and we all got into our cars and buses and walked and got to his favorite bar where he was going to entertain us and have us for drinks, and we walk into the bar and there's a great big confederate flag on the back of the bar that everybody can see as you walk in. And it was a very uncomfortable moment . . . I think that was the worst moment at Columbia.

> Derrick Burrows

Another incident that became part of the ethnic minority recruit's folklore was narrated by Hamilton, who described an experience of being stereotyped as underprivileged:

> One of the professors . . . offered me a job . . . building a log cabin on Long Island. I thanked him and told him that, "No, I couldn't work for free anywhere." And just that to be working on log cabins—I wanted to get involved with working on something in the inner city; I wanted to get involved with construction, maybe in the Harlem area. And his remark . . . to me at that time was, "I've given you an opportunity to taste steak, and you want to eat hamburger." To me, that was a remark that stuck with me, because my parents, my grandfather, was an entrepreneur, and we had a restaurant in Atlanta. And I had always had the best of food to eat. And so, by him thinking that he was offering me something that he thought I would not be able to get anywhere else, unless I took this job building these beach houses, I was so furious about it, I went to the dean. . . . And of course, the dean there, Dean Smith at the time, told me that I needed to just go back and do what I was doing, that I should be thankful that I was there because my parents were not paying one dime. So that was the kind of experience that stuck out in my mind. After that, I felt like, no matter what I did, I had to represent who I was. Just because I made a decision that I didn't want to work on log cabin beach houses and I wanted to work in the inner city, that I wasn't going to miss anything in life.

> Mark Hamilton

Retelling this story, Manning said that the professor "was trying to teach him how to eat steak instead of hamburger. And I just thought that was a very out-of-place comment to make. The comment assumes that a minority student doesn't know anything about steak." Jackson reported the third incident, describing the cruel comments of a teacher who apparently met with some ill fate in due time:

> I had one teacher—this was not in design studio, but it was in a perspective drawing class—and I basically couldn't understand something he was teaching and he said, "If you can't understand that, then there is something psychologically wrong with you." That stands out in my mind. All I have to say is that what I wished for this teacher happened. That comment, I think, was racially based, but there's no way of proving it. Because I don't know if

he spoke to other people that way. A lot of the architecture studio critics were equal-opportunity bashers. But this particular professor had a certain amount of venom in his statement.

James A. Jackson

You can well imagine how unsettling these incidents were to the ethnic minority recruits who experienced them, whether directly or indirectly by word of mouth. Their snowballing recruitment program had brought them into what had been the exclusive preserve of privileged white males, where insurgency had shaken loose old notions of white supremacy. Now these notions were seeping back in to reclaim the ivory tower. Understandably, the recruits did not willingly abandon their Italian Renaissance shantytown where they had their own separate desks and could work 24/7 to create "a real sense of possibility." No, the recruits did not walk quietly back down Avery's curving marble stairs and out its massive oak doors.

Going on the Offensive

BPRSFAO amassed an extraordinary power base within the School of Architecture as its membership mushroomed to include three administrators, seven faculty and staff, three alumni, and forty-four students. At the apex of the arc of insurgency, this extremely well-organized group was able to influence student admissions, faculty and staff hires, and the curriculum. However, when ethnic minority student enrollment plummeted, BPRSFAO became alarmed that the school's affirmative action efforts were coming to an end, whether due to financial limitations, lack of commitment, or outright racism. The organization went on the offensive, its strategy for keeping the recruitment program alive taking the form of demands—some unfortunately unfounded.

CHALLENGING THE DEAN'S SEARCH

The School of Architecture's first racial struggle occurred in reaction to an announcement by the external administrator that a dean search committee would be formed. In a fierce exchange of letters, BPRSFAO demanded that the university president include on the committee a "body" of five persons to represent its constituency and, along the way, aired grievances about central administration's heavy-handed management of the school.[63] Backing up its claims with meeting minutes, it accused the external administrator of deliberately distorting reality (or lying) in his communications to the school community about the search,[64] and it also accused the president of subverting a search in the planning division by unilaterally appointing a junior law professor as its part-time chairman.[65] When the president insinuated that the organization's pursuit of "narrow interests" could compromise the university's ability to attract a first-class leader to the job,[66] BPRSFAO shot back that its constituency had "broad-based" support in the Harlem community.[67]

The president did not concede to BPRSFAO's demand that he include a body of its representatives. Yet he ultimately appointed a thirteen-person search committee that included four of the organization's six nominees. He also appointed Professor Charles V. Hamilton,[68] the African American political scientist hired to fill one of Ford's endowed chairs in urban and minority affairs, a position that had made him one of the first blacks in the country to hold an endowed chair at an Ivy League university. As coauthor, with Stokely Carmichael, of the 1967 best seller *Black Power: The Politics of Liberation in America*, Hamilton was a highly visible public intellectual known for his advocacy of the black solidarity movement.[69] Surely no one could have been a better spokesperson for the interests of BPRSFAO and the Harlem community than Hamilton.

That the president appointed a search committee in which five of thirteen members (38 percent) were black and Puerto Rican spoke volumes to the respect BPRFSAO had garnered. It also foreshadowed the racial struggles that would continue as the arc of insurgency tumbled downward.

LODGING UNSUPPORTED COMPLAINTS

The School of Architecture's second racial struggle was instigated by the assistant to the dean for minority affairs, Hiram E. Jackson III, who proved an inexperienced executor of the BPRFSAO legacy. Hired with Urban Center funds early in the school's experimental operation, Jackson had earned undergraduate credits at the University of Michigan and at Columbia but held no degree. Yet his job description put him in charge of such upper-level academic tasks as supervising the research of ethnic minority students and evaluating their academic performance to ensure that the faculty treated them objectively.[70] Perceiving Jackson's inflated status, individual members of BPRFSAO began seeking counsel that he was ill equipped to provide. Among them were three students who complained to him about the PhD in Urban Planning program two years into his tenure, after he had built a reputation as a fierce advocate of black power.

Instead of verifying the students' complaints, Jackson passed them on as fact to the university president. In a five-page letter, he asserted that Rapkin was treating the students unfairly "*primarily on racial and ethnic grounds.*"[71] He also asserted that a subcommittee overseeing the program was not functioning and therefore was delinquent in making recommendations on student fellowships—the only accurate part of his letter, which unfortunately called attention to the dean's growing list of administrative blunders. Jackson demanded that Rapkin's advising of black and Puerto Rican students "be transferred *immediately* to another advisor or advisory group" and then offered several audacious recommendations on how the Graduate School of Arts and Sciences (GSAS) should operate the program.[72]

A response to Jackson's letter, drafted by the GSAS dean, indicated that the president should rebut the numerous matters of fact in the complaint and then agree wholeheartedly that the PhD in Urban Planning program had a range of problems, including a nonfunctional subcommittee and a student body that had outgrown the number of faculty advisers.[73] The GSAS dean proposed that the president assure Jackson that this part of his complaint would "have [his] continued attention, as well as that of the dean of the Graduate School."[74] And that is precisely what happened.

However, Jackson's damage to the Division of Planning did not end there. In addition to forwarding unsubstantiated complaints from students to the president, he was on the front lines of making demands that the recruits be treated differently. Arguing that ethnic minority students, himself included, had needs that entitled them to special treatment, he convinced the Admissions Committee that his undergraduate credits qualified him to enroll in the MS in Urban Planning program even though admission required a bachelor's degree.[75] Not satisfied with this concession, Jackson pushed further, convincing Dean Smith to ask university administrators to approve his hire as part-time assistant to the dean *and* part-time research assistant to Ben Robinson, while he was enrolled as a full-time graduate student. He further convinced Smith to ask the university for $5,000 above the school's budget to cover his fringe benefits.[76] As you might imagine, university administrators flatly rejected Smith's proposal,[77] but these absurd demands layered upon unfounded charges of racism attracted scrutiny of the understaffed Division of Planning. Hiram E. Jackson III, hired to advance ethnic minority affairs, unintentionally helped bring the end of the arc of insurgency ever closer.

Adopting New Rules

After Smith resigned, the faculty charged an ad hoc committee with revising the long-disputed interim rules.[78] Over the course of the year, the faculty debated new rules (written by the Planning Division Council) that laid out a governance structure and day-to-day operations. Notably, the new rules maintained the spirit of democratic governance, stating "that all segments of the School of Architecture should have as active participation in the affairs of the school as legal, educational, and practical considerations permit."[79] In particular, they contained four major wins for the now-vanquished insurgency. First, the new rules legitimized the school's internal divisional structure with its councils, chairmen, and director of an institute. Second, they legitimized the part-time faculty, who could be nominated as voting officers of instruction if they had "demonstrated deep commitment to the educational goals of the school and becoming involved in its day-to-day operations."[80] Third, they legitimized student participation in subcommittees (and voting on preliminary decisions). And fourth, they legitimized an ethnic minority student and faculty presence in the school, specifying their representation on all standing committees.

Notwithstanding these considerable wins, the new rules re-centralized authority. The broadly representative, division-based Executive Council and the faculty caucus, which had been convening monthly, were replaced by a Committee on Instruction. The dean would chair this all-powerful committee of elected faculty and students, which would control all the other standing committees. The full faculty would return to meeting just three times annually to ratify the reports of standing and ad hoc committees, and the dean would maintain ultimate authority for the budget. In short, the new rules specified participative governance within a decision-making structure emanating from the dean who, apart from the university administrators, remained the school's sole statutory administrator.

On May 12, 1971—almost exactly three years after adopting the "May 17th Resolution"—the faculty reconvened its sixty-seventh meeting. Professor Mario Salvadori—who had once vowed that "he would resign and the faculty would be destroyed if the [interim rules] were disregarded"[81]—gave the new rules a symbolic stamp of approval, offering a motion that they be adopted with the understanding that a new dean could initiate revisions. After the usual wordsmithery, the motion barely passed (six in favor, four opposed, four abstentions). Progressing immediately forward, the faculty referred to the new Committee on Instruction a proposal to convert the undergraduate professional degree program in architecture to a graduate program.

And so ended the School of Architecture's experimental operation as its arc of insurgency hit rock bottom. Now the school would begin transitioning to a future where things would be "as they used to be"[82]—but not before the BPRFSAO made a last-ditch effort to prevent the great oak doors from slamming shut on the ethnic minority recruits.

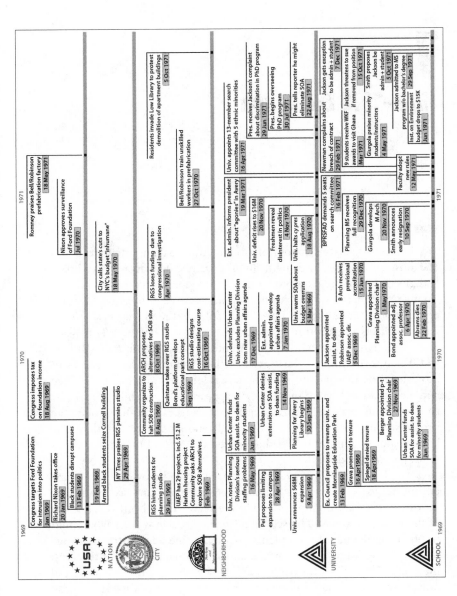

Figure 22. This timeline schematizes the events that occurred along the arc of insurgency from its peak in 1969 to its extinction in 1971. (For a larger version of this image, download the file at http://fordhampress.com/media/mconnect_uploadfiles/s/u/sutton_art_1.zip.)

7

1972–1976 Extinction

The pressure at the School of Architecture to find a new dean was unspeakable, and it came from all quarters. The accrediting board had given the architecture program just two years to fix serious administrative malfunctions, the external administrator had threatened receivership should the search for a new dean fail, and the university president had leaked his intention to eradicate the school altogether. The Black and Puerto Rican Student-Faculty-Administrators Organization (BPRS-FAO) had turned up the heat even further, mounting fierce battles to protect its constituency from extinction as scholarship funding vanished and old notions of white supremacy reappeared. Meanwhile outside the gates of Columbia's ancient Athenian agora, a fiscal crisis had stoked the fires of social conservatism both nationally and locally, extinguishing the humanistic sensibilities that had anchored the School of Architecture's social justice agenda.

Though the school's experimental operation had provided untold opportunities for a record-breaking number of ethnic minority recruits, its shortcomings were undisputed—and the recruits had been vocal critics of those shortcomings. The school needed a miracle worker who could fix its many debilitating problems—its byzantine administrative structure, ongoing internecine warfare, and occasional cretin-like teaching methods. The school needed someone who could put an end to the university administrators' heavy-handed management of its day-to-day affairs. More urgently, the school needed someone who could secure accreditation for the architecture program. As you will see, the dean search produced just such a miracle worker who undertook sweeping changes with the speed of light. However, you should keep in mind that these changes happened within a society that had turned away from the dream of educational equity that had propelled the recruits into the school. The changes fixed very real problems, but they also distanced the school from the realities of race and poverty, thus propelling the recruits back out of the school. By the time the accrediting board gave the architecture program its stamp of approval in 1976, the ethnic minority recruitment program was well on its way to extinction.

Dismantling a Dream

With the BPRSFAO standing guard to make sure central administration followed democratic procedures, a do-or-die dean search got underway. The president chose wisely in picking Alexander Kouzmanoff to lead the committee. Kouzmanoff was hired in 1952 during the school's Beaux-Arts era, but he was also in Avery the night of the bust, helping the insurgents move the school toward its transgressive era. A practicing architect, chairman of the architecture division, and a favorite among students, especially the ethnic minority recruits, he knew his way around academic minefields.

Cognizant of explosive internal and external pressures, Kouzmanoff seized the moment, preparing an elegantly worded letter to the president that probed the parameters of the search. He asked about the particulars of the job (salary, responsibilities, starting date) and the search (timeline, selection procedures, budget). He also asked about the school's long-range future as well as its prospects for growth and for influencing campus planning. In short, Kouzmanoff politely demanded to know what the school had to offer that would entice a strong candidate to the job.[1] He ended his letter by inviting the president (or the external administrator) to attend a committee meeting as soon as possible.[2] With his well-mannered prose, Kouzmanoff threw down the gauntlet, demanding that university administrators commit to a strategic direction for the school—a commitment they had sidestepped with Dean Smith.

The approach worked. For the first time, the dean search ended not only in a choice candidate but also in an acceptable contract offer. A little over a year later, in spring 1972, James Stewart Polshek was named to succeed Smith as dean. Polshek had been a reluctant candidate, but committee member Max Bond persuaded him to apply.[3] An uncanny curator of talent, Bond believed that Polshek had the requisite miracle-worker personality and portfolio. He was good-looking and younger than the other tenured faculty. He had a winning smile and the signature bowties that seemingly all successful architects wear. He had the assertiveness of a Yale alumnus with a blossoming reputation among the upper echelon of the New York City design community. Yet he also had the humility of a midwestern native that would help him navigate the perverse politics of the school and university.

To secure Polshek as dean, university administrators reversed all the off-putting policies that had eliminated other distinguished candidates in past years. Recognizing the need "to try first for something more than a manager to reclaim our school,"[4] they met all of Polshek's conditions of acceptance. With dean designate Polshek in attendance, Mario Salvadori drew upon his skills as a spellbinding lecturer to lead the faculty in a tribute to Smith at his last faculty meeting, noting that "it is with infinite gratitude that we remember the role paid by Ken in the transformation of the school."[5] Not everyone may have agreed with the tribute; nevertheless, this typically quarrelsome faculty rose in unison to applaud Smith as the doors began closing on the ethnic minority recruits.

Dean Polshek's Rapid-Fire Changes

Dean Polshek undertook a slew of changes that completely revamped the school's identity and degree offerings, some transpiring effortlessly, others causing a great deal of angst. The "dowry" of his hire included new faculty lines, a graduate professional degree program in architecture, access to the endowments that were on hold, time for his own practice, and an appointment as the president's adviser on campus planning.[6] These perks in hand, Polshek moved to address the school's most urgent malfunction: architecture's provisional accreditation.[7]

Just before Polshek was named dean designate, a subcommittee of the accrediting team had returned to review the program's progress; its speedy return confirming the graveness of the situation. Unfortunately, the follow-up visit occurred at an inauspicious moment when almost half the architecture students had received warning letters about their performance during the design studio meltdown that had eluded the initial team. Observing the programmatic disarray, the subcommittee added to the board's initial request other requirements related to the curriculum, budget, and staffing. Polshek moved swiftly to alleviate the board's concerns, issuing a report that described a reorganized curriculum, new faculty lines, immediate and long-term facility upgrades, faculty salary increases, and a close working relationship with the university president on campus planning. After university administrators toned down some of Polshek's claims of success, they dispatched his report to the accrediting board president, who unhesitatingly lifted the program's provisional status. With outside oversight in abeyance, Polshek proceeded with a change that had devastating consequences for the ethnic minority recruitment program—eliminating the undergraduate degree.

ELIMINATING UNDERGRADUATE EDUCATION

Polshek made a strong case for converting the undergraduate degree in architecture into a graduate degree, arguing that it would bring the architecture program in line with other East Coast architecture programs at Harvard, MIT, the University of Pennsylvania, Princeton, and Yale. Citing escalating costs as the most compelling reason for the conversion, he worked with the all-powerful Committee on Instruction to reconfigure the five-year bachelor's program as an intensive three-year master's program. Polshek's move toward "new ideas in [graduate] education"[8] also brought about a reassessment of the evening program, which the 1970 accrediting team had lauded both in terms of its design excellence and because it provided "an important alternative for disadvantaged students."[9]

Polshek appointed an ad hoc committee to evaluate the evening program, which determined that it exhibited "a general feeling of lower status"[10] and was thus incompatible with the move toward graduate education. Ignoring the implications to low-income students, the committee (with Bond's blessing) recommended that the program be closed. To alleviate concerns about "students unable to afford the necessary time and money to complete their studies in three years,"[11] the committee also proposed a graduate work-and-study program with attendance during summers and evenings. The faculty voted to close the old evening program but never proceeded with its replacement.

Polshek then proposed, and the faculty supported, renaming the school as the Graduate School of Architecture and Planning (GSAP), eliminating the tiny Division of Architectural Technology, and creating an MS in Historic Preservation for a program that opened in 1964 but lacked a distinct degree.[12] With these changes, Polshek inadvertently restructured GSAP as the preserve of an elite student body—one that would not include the ethnic minority recruits. Another round of changes would further distance GSAP from its momentary moorings in social justice.

ELIMINATING COMMUNITY ENGAGEMENT

With graduate education firmly in place, Polshek set about firing and hiring faculty. He asked for the resignations of two untenured faculty, both
favorites of the recruits. One was Victor F. Christ-Janer, lauded by James
Hamlin for replacing reviews with roundtables and for taking "the whole
class out to dinner at a Chinese restaurant . . . on an informal basis." The
other was David Seader, the school's second African American faculty
member, described by Craig Shelton as "a really cool guy who could
relate to us because he was just as radical, I guess, as we were." In their
stead, Polshek appointed two tenured faculty members with Ivy League
pedigrees and used his vast professional network to recruit three young
turks with budding reputations. Together these five new faculty members
helped eliminate the social justice vision Abrams had put in place, which
was already in jeopardy due to snowballing problems in the Division
in Planning. Chester A. Rapkin's resignation put these problems over
the top.

An extremely popular teacher, Rapkin was running the PhD in Urban
Planning program almost single-handedly by 1973, advising sixteen of the
eighteen students who were at candidacy level.[13] And though he never
chaired the division, university administrators frequently called upon him
for personnel advice as if he were the chairman, due to his stature in the
field and longevity in the division. A two-year Urban Center grant to the
institute to inventory Harlem's housing stock had produced two doctoral
dissertations and a master's thesis. However, after four years, Rapkin still
had not produced a final report, which put the institute's grant management under scrutiny by the Urban Center.[14]

Rapkin asked Polshek for a sabbatical leave, arguing that he needed
to be "free of teaching obligations for the semester"[15] to complete this
report and other institute research projects. However, prior to Polshek's
arrival, university administrators had already written off the institute due
to Rapkin's failure to bring in external funding, but more importantly
due to the institute's now out-of-fashion commitment to addressing the
problems of race and poverty. In correspondence among themselves, they
had noted the impediment the institute posed to achieving the university's color-blind vision of urban studies, noting that "the university's
commitment to research in problems of urban environment, both locally
and comparatively, is not represented by the institute. Perhaps, it is even
thwarted by the institute, given the close connection with the School of
Architecture. More interdisciplinary involvement in this area of research
might be encouraged by another vehicle. . . . In addition, the institute

has caused conflicts, some destructive, others constructive, between those interested in a full pursuit of knowledge in this area. A different apparatus, less attached to one school, might minimize the destructive aspects of this conflict."[16]

When university administrators were negotiating Polshek's dowry, they likely indicated that he could eliminate the institute and make a fresh start in establishing a research agenda.[17] Certainly this would be the sort of perk a dowry would include. Perhaps Polshek communicated this intention to Rapkin, or perhaps Rapkin perceived that research priorities were not shifting in his favor. In any event, Rapkin resigned six months after Polshek's arrival to accept a position at Princeton. His departure freed Polshek to eliminate the institute and the Urban Action and Experimentation Program (UAEP), the school's interconnected applied research and community outreach programs that had been a home base for the ethnic minority recruits. In their place, he established what would become the Temple Hoyne Buell Center for the Study of American Architecture[18]— an institution far removed from the gritty realities that were becoming ever more urgent in Harlem.

Resistance to Change

Polshek's rush to fix the school's problems responded to urgent internal and external pressures, but his shortcuts in democratic governance stirred up grievances among faculty, students, and even some university administrators. Protesting their lack of meaningful involvement in formulating new initiatives, faculty complained about being asked to vote on ad hoc committee proposals without having written information to consider in advance, about the lack of student involvement in governance, and about exclusionary Kinne Award policies that seemed to violate the donor's contractual agreement. They pressed for more frequent, informal meetings so they could discuss changes prior to the rapid-fire formal faculty meetings.

After Polshek (still only dean designate) notified the untenured faculty that their appointments would not be renewed, he got a taste of the leap-frogging skills that students and faculty had honed over the years. Accusing Polshek of "totalitarian approaches and arbitrary decision making,"[19] faculty wrote letters of dismay to university administrators and students threatened to seek relief from the University Senate. Polshek made some concessions but stood his ground on major changes, with strong backing from central administration. However, university administrators had their own concerns about his decision-making shortcuts. In particular, they admonished the new dean about what they perceived as his do-then-ask-forgiveness approach, including making faculty appointments in violation of university statutes,[20] listing degree programs in the school's bulletin that had not been approved by the University Senate,[21] and making decisions about the PhD in Urban Planning program without approval of the Graduate School for Arts and Sciences (GSAS).[22] At a meeting held to issue statutory approvals for last-minute changes in GSAP, a Senate committee summed up its exasperation with the school's rule breaking: "We note that very strong feeling was expressed . . . about the extent to which the School of Architecture has announced decisions, published bulletins and brochures, and then asked for statutory approval by this committee and by the Senate."[23]

A Diversion from the Inevitable

Admonishments aside, GSAP was barreling ahead and a $5.4 million expansion of Avery Hall diverted attention from the unpleasantness of change and toward long-awaited improvements in the school's facilities. An ad hoc committee chaired by Polshek laid out a program that called for both new and renovated space. In an ingenious scheme, a grassy quadrangle formed by Avery Hall, two other academic buildings, and St. Paul's Cathedral would be excavated to a depth of twenty-seven feet to create subterranean space. Designed by Kouzmanoff, who hired three recent graduates (this author included) to assist in his office, the first below-grade level would house a library containing the world's most significant assemblage of books on art, architecture, and archaeology. The library was to have large light wells penetrating a new brick-paved quadrangle, but those wells would eventually be eliminated due to waterproofing concerns. The second below-grade level would house new classrooms, offices, galleries, study areas, and a large auditorium containing the university's most advanced audiovisual equipment (see 12/2/16 23). In addition to this newfound space, extensive renovation of the existing sixty-two-year-old Avery Hall would create redesigned studios and administrative offices.

According to Polshek, Avery's expansion would "contribute to [the school's] ability to train a new generation of architects, urban designers, and top professionals with a concern for intelligent use of the environment."[24] Ingenious though it was, the completed expansion would not contribute to the planning division's ability to expose students to an increasingly out-of-fashion social justice agenda. Nor would it contribute

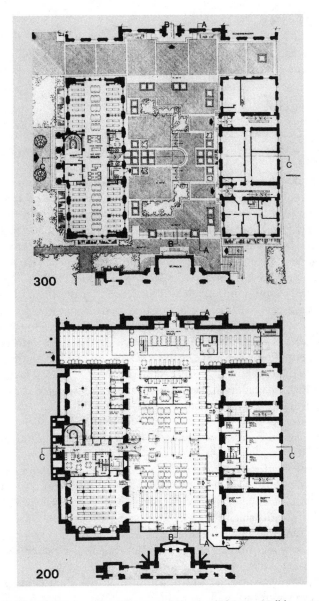

Figure 23. This photo shows how Kouzmanoff expanded Avery Hall by creating two subterranean levels under a quadrangle located to the east of the building. The plans for the 300 level (showing the existing library and new brick-paved quadrangle) and 200 level (showing the new subterranean library space) were drawn by the author. The plan for the 100 level (with new subterranean classroom space) was drawn by another recent graduate. (Photo courtesy of Sharon Egretta Sutton.)

to the advancement of the ethnic minority recruits who fought a losing battle against the changes that eventually eliminated them.

Dean Polshek's Encounter with Race

Prior to Dean Polshek's arrival, the Division of Planning had "one of the most active and successful programs in the university involving minority students."[25] The division succeeded in recruiting and retaining ethnic minority students despite having gaping holes in its faculty, despite being pressured to provide specialized planning courses to students in other divisions, despite teaching community-engaged studios that were labor-intensive and often political minefields. Its commitment to affirmative action was evidenced by an ethnic minority enrollment that peaked at 22 percent during the 1975–76 academic year.[26] It was evidenced by the many new courses the division developed that focused upon planning for minority communities.[27] It was evidenced by the financial support the division secured for ethnic minority recruits from the Urban Center, the Mellon Foundation, and the Leola W. and Charles Hugg Trust. It was evidenced by the internships the division arranged with the U.S. Department of Housing and Urban Development (HUD), the New York State Urban Development Corporation, the New York City Department of City Planning, and the Architects' Technical Assistance Center. The planning division had excelled in recruiting ethnic minority students, offering financial support, a relevant education, and real-world work experiences, while also engaging recruits in service to the surrounding communities.

Polshek envisioned that the planning division would continue its commitment to educating culturally responsive city-making professionals. In his five-year plan, he declared that "the student body [should] reflect the community with which the profession must work and on whose welfare it may so directly impinge. This means, for the Planning Division of Columbia, active recruitment of eligible black, Spanish-speaking, other minority, women, and financially poor students."[28]

This commitment came with a major liability. With its larger percentage of ethnic minority students and more aggressive engagement in urban and minority affairs than the architecture division, the planning division became a hotbed of racial conflict. When ethnic minority recruitment ebbed and UAEP vanished into thin air, Polshek became the bull's-eye in this conflict. Calvin Page recalled a volatile encounter early in Polshek's tenure:

I was, as I said, the head of the black student group and we had some complaints, and I forget what the complaints were, you know, this, that, and the other. And so we took them in to our new dean who was James Stewart Polshek, you know. . . . There's a list of demands and we went in there and I was the leader and I had my little group in there and you know, also, what was supposed to happen was we were supposed to have these negotiations, you know. And this wasn't something we'd call and say, you know, like, "let's have a negotiation at three o'clock," or something, you know. I mean, we stormed into his office, you know, and he was, therefore, you know, required to sit and listen to our demands and then he was gonna be required to negotiate or else, you know? So we had one of those little events and I'll never forget—he didn't want to budge. And so then, you know, me being the militant, I started giving him all the background and what those terms mean and all that, you know. I said, "Well, you know, we're gonna have to create a boycott/shutdown, you know, and in other words, we're gonna to shut this place down, you know, starting with you. You know, you're not going anywhere." You know, we were gonna keep him in his office, you know, and we had the numbers behind us and whatnot. I'll never forget that moment . . . Lou Schiller . . . almost panicked. I mean, she was like, "Oh my God, no!" you know, she said, "Please!" And I'll never forget, instead of her trying to ask me to back down, she asked Jim 'cause Polshek was new. I mean, when I say "new" I mean relatively new. I mean, he had just gotten there—I mean we were only there for two years or so, but you know, she was like, "Jim, no! no! no! Let's just wrap this up."

Calvin Page

Getting Dean Polshek's Attention

After that near disastrous encounter with Polshek, BPRSFAO took a more reasoned approach, seeking legal assistance to get action on its demands. At the end of Polshek's first year, two black female planning students registered complaints with the organization, one who received an incomplete in a course and another who did not receive a Kinne Award. The woman who received an incomplete claimed that, after the instructor said she had passed the course, the acting chairman notified her that she would receive an incomplete until she carried out makeup work. The woman who did not receive a Kinne Award claimed that she was in a class that was "almost fifty percent black in a white university that sits in the heart of a black community"[29] but that no black students had received the award.

The BPRSFAO cochairs registered these complaints with Polshek and, when he did not respond, they contacted a Harlem attorney who had just been elected councilman for city's Fifth District and who was known as the "people's lawyer" for his dedication to Harlem clients.[30] The attorney reiterated the complaint, copying his letter to Polshek to the city's top black leaders, and also to various university officials. With that salvo, BPRSFAO had gotten Polshek's attention; he knew he could not simply ignore this determined and politically astute organization.

Racial tensions escalated during the next academic year, due to decreasing financial aid and waning recruitment efforts. The BPRSFAO cochairs registered another complaint with Polshek, demanding scholarship support and university-sponsored married student housing for its constituents. This was the first complaint that shifted away from seeking fairness for individual students and back to the compelling societal reasons for achieving educational equity that had underpinned the insurgency. Noting that, though a laissez-faire attitude pervaded the larger society "in regards to the enrollment of minority and low-income students . . . the crisis that pushed the need for affirmative action programs is still with us."[31] The cochairs then challenged Polshek to ensure that the school had the human and intellectual capital to address that crisis, declaring that "the Graduate School of Architecture and Planning educates those professionals who should be in the forefront of confronting and resolving the mass of social and economic inequities that continue to plague our society. Thus talent and diversity are critical to this school's life. Lack of opportunities for [the] minority and non-affluent to attend this school automatically places this school outside the leadership arena in urban development and societal growth."[32]

Again BPRSFAO had gotten Polshek's attention, and he responded with grace. His approach was one of evenhandedness in uncovering the facts before attempting to adjudicate conflicts. He met for two hours with BPRFSAO officers in the attorney's "Striver's Row" offices in Harlem, discussing the charges lodged by the two black female planning students. He got valuable information from a student services staff member who conducted a third-party investigation of the situation. He charged the "angel of mercy" Loes Schiller with developing statistics on the distribution of scholarship awards. Armed with the facts, Polshek then set about negotiating concrete solutions that considered multiple perspectives. He was firm in discussing the maltreatment of black students with the planning faculty and their culpability in sending those students conflicting messages. At the same time, he supported the faculty's right to evaluate student performance. Once the woman who had received an incomplete made up her work to their satisfaction, Polshek arranged for her to receive a Kinne Award, which mollified the second woman who was concerned that no black students had received the award.

After learning that the school's assistant dean for urban and community development was fanning the flames of some of the student discontent, Polshek fired him, hired a replacement, and charged her with addressing the discontent. He also initiated conversations with the director of university housing to secure an increased allocation of married-student housing for the school. And he shared Schiller's statistics on scholarship awards with BPRSFAO. The data revealed that, at a little over 14 percent of the total student population, ethnic minority students had received 41 percent of the available financial aid.[33] After explaining that support for all students had decreased due to decreased funding and increased tuition, Polshek cautioned BPRSFAO leaders that the school had obligations to support "other highly qualified candidates who are Caucasian, Asian, and from other foreign countries."[34] Nevertheless, he committed to continue the financial aid discussion with them.[35]

In addition to evenhandedness, Polshek demonstrated a capacity for laughing at himself, chuckling while saying that, in responding to the recruits' complaints, "I mumbled and stumbled to such an extent that I even began to laugh at my own unusual inarticulateness."[36] However, Polshek's volatile encounter with race eventually dissipated due to a precipitous decline in the number of ethnic minority students. When the accreditation team returned in 1976, it noted that the graduate architecture program attracted middle- and upper-middle-class students capable of paying high tuition. Female enrollment had climbed to 33 percent from 19 percent in 1970, making leadership on gender diversity in architecture education one of Polshek's most notable accomplishments. However, ethnic minority enrollment had declined to fewer than 10 percent, including an increased number of international students of color rather than the historically marginalized U.S. ethnic minority students.

In the face of a declining ethnic minority presence, Polshek appointed a succession of four black urban planners as assistant deans for minority and urban affairs. Though Abigail Abruña noted that they were "instrumental in sort of pulling us together as a group," the appointments were too little, too late. Graduate school status, rising tuition costs, and the absence of the institutional recruitment and fund-raising strategy that Urban Center director Frank Williams had urged ultimately stamped out the school's audacious attempt to educate, in significant numbers, ethnic minority students.

Dean Polshek's Encounter with Elitism

The planning division's engagement in urban and minority affairs reflected an extraordinary commitment to recruit and retain a culturally diverse population.[37] It also reflected an orientation to engage students in addressing the "problems of racial discrimination, poverty, injustice, pollution, sexism, and democracy because these are the real problems of cities."[38] At the outset of Polshek's tenure, the ethos of graduate education in an elite research university would stifle the division's orientation toward hands-on engagement with real urban problems.

GSAS's review of the PhD in Urban Planning program began collegially enough under Smith's leadership. A subcommittee, whose members were all closely affiliated with the profession of planning, had determined that the program was in good health in 1972. However, after Rapkin's resignation left only one tenured faculty member in the division to advise thirty-two doctoral students, GSAS administrators "discouraged" applications, creating a crisis. After a year's delay, GSAS administrators appointed a new subcommittee without consulting Polshek about its membership. Unlike the profession-oriented initial subcommittee, the new one consisted entirely of theoreticians who were unfamiliar with planning as a profession. Furthermore, what had started as the review of an *existing* doctoral program morphed into the formation of a *new* program.

By this time, Polshek had recruited Peter Marcuse[39] from UCLA to rebuild the program from the ground up. Marcuse had earned a PhD in social policy planning at UCLA and had also worked as an attorney in housing, labor, and real estate law, so he brought a distinctive vision of planning to Columbia—one not dissimilar to the vision Abrams brought ten years earlier. Marcuse became the point person, along with Polshek, in negotiating with an increasingly hostile GSAS subcommittee.

The main points of contention between GSAP and GSAS centered on the degree to which the new program should be independent of, or embedded in, existing social science programs and, relatedly, who should teach the all-important research methods courses. Marcuse argued that the new program could not rely upon other disciplines because it needed the "specific problem-solving and intervention-oriented approach required by planning." He envisioned drawing a core faculty for a new, high-quality professional program from the Faculty of Architecture. GSAS administrators—who frequently referred to the school by its old name rather than as the Graduate School of Architecture *and Planning*—disagreed. They chastised the Marcuse/Polshek team for failing to identify expertise in other departments, demanding that the team search campus-wide for possible collaborators.

Over time, the gap between these conflicting visions of the new urban planning doctoral program hardened. Then one of the ad hoc committee members belatedly "discovered" the planning division's statement of philosophy.[40] In contrast to academia's elitist traditions of neutrality, the statement unabashedly declared "a shared concern for social justice" and a "desire to alleviate the acute social problems caused by inequitable income distribution; racial, ethnic, and sex discrimination; ineffective democracy; restraints on individual growth and freedom; and pollution of the physical environment."[41] Seemingly unaware of the threat it posed to the status quo, Polshek incorporated the statement into GSAPs five-year plan and presented it to university administrators.

Upon discovering the statement, subcommittee members inundated GSAS and university administrators with long letters saying it threatened "the search for truth that has until now been the *raison d'etre* of the university."[42] The parsing of the statement became so intense that GSAS administrators considered that "it would be an appropriate subject of university discussion and [asked] that it be taken up at an early meeting of the Thursday seminars on general education."[43] Had these letter writers known more about the planning profession, they would have realized that planners are obliged, by virtue of their social contract with the public, to "expand choice and opportunity for all persons, recognizing a special responsibility to plan for the needs of the disadvantaged and to promote racial and economic integration."[44] Lacking a professional practice perspective, GSAS administrators concluded that the planning division's ethical commitments were inappropriate in a university.[45]

Noting their "general lack of understanding of the role of planning or its substantive or methodological content,"[46] Polshek drew upon his extraordinary problem-solving skills as a practicing architect to address the problems that were blocking approval of the new doctoral program. Not only was every remedy he proposed (save one minor point) rejected by GSAS administrators, but GSAS administrators even refused to agree upon a target date for completing the review. The Marcuse/Polshek team had hit a "brick wall of technicalities . . . in [its] efforts to pump some life into a field which thrives on social consciousness";[47] however, just one week later it would hit the inner layer of this solid brick wall.

Attempted Hire of Frances Fox Piven

The Marcuse/Polshek team had agreed that the planning division would not be another technically oriented trade school "teaching the methods and canned knowledge whose conspicuous past failures were nowhere more evident than in New York City."[48] The division would, instead, explore new territory and challenge traditional planning approaches. Having agreed upon a focus and direction, the team set about recruiting Frances Fox Piven from Boston University, believing that she possessed the kind of forceful, broad-ranging perspective to help the division act upon its stated philosophy.[49] Piven had been a tenured member of Columbia's Faculty of Social Work when she used Ford funding to coauthor *Regulating the Poor: The Functions of Public Welfare*, an award-winning publication that is now in its second edition and still used in colleges and universities throughout the country.

Prior to relocating in Boston, Piven had been an inspiration for the ethnic minority recruits at the School of Architecture. James Hamlin recalled that she "kind of worked on [him] for a year and a half" to convince him "to come to Columbia" after meeting him at a conference in San Francisco. Philip Bertoli-Pearson recalled Piven's book and how she inspired the radical tactics he used to help Puerto Rican gang members bring about change in the streets of East Harlem:

> We were trying to make a statement, you know, with Frances Piven, she was a star, she was huge—she's a superstar in the welfare rights movement. She wrote a landmark book called *Regulating the Poor*. And she was a professor at Columbia who spent the whole year fighting Columbia because she refused to sign the contract because she had to sign a pledge of allegiance to get paid. She said, "No, that violates my freedom of speech." If you had such a radical professor, wouldn't you want to make change also?
>
> Philip Bertoli-Pearson

In July 1974, when university administrators learned that Polshek wanted to appoint Piven, they warned him in the strongest possible terms that doing so "might well threaten the continued existence of the doctoral program in urban planning." Ignoring this threat, and with the enthusiastic support of students and faculty in the planning division, the Marcuse/Polshek team submitted Piven's credentials to an ad hoc committee of GSAS in September 1974.[50] Nothing happened with the nomination for six months as the tug-of-war proceeded over the competing GSAP/GSAS visions of the doctoral program. Meanwhile, an ad hoc committee approved Marcuse's "especially difficult and delicate"[51] tenure appointment, freeing GSAS administrators to act upon the Piven appointment. Disgracefully, they set a deadline of just seven business days for receiving her peer review letters. Even more disgracefully, they sought letters from faculty in many different disciplines but none from faculty in social work, even though Piven had been tenured there and even though most of her peer-reviewed publications appeared in social work journals.

Piven's peer review letters, which were being written at about the same time as the ones objecting to the planning division's statement of philosophy, were remarkably similar to one another. In near unison, letter writers disparaged her dearth of scholarly publications, lack of systematic data collection, and partisan point of view, maintaining that she was engaged in political advocacy, not research. At least one person linked her candidacy to what he regarded as the "corporate view on public issues" expressed in the planning division's statement of philosophy.[52] He reasoned that "if Columbia University indeed wants this kind of program, Professor Piven seems qualified. If not, then I am doubtful about her qualifications."

The most outrageous response was from a reviewer who noted his difficulty in assessing Piven's credentials because "the urban planners have not succeeded in delineating their field; thus it is difficult for me to judge what they are qualified to do."[53] Whether the reviewer was referring to *all* urban planners or just to those at Columbia, this statement certainly provides ample evidence of Polshek's claim that the theoretician faculty who were empowered to recast the doctoral program lacked any understanding of planning as a discipline and practice. Notwithstanding its utter lack of qualifications in the matter, the ad hoc committee rejected Piven's appointment at its first and only meeting.

Dean Polshek's Line in the Sand

Dean Polshek spent five weeks preparing his response to the double whammy of having the doctoral program direction thwarted and the Piven appointment denied. In a no-holds-barred letter, he accused GSAS of stymieing the reasonable development of GSAP through the abuse of statutes and policies originally conceived to serve legitimate purposes, compromising the school and his ability to make the changes necessary for its survival.[54] He demanded—and got—a public statement of support from central administration for the Division of Planning, for the doctoral program, for himself, and for Marcuse. While disagreeing with Polshek that the ad hoc process was corrupt, central administration agreed that the membership of the ad hoc committee should be reconstituted with Marcuse's input and that a timely review would be completed so a full complement of ten students could be admitted in autumn 1976. More important, it yielded on a very significant point, admitting "a tendency to scrutinize the PhD degree programs of the professional schools with even more than the usual high standard of care, precisely because the Graduate School has less experience and perhaps less expertise in these areas."[55]

Apologies aside, the review of the PhD in Planning program proceeded and eventually its critics prevailed in upholding Columbia's elitist approach to doctoral education. This approach was not to educate change agents, as the planning division had been doing, but "to educate people who will 'make formal contributions to knowledge.'"[56] After the planning division adopted a thoroughly sanitized program description and statement of philosophy, GSAS administrators approved an incoming class of up to eight students. However, the division received only two acceptable applications, and GSAS was unable to offer any fellowship support as all its funds were "committed to programs already underway." And so ended the planning division's orientation toward addressing pressing urban and minority problems. The evolutionary arc of insurgency had returned to the status quo. The fiscal crisis buttressed the status quo even more securely, eliminating funding for the ethnic minority recruits and wiping out the kind of work most wanted to do.

Fiscal Crisis and the Dismantling of a Dream

Facing the prospect that New York State would accumulate a $1.5 billion deficit over a fifteen-month period, Governor Nelson A. Rockefeller proposed a budget in 1972 that included a $408 million tax increase, cutbacks in programs and services, and postponement of some debt payments. New York's fiscal crisis was due to the simple mathematics of expenditures that had risen 100 percent in five years, primarily for support of education and government programs, and tax revenue that had fallen by almost 30 percent in the previous two years.[57] Declaring that the Nixon administration would soon undertake "radical and revolutionary changes" to ease "the plight of the overburdened taxpayer,"[58] Governor Rockefeller laid the groundwork for the soon-to-come trickle-down policies of the Reagan administration. He made clear that New York's commitment to equal opportunity had resulted in the nation's highest combined state and local taxes, which if further increased would drive out the jobs and industries that buttressed the state's economy.[59]

A nationwide fiscal crisis resulted in a housing crisis, and at the core of the housing crisis was the energy crisis; New York City was especially hard-hit by this triple whammy. Due to the increased price of foreign oil that the city depended upon, New York's fuel and utility costs were twice those of other cities, accounting for 20 percent of monthly housing costs. Tenants could not afford to pay these higher rents, especially given the city's higher-than-average unemployment. However, landlords were also hit hard by increasing maintenance costs,[60] leading some to allow their properties to deteriorate, lease them to unsavory characters, or abandon them entirely. The energy crisis also increased construction costs, profoundly affecting the building industry. Rising construction costs combined with disappearing bond markets and shrinking investor capital to produce a significant decline in building starts, which meant that practically all the city's architecture firms were laying off staff. For example, the New York chapter of the American Institute of Architects estimated a 55 percent downturn in work over an eighteen-month period between 1973 and 1974.[61]

New York's fiscal crisis hit the ethnic minority recruits full force. They set out looking for entry-level employment just as architecture firms were hemorrhaging jobs, often facing the additional burden of workplace discrimination. Not only had the housing work vanished that most of them envisioned as the core of their careers, but jobs doing anything in architecture were practically nonexistent. Job prospects for those who lacked practical experience prior to entering Columbia were hopeless. The crisis heightened the recruits' awareness that they were leaving Columbia's ivory towers to enter a vastly different reality. Or as Jimmie Lee Jacobs put it, "Perhaps that social experiment at Columbia . . . doesn't transcend out into the workplace of even your most worldly cosmopolitan city like New York."

Disappeared Dreams of a Democratic Society

The no-new-taxes mode of governing—in combination with the energy crisis, lack of decent housing, and loss of blue-collar factory employment—would soon result in the devastation of poor communities across the nation. Black and brown ghettos in New York City and other postindustrial cities offered iconic images of the burnt-out, abandoned inner city that fueled the public's imagination about the "black 'welfare cheats' and their dangerous offspring" who were ripping off "overly generous relief arrangements."[62] The images came full circle to reinforce the prevailing no-new-taxes mode of governing. When a rumor began circulating as early as 1972 about an eighteen-month moratorium on public housing and interest subsidy programs, a national coalition of housing organizations descended upon Washington, D.C., in an attempt to revitalize the government's investment in housing.

The group issued a sharp rebuke of the Nixon administration's reported intention to "substantially curtail, if not totally eliminate, this nation's federal commitment to a decent home and a suitable living environment for every American."[63] The coalition complained that Nixon was unilaterally altering long-standing policies and programs, predicting that his cutbacks would lead to a return of the urban riots. The rumor gained traction over the course of the year as George Romney, the outgoing secretary of HUD, maintained that the government should get out of the housing business. Alarmed, a group of thirteen mayors, including John Lindsay, convened in Washington and issued a more expansive warning that "the loss of new housing would result not only in heightened inner-city tensions and frustrations but also in the loss of jobs and tax revenues."[64]

By 1975, New York City was losing twelve thousand units of existing housing stock annually to abandonment and tax delinquency, some of it not only sound but of irreplaceable turn-of-the-century quality. The fiscal crisis had also halted all new housing construction: "The magnitude of the housing disaster, in terms not only of shelter but of the destruction of neighborhoods, [could] hardly be grasped."[65] As an alarming gap developed between wages and the cost of shelter, many families began losing their homes, with small children becoming the fastest-growing segment of a rapidly growing homeless population.[66] Columbia's 1968 insurgents would have been enraged by such violations of the social and spatial fabric of the city, and likely they would have been motivated to take action.

However, according to a *New York Times* survey, a different type of student now attended the university. Interviews with a cross-section of the 705-member Columbia College class of 1974 found that, on the whole, the freshmen saw "little prospect for significant social or political reform and less cause for getting personally involved" in politics or movements,

nationally or on campus.[67] A few years later, the president's commencement speech confirmed this sentiment, declaring that students had grown
weary of social protest and were searching "for the half-forgotten joys of
an earlier time. . . . The decade of the 1950s, which our students now
find so fascinating, was an era of golden optimism for faculty and administrators as well. Those were the days before student unrest and profound
public skepticism. . . . During the intervening years all of us have had to
endure unanticipated anxiety and bitterness. We seem to have come out
on the other side far wiser, a bit sadder, and filled with nostalgia for things
as they used to be."[68]

A different type of student also attended GSAP. When the accreditation team returned in 1976, it found a changed architecture program. Its
report noted that Polshek had undertaken major changes and that central
administration, pleased with what he was doing, had provided him with
support both academically and financially. It also noted an overemphasis
upon design and the "heroic architect," and a student body with a voice
in their education but a passive outlook on the social world.

Within this changed context, the architecture students participated in
an urban design studio that functioned as a real-world planning office. In
"a deliberate departure from the usual imaginary schemes used as architectural school projects," students undertook actual city projects that had
been shelved due to the fiscal crisis.[69] The pedagogy in the new program
was unlike the empowerment approach taken during the school's experimental operation of helping poor communities formulate their own
solutions to problems; nor was it like Charles Colbert's earlier outreach
approach of offering services to various city and community clients. Instead, the new urban design studio modeled a Beaux-Arts atelier-style
pedagogy. Hidden away in Avery's attic—the space where BPRFSAO
once held meetings and Kinne awardees once mounted an exhibit of
their study tour to Ghana—gathered a distinguished jury consisting of a
city planning commission chairman, a builder, a lawyer, an architect, and
other professionals. The studio critic introduced the students' charge by
saying, "We want you to look at these as real projects, since that is the
way we have run the program—students taking on real work and hopefully providing solutions which the city in its present state can still afford
to carry out."[70]

Presuming the privilege of knowing how the proposals would work for
the affected communities, the jury used the students' projects as a spring-
board for debating theories of urban design. Over almost twelve hours,
they engaged in a highly theoretical insider debate, discussing such issues

as preserving old buildings versus clearing a site of existing buildings, focusing upon individual building needs versus a building's fit with its surroundings, and letting the city determine the direction of development versus letting the marketplace determine it, even debating the definition of urban design.[71] The students, decked out in the shirt-and-tie uniforms of the business world, received the executive training that would groom them as partners in large, white-owned architecture firms. During this high-level marathon simulation of real-world professional practice, students learned the social graces and cultural norms that would prepare them for practicing in elite society, though Polshek certainly did not perceive that eventuality. "I am very excited about the way this program has brought the realities of professional practice, of politics, of economics into the school. I don't want this program to have the aura of a finishing school."[72]

As Columbia students sought out the tranquility of an earlier era, the devastation of poor communities spread like fungus. Nevertheless, the worries of officials about a surge in inner-city tensions and rioting proved unwarranted as Nixon was on top of the problem. In his presidential campaign he had "explicitly called on voters to reject the lawlessness of civil rights activists and embrace 'order' in the United States."[73] Once elected, he enacted his law-and-order policy through a war on drugs, indiscriminately sweeping potential black and brown rioters into an unending criminal justice system—permanently disenfranchising them from voting or demanding equity. Many of the ethnic minority recruits had dreamed of using their city-making skills to help the poor revitalize their rat-infested but beloved communities. In the place of these dreams were violent scenes of SWAT teams raiding apartment buildings, moving their unemployed residents out of sight, into a growing prison population. The will to rebel against injustice had been broken. In its place was a "strange Proustian searching . . . for the half-forgotten joys of an earlier time."[74]

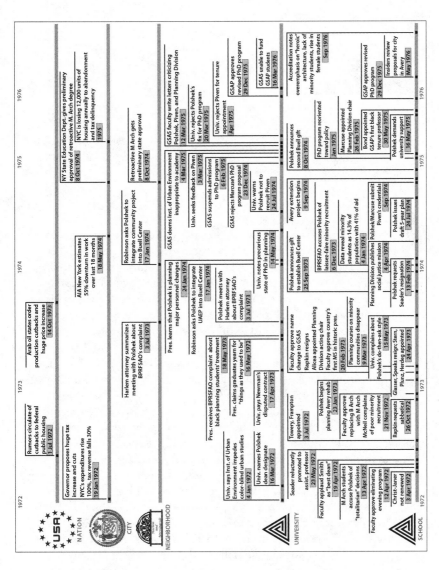

Figure 24. This timeline schematizes the events that occurred between 1972 and 1976 when society and GSAP turned away from the dream of educational equity that propelled the ethnic minority recruits through Avery's oak doors. (For a larger version of this image, download the file at http://fordhampress.com/media/mconnect_uploadfiles/s/u/sutton_art_1.zip.)

8
Alumni Years

Mark Hamilton graduated in 1978 as the last member of the oral history cohort to straggle out of Avery before its massive oak doors became all but padlocked for U.S.-born persons of color. He was among the twenty-six (out of a total of forty-nine) ethnic minority recruits who graduated after the fiscal crisis hit full force in 1973. Actually, the crisis began gathering steam in 1969 and overshadowed all of their early careers. The ethnic minority alumni left Columbia believing that their technical skills, intellectual prowess, and Ivy League pedigrees would surely heighten their marketability in America's newly desegregated workforce. Instead, Hamilton and his peers found themselves in overwhelmingly white city-making professions, equipped with the same education as their Caucasian counterparts, but having to prove themselves "over and over again."[1] Throughout their careers from the early 1970s into the beginning of the twenty-first century, they would witness precious little progress at the intersection of race, urban development, and higher education. The shift toward more conservative antigovernment ideas that the fiscal crisis birthed and Ronald Reagan accelerated[2] all but eclipsed the social progress they had witnessed as students.

With the ideals of black power disappeared, adaptation to white society necessarily defined the oral history cohort's careers. However, over a thirty-five-year period, societal limitations also helped them shape distinctive career trajectories that, in turn, informed new directions in city-making practice. Nor was social progress completely stunted. Not only did new opportunities for city-making practice emerge, but the innovations that occurred during the School of Architecture's experimental operation also lived on and, over time, informed best practices in architecture education and university/community relations. To understand the long-term effects of events past, you will need to enter the dark ages that descended upon the nation in the 1970s, stunting social progress within the city-making professions. You will also need to dig a little deeper into the peculiarities of the clannish field of architecture, because the idiosyncrasies of its professional culture are precisely what made access for the members of the oral history cohort so arduous, especially given the dark ages overshadowing the country.

A Dark Age for Social Progress

At the same time that the federal government dismantled its housing programs and reduced support for the development and maintenance of physical infrastructure, conservatives attacked affirmative action, leading to "major reductions in grants, scholarships, and guaranteed loans for underrepresented students."[3] As options vanished for achieving educational equity, and as black and brown rioters encountered an increasingly militarized police, the youth who had so inspired the ethnic minority recruits turned their frustrations inward to drugs and black-on-black crimes. Their deviance from an increasingly mean-spirited, mainstream society reawakened centuries-long stereotypes of black inferiority.

Working with the Urban Action and Experimentation Program (UAEP), the Architects Renewal Committee in Harlem (ARCH), and the Real Great Society in East Harlem (RGS/Uptown) during their school years helped the recruits understand how racial politics had affected their chosen fields,[4] allowing them to bring their professional studies together with their sense of cultural identity. The shift in mentality from empowering the colored masses to punishing them for being poor contributed to the demise of UAEP, ARCH, RGS/Uptown, and the many other community design centers that advocated for the disenfranchised. The disappearance of an empowerment approach to city making in the early 1970s thrust many of the ethnic minority alumni into a career-long struggle to negotiate a disparity between their professional aspirations and their aspirations "as people of color concerned about community."[5]

Lacking opportunities to work in communities of color, the alumni found themselves isolated—lone wolves in a white world. In contrast to

their heady experiences of camaraderie in Avery that buffered discriminatory behavior, they entered chilly city-making professions that were
totally absent an ethnic minority presence. In particular, the white gen-
tlemen's field of architecture remained a "pristine island, disconnected
from the social contexts and mundane realities of daily life."[6] Despite the
efforts to improve cultural diversity that Whitney M. Young, Jr.'s fierce
speech triggered at the 1968 American Institute of Architects (AIA) convention, architecture did not witness a growth in underrepresented populations anywhere near that witnessed in other professions like medicine,
law, and accounting.[7]

For example, in 2004, African Americans constituted a little over
12 percent of the population. However, they made up just 1.5 percent
of over one hundred thousand registered architects—among them fewer
than two hundred black women—and a mere 1 percent of the AIA's
fifty-two thousand members.[8] In accredited schools of architecture, black
faculty members numbered only about one hundred, with black students
constituting a mere 6 percent of the population—half of them enrolled in
historically black colleges and universities (HBCUs). Unlike the School
of Architecture's ethnic minority recruits, few of these students became
architects. Over 68 percent of black architecture graduates left the field
for other lines of work due to "a mix of reluctant patrons, unsupportive
majority firms, social attitudes, and low pay."[9] Clearly, racism plagued Columbia's black alumni, especially at the outset of the careers. As Jimmie
Lee Jacobs recalled:

> I could never figure out, especially early in my career, was there
> something wrong with me? Why weren't they hiring me? . . . I
> started to confer with some of the other kids that I went to school
> with at Columbia, and I wanted to know . . . was there something
> wrong with me? And they began to tell me, "No, it wasn't me; it
> wasn't me." . . . We're still treated grossly unequal and unfairly.
>
> Jimmie Lee Jacobs

Kevin Alexander Kersey, who had pursued advanced studies in London, also experienced racism as he sought employment early in his career:

> I could not get a job when I came back to the United States . . . I
> had leads on jobs. I mailed out close to four hundred résumés when
> I got back to the United States—and all rejections. That hurt. A
> lot. I had a few contacts and I went for a job interview that I heard
> about. I went, I told another fellow about it who's white. He got

the job; I didn't. That's when I stopped looking for work. That hurt a lot. That's America in 1975.

Kevin Alexander Kersey

The black planning alumni did not fare much better. With its roots in Progressive Era social reforms, planning has the explicit commitment to social justice that some Columbia officials found so unsuited to academia. The American Institute of Certified Planners (AICP) Code of Ethics recognizes planners' dual responsibility to address the needs of disadvantaged communities while also increasing the number of planners from underrepresented groups. An enrollment in 2009 of 12 percent full-time African American students in accredited planning schools reflected this ethic (though paling in relation to the peak in Columbia's planning division of 22 percent). However, higher up the ladder, less than 4 percent of APA (American Planning Association) and AICP members were African American. To address the field's low ethnic minority representation, APA held a national convention to explore barriers to demographic diversity and, according to James A. Jackson, its "African American and Latino members formed a committee to discuss . . . the shortage of our numbers in planning and what we could do to attract people or promote people in the planning profession." Limited opportunities for ethnic minority planners to advance as professionals surfaced as a serious problem—one that clearly affected Columbia's ethnic minority alumni as they tried to move into mid-level positions.

AIA also explored barriers to demographic diversity, commissioning a survey of thousands of practicing architects, architecture educators, interns, students, and non-licensed designers. By far the largest study ever conducted on the city-making professions, the survey revealed deeply entrenched barriers to ethnic minority representation, with social isolation and all its ramifications standing out as one of the most profound.[10] As "only ones" working in majority firms,[11] ethnic minority city-making professionals reported that they either learned to suppress parts of their identity or alternatively to draw upon flamboyancy—that is, "using one's visibility to establish one's presence in the minds of colleagues and clients."[12] In particular, African American architects complained of being closely scrutinized, of having to exert extra effort, of being rejected by prospective black clients in favor of majority architects, and of not having champions who could channel privileges and even ordinary opportunities their way.[13] Clearly, social isolation plagued Columbia's ethnic minority alumni.

The alumni who gained enough experience to establish their own firms encountered the triple bind of being certified to participate in government work. First, the set-aside programs gave their firms a revenue stream, but "the quality of their work . . . was often perceived to be inferior, whether they did a brilliant job or not."[14] Second, these projects had low budgets, "unadventurous clients," and a dearth of "opportunities to do pioneering work, attract attention, make the professional journals, and recruit the most talented staff."[15] Third, their firms were falsely perceived as not needing private work because they were overwhelmed with government contracts. But the nail in the coffin was a case in Washington, D.C., in which prominent white architects sued struggling black architects for pursuing a set-aside project, accusing them of "participating in a 'crass political process' in order to effect 'merit-based' architect selections."[16]

The social isolation of Columbia's ethnic minority city makers, their lack of opportunities for community empowerment, and their no-win relegation to government set-aside programs were magnified by their concentration within cities that had high ethnic minority populations. Not surprisingly given the country's racist history, cities with large ethnic minority populations also had "debilitating problems of vacant land and buildings, unemployment, and poverty . . . and even more crippling fiscal problems."[17] Put another way, cities that experienced the greatest disinvestment also had the highest average black populations, including Gary, Indiana; Detroit, Michigan; Cleveland and Cincinnati, Ohio; and Trenton and Camden, New Jersey.[18] Predictably, states with the most disinvested cities also all had a higher-than-average concentration of registered black architects, with Maryland being the highest at 4 percent. At the same time, booming cities like Seattle, Washington, and Portland, Oregon, had very low black populations and were predictably in states with a lower-than-average concentration of registered black architects (a mere 0.4 and 0.2 percent, respectively).

Thus Columbia's ethnic minority city makers were often working in "neglected places of poverty,"[19] unwilling witnesses to "a fatal combination of isolation, neglect, and intrusion"[20] in the marginalized communities of color in which many of them had grown up. There they struggled "with inferior resources and less glamorous commissions—in order to be accepted by clients on the same basis as majority firms."[21] And yet, as you will see, these alumni used the gift of their Ivy League education to beat the odds and achieve success in all sectors of the workplace, often crafting unique careers along the way.

Distinctive Career Trajectories

Here you will follow the cohort members through three stages of their careers: early, middle, and advanced, spending the most time on their advanced years. Your exploration will be mostly about career paths in architecture simply because, though one-third of the cohort members earned degrees in planning, only two of them chose to work solely in planning. As you will see, the achievements of the cohort require absolutely no disclaimer—they are worthy of what would be expected of the graduates of an Ivy League school of architecture. However, recognizing architecture's obdurate elitism, its 68 percent attrition rate for African American graduates, and its vulnerability to fiscal crises, you should be even more impressed.

Early Career Years during the 1970s

Though the late 1960s had catapulted the ethnic minority recruits into unimagined opportunities within Avery's Italian Renaissance shantytown, the 1970s thrust them back into a world filled with obstacles. Runaway inflation and high interest rates resulted in unemployment and a skyrocketing cost of living. National panic built as food and gas shortages punctuated ugly school desegregation and anti–affirmative action struggles in both the South and the North.

When President Gerald Ford denied New York City's plea for federal assistance to stave off impending bankruptcy, the front page of New York's *Daily News* carried the headline "Ford to City: Drop Dead," heightening the city's sense of panic. Though Ford would deny ever saying these words, his implication of a tough stance on the city's economic woes forced officials to make draconian cuts in services.[22] Within this context of national and local panic, one by one the ethnic minority alumni left the security of Columbia's ancient Athenian agora with little preparation for the world of work. Especially lacking was their understanding of the licensing process that controls entry into the city-making professions. As August André Baker explained, "I don't ever remember being encouraged to get [professional certification], being prepped for it. I don't remember there being classes or opportunities to take the exams, practice exams, or any of that." However, passing the Architecture Registration Exam (ARE) was as important to the career trajectories of the ethnic minority alumni as was earning their Ivy League degrees.

To become eligible for the ARE, novice employees must work for several years under a licensed architect, a period of employment that can be challenging under the best of circumstances. For recent graduates, especially those with minimal technical skills, "the architectural labor market most resembles the market for unskilled labor . . . low wages and high turnover."[23] Job security is nonexistent and assignments such as correcting working drawings and model building can be mind numbing. Further, industry expectations for speed and efficiency contrast with academic expectations for exploration, making the transition to work from school rarely graceful.[24] Add race and a fiscal crisis to the mix and you can sense what cohort members faced. However, as you will see, they demonstrated unflappable Ivy League ingenuity in navigating this challenging period. Some left the country, others were exceptional enough to rise above the fray, still others became rainmakers or shifted gears, with quite a few augmenting their incomes with part-time teaching.

NAVIGATING EARLY CAREER YEARS

Those who fared the best during their early careers were the five who went abroad, which allowed them to move into more responsible, nurturing positions than they would ever have gotten in this country. These cohort members returned to their homelands, set off to pursue their dreams of nation building in the newly liberated continent of Africa, or joined the Peace Corps. James A. Jackson recalled his superior experience when "I was in the Pacific in Micronesia and I was an architect there and I worked on low-cost housing and projects like that. And I even had a building built, which I haven't seen."

Seven cohort members were exceptional enough to find work despite the turndown in architectural employment. They either graduated with significant work experience, had a specialty that helped them "stand out from the crowd," or entered the job market after the crisis began to subside. However, William Manning managed to secure entry-level work even though he lacked experience and entered the job market at the height of the fiscal crisis, perhaps because his upper-middle-class background shielded him from the discrimination others encountered.

Unable to find satisfactory work as employees, three cohort members became rainmakers, generating their own jobs and then arranging for registered architects to supervise them. For example, Bruce Fenderson described the peculiar experience "of generating contracts and hiring a registered architect to work for me and then sort of studying under him while he was working for me, which was rather odd." Eight others simply shifted gears when faced with architecture's discriminatory practices and lack of work. They found work in planning agencies, went back to school to earn advanced degrees, went into construction, or took up landscape architecture. In explaining his shift of gears, James Hamlin said that he "interviewed at a lot of the big offices in New York City and found them to be just a bunch of stuffed shirts"—that is, he encountered a bunch of racists.

Then again, eight cohort members augmented their incomes with part-time teaching. Jimmie Lee Jacobs recalled being prompted to do so by a mentor who had asked, "'Why don't you go and teach?' I hadn't considered teaching and then I considered teaching, and eventually I was able to get a part-time job teaching . . . and that kind of stabilized me a little bit so I could pay my rent." These cohort members began teaching abroad or at HBCUs and urban institutions that had a reputation of being open to hiring ethnic minority faculty, including Pratt Institute in Brooklyn, the University of Detroit, UC Berkeley, and even Columbia.

Regardless of the path taken during the early years of their careers, cohort members had to navigate the difficult transition to work from school as "only ones," except for those who left the country. These novices were pioneers as the second generation of blacks to enter the city-making professions. Yet they were also burdened with penetrating the dark clouds of racism and unemployment that loomed over all corners of the city-making workplace.

PASSING THE ARCHITECTURE REGISTRATION EXAM
A primary function of entry-level employment in architecture is to "prepare for registration by performing a range of tasks under the supervision of a licensed architect."[25] At the time, the ARE had an outrageously low pass rate of less than 25 percent, with registrants sometimes retaking parts of the battery of tests year after year. Kirk Bowles described this extreme rite of passage:

> When you pledge, whether it's a sorority or fraternity, or the Marine Corps . . . you've crossed the burning sands, you've stood the test of time. And whether you're an African young man who has to go out and kill a lion with your bare hands, it's your transition to manhood or womanhood or adulthood or whatever applies. The registration exam was like that. It was a five-day exam . . . and the culmination was a twelve-hour one-shot exam requiring you to completely design a building.
>
> Kirk Bowles

Given the diversity of their entry-level jobs—and the lack of technical skills and exam preparation offered at Columbia—passing the ARE
became a bogeyman that blocked cohort members' transition to mid-
career. Eight decided not to go through with the exam, either because
they lacked the appropriate professional experience, decided to prioritize
their families, did not need the credential for the work they wanted to
do, or were derailed by Columbia's lack of attention to getting licensure.

Notably, however, twelve cohort members—50 percent—passed the
ARE, all of them African American (i.e., more than twice the national
pass rate). And three cohort members became doubly licensed in other
fields. Many of these licensed black architects recalled the rigors of the
exam. For example, James A. Jackson characterized it as "a tour de force";
Bowles said "it was hell . . . the most difficult exam that I've ever taken";
Mark Hamilton, who took the exam "over and over and over," complained that it did not test ability but rather required "a memorization of
things"; and Craig Shelton complained that the experience was "gruel-
ing . . . more than I think any other profession goes through in terms of
licensing." In contrast, Laura Marie Swain, who passed on the first try,
was ecstatic about the process:

> I had been a musician so I prepared as I would for any performance.
> I practiced over and over again until I could do all the tests perfectly.
> When I entered that room with all those rows of white men, I
> chuckled to myself thinking, "Okay, boys, just watch me 'break
> a leg.'"
>
> Laura Marie Swain

Clearly, passing the ARE required fortitude. That this small group produced twelve African American architects is nothing short of astonishing,
given the dearth of black architects nationally.

Middle Career Years during the 1980s

Reaganomics overtook the nation beginning in 1982. With unemployment at its highest level since the Great Depression, President Ronald
Reagan sought to stimulate the economy with large tax cuts. He also
froze minimum wages, slashed assistance to local governments, halved
public housing subsidies, and eliminated antipoverty community development programs, his policies widening the gap between rich and poor that
had first surfaced in the 1970s. Thus cohort members transitioned to

their middle years amid increased perks for the wealthy and heightened punishment for the impoverished. During their middle years, novice architects typically gain greater levels of responsibility, advancing based "upon experience, talent, dedication, and personal connections," but "the metamorphosis is slow and sometimes uneven."[26] Normally, individuals begin this period fundamentally undifferentiated from peers with an equivalent amount of experience and end with particular responsibilities that reflect their chosen career paths. Some architects become project managers, others develop specialties, and many "change offices or start their own office."[27]

However, cohort members' path was not typical or normal; they had already learned during their early years that they had to work harder to get the same rewards as their white peers. During their middle years, they discovered that advancement was even more restricted because it depended upon having mentors to help them build relationships and guide them into positions of responsibility. Not having mentors to channel "privileges and even ordinary opportunities"[28] their way meant, in Vernon Walker's view, that "it still wasn't very easy to get promoted—get your career off the ground." Nevertheless, all was not doom and gloom. Throughout the 1970s, opportunities had begun to emerge that blossomed during the 1980s. Most notably, the program the Johnson administration had established in 1968 to help minority-owned businesses was further advanced in 1978 by President Jimmy Carter, who signed legislation that supported the formation of minority-owned and disadvantaged small businesses.[29] This legislation enabled the set-aside programs that helped several cohort members establish their own firms, though with the aforementioned liabilities.

In addition, the energy crisis gave birth to the modern environmental movement and produced new energy conservation measures aimed at reducing dependence upon foreign oil. Legislation advanced by the newly formed Environmental Protection Agency greatly influenced the practice of architecture, creating new opportunities for cohort members to develop specialties related to reducing energy consumption—for example, in the adaptive reuse of buildings and use of passive solar energy. Furthermore, among the outcomes of the civil rights movement was the Architectural Barriers Act, the nation's first effort to mandate building accessibility for disabled persons. This legislation required that any facilities built or altered with federal grants or loans be accessible to all, which opened up another specialty that cohort members exploited.

Finally, the National Endowment for the Arts (NEA) Artists in Schools

program, which had been placing all sorts of artists in elementary and secondary schools since the 1960s, began placing architects in schools in the
1970s. NEA's Architects in Schools program proved a popular option for
teachers because of its unique combination of art and science, and soon
AIA and other organizations adopted the model: "Architectural residen-
cies provide[d] opportunities for teaching math and science, while allowing participants to make some functional and/or esthetic improvement in
the school environment."[30] These programs provided yet another opportunity for underemployed cohort members.

During their middle years, several cohort members began independent
practices, while others developed specialties or were recruited to government agencies. Despite the obstacles, some persisted in climbing the corporate ladder. Still others settled into academia.

NAVIGATING MIDDLE CAREER YEARS
Six cohort members began their own firms during their middle years,
choosing cities with large black populations, including Baltimore, Cleveland, Detroit, New York City, and Paterson, New Jersey. Sylvia K. Atkinson recalled why she made this choice:

> Realizing that I knew more than some of the people I trained who
> got promoted to management positions, and that I wasn't getting
> promoted to management and it didn't look like I was going to. . . .
> A woman, whom I had trained that I had brought into another
> firm, a white woman . . . was an associate and I wasn't, but I felt
> that I was just as aggressive as she was, and I was just as smart and
> I worked as hard, but I didn't feel that I was seen the same. And
> then when I looked around, there were many women who were
> becoming associates in the firms, but there were no black people,
> men or women, in New York City at that particular time.
>
> Sylvia K. Atkinson

Three of these entrepreneurs formed partnerships with more experienced architects. As Calvin Page explained, "I opened up in the old ar-
cade in downtown Cleveland and that was going fairly well except that
I had hoped to actually get some larger projects. So I decided to collaborate with a larger architect, in fact a black architect . . . [with] a fairly
prominent practice."

Emerging trends offered eight cohort members excellent opportunities for developing specialties. They became involved in the nascent envi-

ronmental movement, were drawn to the military's need to house a new type of personnel, and developed specialties in rehabilitation and energy conservation. As Laura Marie Swain explained:

> I had what I referred to as my "roof repair" practice. I did retrofits of school buildings for an engineering firm to make more energy-efficient windows and doors, roofs. I converted old buildings. . . . Sometimes I did small renovations so artists could live legally or illegally in abandoned industrial buildings. Whatever I could get. Once I even designed a solar house but the clients chickened out and it never got built.
>
> Laura Marie Swain

Others took advantage of affirmative action programs in government agencies. For example, Kirk Bowles accepted a government position where he worked "for about twelve years in the late seventies all through the eighties, [designing] housing for low-income urban people who could not have afforded it otherwise." He recalled doing "many projects here in California and around the country. I probably finished about four or five thousand units of housing."

Still others found a lifeline in the NEA's Architects in Schools initiative during their middle years. For example, Jimmie Lee Jacobs recalled participating in an AIA-funded residency in New Orleans:

> I did a three-year residency at a high school in New Orleans. . . . We tried to . . . expose students and teachers and administrators alike to the skills, knowledge, and nomenclature of the design professional. . . . What I attempted to do was to work with a group . . . of volunteer teachers in a variety of disciplines to show the applicability of a design professional's skills in their coursework, and at the same time try to affect some physical change aesthetically in the needs . . . of the school.
>
> Jimmie Lee Jacobs

However, John Little felt that exposing "kindergarten children through college age" to architecture was what he was supposed to be about "in terms of both reaching back and encouraging other folks . . . just trying to give them more of an advantage."

In contrast to the freewheelers, three cohort members tried working in large for-profit and nonprofit corporations during their middle years. However, only John LePoi—unimpeded by discrimination in Trinidad—

was right on schedule, moving up a traditional career ladder from entry level to, in his words, "increased responsibility and recognition, dealing with clients, a lot of supervision, being in charge of a small group." The other two struggled to advance, as Vernon Walker explained:

> I got frustrated with city planning because I found out it was one of the most political organizations in the city and it became very stifling because of the discrimination. I was rejected for about three or four promotions because—I'm very sure—because of discrimination, because I was also recommended for a couple of those positions by people who were on staff.
>
> Vernon Walker

Finally, six cohort members entered the academy full-time during their middle years, three armed with doctoral degrees. Most notable was Frederick Gutiérrez, who had enrolled in Columbia's PhD in Urban Planning program in 1969. He worked as a teaching assistant, research assistant, and then—when Rapkin resigned—interim chairman. As the program approached closure by the Graduate School for Arts and Sciences, Gutiérrez had the good fortune of being "invited to direct a research center—the Puerto Rican Research and Resources Center in Washington, D.C.—and also to begin planning a Puerto Rican college in New York City." He returned to Columbia and completed his doctorate before launching the new college and becoming its president.

Thus cohort members were able to move forward during the middle years of their careers, primarily by overachieving in comparison to their Caucasian peers, with half becoming licensed professionals (three doubly licensed) and seven earning advanced academic credentials. Superior qualifications, in combination with affirmative action and persistence in taking advantage of emerging trends, enabled their continued progress as lone wolves.

Advanced Career Years during the 1990s and 2000s

When President George H. W. Bush took office in 1989, he inherited a huge federal deficit. Though vowing not to change the trickle-down policies of his popular predecessor, ultimately Bush was forced to combine government cuts with tax increases.[31] Still, the deficit grew so that when President Bill Clinton took office in 1993, he famously promised to focus "like a laser beam" on the economy. To the horror of many of his supporters, Clinton adopted additional tax increases and expenditure cuts which, despite predictions of doom, succeeded in not only lowering the deficit but in creating a huge surplus.[32] Thus cohort members came into their own amid a booming economy, securing "significant commissions, public recognition, and a widening sphere of influence."[33] Eight wound up as firm principals, eight as administrators, two as planning officials, and six as academics. In addition to their appointments in industry, the government, and academia, three alumni developed distinction as fine artists.

Apropos their Ivy League credentials, Columbia's ethnic minority alumni won the respect of fellow city-making professionals, capturing awards and important commissions, administering large projects, founding programs, giving lectures, and assuming leadership positions within professional organizations. Yet practically all continued to seek an improved quality of life in disadvantaged ethnic minority communities. A few stories will show you the depth and breadth of their accomplishments.[34]

AN ADMINISTRATOR'S STORY
Bruce Fenderson (*Columbia* 1970) spent most of his career advocating for environmental and racial justice. After founding a nonprofit organization on the West Coast, which he characterizes as "one of the first environmental justice organizations in the country," he convened an alliance of one hundred jurisdictions to develop a sustainability initiative for the region. Fenderson then led a community reinvestment initiative, creating public/private partnerships that provided community resources in order to promote environmental equity. As chair and principal officer of another reinvestment initiative, he advocated for affordable multifamily housing near transportation hubs, and championed equitable transportation, housing, and land-use planning as a means of reducing greenhouse gas emissions.

Later on, Fenderson moved back to the East Coast to join the staff of a large foundation's environment and community development unit, where he supervised the global portfolios of program officers. In particular, Fenderson was responsible for developing strategies that could attract investment in low-income communities without displacing them, create affordable housing near public transit, and encourage financing of reliable public transportation. To disseminate the groundbreaking work of his grantees, he is overseeing publication of an eight-volume book series that contains practical case studies. In characterizing the focus of his work, Fenderson explained:

At some point in my career, I began to understand the importance of environmental consciousness. And so the kinds of projects that interest me the most are projects that incorporate an environmental perspective, a concern for social and racial justice, and a concern for the shaping of our American cities.

Bruce Fenderson

ANOTHER ADMINISTRATOR'S STORY

August André Baker (*Columbia* 1972) worked in public policy planning, served a sixteen-year-term as a planning commissioner, and then went to work as a community liaison in a preeminent African American university. This institution had been in a Columbia-like struggle with its predominately African American neighbors, "purchasing properties in contiguous city blocks, as real estate became available," to accommodate hospital expansion. "Once purchased, [the university] boarded up the existing structures (most of which were row houses). . . . Tempted by these neglected structures, homeless people and local drug dealers moved into these abandoned properties."[35]

After a long battle with residents, the university eventually established a community association and appointed Baker as its first director. To stimulate reinvestment, she created public/private partnerships between an array of federal and local government agencies and local community development corporations; leveraged university resources to create home ownership opportunities for low- and moderate-income families; facilitated infrastructure improvements in landscaping, traffic calming, and street lighting; and constructed both new and renovated homes. With these strategies, Baker was able to reverse the neighborhood's widespread disinvestment while building trust. As she explained, "Over the past sixteen years, our neighbors have gone from being openly hostile to being cautiously optimistic."

Today the neighborhood has the combination of market-rate and subsidized housing that assures a mixed-income, culturally diverse community. Under Baker's leadership, this unique town/gown partnership restored "the area to its former grandeur as a handsome residential neighborhood."[36] In her view:

What is so significant about this [project] is that right in the midst of rapid gentrification . . . we were able to anchor a low- and moderate-income presence, so that [these groups] didn't get just completely displaced by the increase in land values and property values. And so for me, that was a significant contribution that we were able to make. It placed [the university] on the right side of the issues for the right reasons, and it helped us to retrieve a sagging credibility that we had with our neighbors who were not happy at all with us because of the way in which we had been land banking for about twenty-five or thirty years and really causing some of the marginalization of this neighborhood.

August André Baker

In addition to overseeing brick-and-mortar redevelopment, Baker also places students in service positions in the community and teaches at a community art program. These combined planning and artistic involvements help Baker realize her long-held commitment to "nation-building," which she defines as not displacing the historical residents of a community, while helping them find joy in creative pursuits. As she explained, "those are the kinds of things that help make the work that I've been doing important and add meaning to it. . . . To be able to wed your passion and your lifework is a blessing—a major, major blessing."

A FIRM PRINCIPAL'S STORY
Sylvia K. Atkinson (*Columbia* 1971) is principal of the largest continuously operated, black female–owned architecture firm in the country. When asked what type of work interests her, she responded:

When I decided I wanted to do architecture . . . I guess I knew what I didn't want to do. I wasn't really interested in doing shopping malls, I knew I didn't want to do high-rise office buildings . . . I'm not really interested in stores; not really interested in churches—not really. But I'm interested in projects that have something to do with creating spaces that somehow help people or reshape them or make them better.

Sylvia K. Atkinson

Atkinson's portfolio exemplifies this philosophy, encompassing schools, cultural facilities, and housing for disenfranchised populations. Of particular note is her work in "green building" design, an approach to using resource-efficient materials to reduce energy consumption throughout the life of a building. She designed the first green school for an East Coast school district and an eight-story mixed-use building in a historically African American neighborhood, where she also renovated numerous

abandoned townhouses and apartment buildings. However, one of Atkinson's most significant projects is an African American national monument, where she designed an exhibition space suited to both visitors and
researchers. The 15,280-square-foot monument marks the earliest known
burial ground for blacks and contains the remains of 419 Africans who
were entombed there in the seventeenth and eighteenth centuries.[37] The
project resonates with Atkinson, both professionally and personally, not
only because of the design recognition it has received, but also because of
its relevance to the African American experience. She is proud to have
contributed to a project that safeguards and passes along the history of
New York's African-descended people.

A fellow in AIA, Atkinson seeks to design spaces that encourage positive social interactions and improve the quality of people's lives. She is
committed to advocating for the underrepresented and to designing in a
way that conserves energy, all the while making sure that her firm thrives
financially and completes high-quality work.

A PLANNER'S STORY
As director of a planning office in a large East Coast city with a significant black population, James A. Jackson (*Columbia* 1966) invested his
energies in revitalizing public space as a means to improve deteriorated
communities. For example, he and two colleagues started a street festival
in a commercial area of the city that was blighted with faltering mom-
and-pop businesses. The festival snowballed into an annual event that
now attracts throngs of people who partake of the area's live music and
authentic cuisine. In another instance, Jackson integrated federal funding
for a transit station with private monies to make the streets of a seedy
downtown neighborhood safer and more inviting to tourists and residents
alike. Drawing upon art and architecture as a means of promoting community vitality, he once collaborated with theater owners, performers,
attorneys, architects, and developers to establish a theater district, and then
he drafted design guidelines that preserved the area's unique architecture,
signage, and lighting. At the same time, Jackson also invested in promoting zoning regulations that preserve the city's natural environment,
including its trees, topographic elements, wetlands, and public parks.

At one point, Jackson attended night school to earn a degree in hospi-
tality management as a means of honing his managerial skills:

> And I can tell you how it has served me. Although it seems totally
> different, it was the management part of it that was very useful. Be-

cause it helped me—even though I never went into the field, other than doing some catering. . . . What I learned about management was very helpful and I was able to translate that into the work that I did running an office.

James A. Jackson

Over the course of his career whenever he had the opportunity to hire candidates of color, Jackson made a special effort to support their career goals. Realizing that he could offer the mentoring many people lacked, he came to treasure his manager role:

[Managing was] probably the most satisfying part of the work. It wasn't something that I necessarily thought of when I got into the profession, that I would be a manager, and as a matter of fact I went into management sort of kicking and screaming because my perception of a manager was somebody who told you to do something that you may or may not have wanted to do.

James A. Jackson

Jackson looked for people with strong interpersonal skills "who would serve the department well and serve themselves well." Then he worked with his protégés, grooming them "to move on to good positions." At the time of the interview, Jackson was utilizing his love of mentoring in a program for employees of nonprofit and public service organizations.

A FINE ARTIST'S STORY

At the time of the interview, Carlos Méndez (*Columbia* 1970) was working simultaneously as a fine artist, architect, and professor/administrator. Within these shifting professional roles, his work as a sculptor and art activist takes center stage. Méndez has completed commissions for numerous large public installations, the most prominent being a monumental sculpture that celebrates the fifth centennial of the Spanish colonization of the Americas. Another commission resulted in garden sculptures that the main public university system in Puerto Rico displays in public spaces throughout its campuses. Méndez has received several international prizes, most notably a gold medal from the International Art Competition in Faenza, Italy. His art installations are gestural—some large, others more intimate—and reflect Méndez's interest in people as both the makers and destroyers of their surroundings. His installations can be found in public collections in Europe and in the United States, including in mainstream museums.

However, Méndez goes beyond doing his own work to promote a community of artists:

> [I see art] as a way of reinforcing our national identity as Puerto Ricans. And that has sort of always been in the background . . . I've been involved in a lot of institutions here that promote the arts . . . because I think one of the issues here is how the culture gets in the hands of the artists who promote the culture.
>
> Carlos Méndez

For this reason, Méndez devotes a significant amount of time to Puerto Rican arts institutions, especially those that advance the ceramic arts, which is considered one of the most recognized mediums on the island. Through his involvements with these institutions, Méndez tries to provide other artists with the space they need to be creative and produce outstanding work that garners international recognition.

AN ACADEMIC'S STORY

At the time of the interview Laura Marie Swain (*Columbia* 1973) was a professor of architecture and planning and director of an applied research center on the West Coast. She described a long climb up the academic ladder that took a turn toward social justice when she received a prestigious national fellowship. As Swain explained:

> This leadership development fellowship . . . lasted for three years and was really the time that I developed social consciousness. I had developed some social awareness as a doctoral student, but it was really this fellowship—you could only get this fellowship if you committed to working across disciplines on important social problems . . . that really cemented my commitment to social justice and also my understanding and ability to work on these issues.
>
> Laura Marie Swain

After the fellowship, Swain received additional funding to develop a program that helped schoolteachers involve children in community improvement activities. The work that came out of this award-winning program was the subject of many different publications and lectures that solidified Swain's reputation as an expert in youth and community development. Then she received an unsolicited foundation grant to study why community service programs were not attracting low-income and ethnic minority youth. Working with a national team of junior and senior scholars, she turned the foundation's framing of the problem on its head. Instead of finding out why community service programs were not working, Swain and her team documented successful programs:

> We spent two and a half years looking around the country and finding a number of really interesting programs with kids fourteen to twenty-seven years old doing a number of different kinds of activities to improve their communities, which we reported. The best thing that came out of it was that someone read our monograph and made a nice little donation to one of the programs. Very impressive.

Laura Marie Swain

When asked what she was most proud of, Swain described having changed hearts and minds during a heated confrontation at a national meeting where architecture educators were considering whether to eliminate architecture's undergraduate degree. Prior to the meeting, presidents of the five professional organizations in architecture had written a manifesto declaring that architecture programs should offer only one degree—the master's degree—so that all architects would have the same education. Attendees at the meeting, including many deans of architecture schools, were discussing whether to support the manifesto. Swain felt strongly that, while the master's degree was appropriate to top-tier schools, second-tier schools should offer an undergraduate option to students who lacked the resources for a lengthy education. She recalled becoming embroiled in the debate:

> I don't remember exactly what I said, but I recall being very passionate that there could not just be one way of being an architect. . . . The person I started really arguing with was someone that I had an ongoing debate with over gender issues that had been very public. So I recall the two of us at either end of this room locked in this almost violent debate over whether there should be one way or many ways to be an architect. It was scary. Anyway, the outcome of it all was that the five presidents decided to put the issue on hold. . . . And then their terms expired, and other people didn't have the same zeal about having one degree in architecture. Besides, the debate had taken on mythic portions, so no one wanted to take it on, so the whole thing died and today there is still the bachelor of architecture degree.

Laura Marie Swain

Canaries in the Coal Mine

The careers of cohort members foretold changes in the city-making professions that would soon be widespread in the postindustrial era, especially in architecture. As the workforce shifted from large bureaucratic organizations to smaller, more versatile operations, architects' domain also shifted due to increasing competition. "Other entities, including accountants, contractors, and developers, have become dominant at the front end of the building process, guiding clients through decisions about such things as location, siting, size, function, and financing, all of which have a tremendous impact on the final outcome of a project."[38]

Bowles noted that the ethnic minority alumni "had to find outlets that [they] did not consider in the past" due to their tenuous position as people of color. However, in time, the erosion of traditional practice led many mainstream architects to consider alternative roles. Some looked abroad, using technology to create distant or virtual offices. Others expanded their services to include "strategic planning, facility analysis, even real estate and development advice."[39] Others established specialized partnerships, and still others "reexamine[d] their practices to eliminate inefficiencies and speed up the process, while still producing high-quality work."[40] Over time, what started for the cohort members as survival tactics became commonplace for mainstream architects.

Distinctive University/Community Partnerships

Similarly, many colleges and universities have evolved community outreach programs that reflect Columbia's experiments in urban and minority affairs—and that reveal the brilliance of the Executive Council's grand scheme for university/community collaboration. As was true when McGeorge Bundy used Ford's assets "to leverage change in America,"[41] colleges and universities today leverage the many grants that are available for establishing partnerships with poor communities.

One type of partnership focuses upon community redevelopment, which either the university or the community can initiate. This approach has a bottom-line benefit as it can heighten a university's "ability to attract tuition-paying students, research-funding corporations, big-name faculty, prestigious conferences, alumni donors, and middle-class patients" for its medical facilities.[42] It can also protect homeowners in deteriorating communities by stimulating multimillion-dollar, long-term investments in revitalization. However, like all market-driven redevelopment, in the absence of a community advocate like August André Baker, this approach has the inherent risk of displacing the most disenfranchised members of a community. The second type of partnership transforms the curriculum by centering student learning in the socio-spatial problems of the surrounding neighborhood, which either faculty, students, or residents can identify. Adherents of this approach point to its extraordinary academic benefits, noting that "communities can provide material, ideas, and opportunities for both research and classroom activities. In fact, the literature on service learning suggests that students learn more through that process than from regular in-class lecturing."[43]

This type of partnership can sustain specific time-limited projects or ongoing ones that occur over many years. Ideally, community and curricular development go hand in hand, transforming both the surrounding neighborhood and the university. In the best of all worlds, a linked approach to community-driven practice and education achieves the Urban Center's vision of turning the university around by transforming "not only the structures of social injustice that produce poverty . . . but also the traditional approaches to learning in the university"[44] that sustain inequity. As envisioned by the revolutionaries in the School of Architecture's experiment, a truly transgressive partnership reinforces "processes where students, faculty, and community people learn together. It moves beyond hierarchies reinforced by the university toward a practice that sees the community people as experts and as partners."[45]

A New Revolutionary Role

You can't replicate now what occurred then, because all of the rules and social dynamics are more complex now. However, the more things change, the more they stay the same. . . . You have to update the entire scenario and evaluate your options accordingly.

Kirk Bowles

Without question, U.S. colleges and universities have made impressive progress in honing mutually beneficial partnerships with impoverished communities since the days of Columbia's insurgency. Still, these achievements pale in comparison to what is needed to address the more complex rules and social dynamics that Kirk Bowles references. Instead of producing socially critical citizens who can advance the tenets of democracy as occurred during the School of Architecture's experiment, higher education is utterly failing to evaluate its options for operating within a context that is, at the same time, new and resistant to change. A democracy requires "limited extremes of wealth and poverty, citizenship oriented toward advancing the public good, equal opportunity structures and practices, and citizens reasonably discerning of the forces that shape their lives."[46] The increasingly destructive forces of corporate capitalism have seriously eroded all these conditions and, like Columbia, too many universities have become part of these destructive forces, operating as private corporations rather than as public-spirited institutions.

Since the early 1970s, corporate capitalism has increasingly turned human and ecological relationships into the prime commodities of a global marketplace, permanently banishing the working poor and un-employed to the outskirts of the "wealthiest and most powerful nation on earth."[47] In response to the brutality of living in rat-infested shanties under the shadow of extreme wealth, a new and virulent rebellion is building among black and brown people across the nation and around the world. For all their good works in poor communities, institutions of higher education have not taken a stand against the "multitudinous oppressive practices manifested through blatant disparity and uneven development patterns, both domestically and internationally."[48] At the very moment that American democracy calls out for an engaged citizenry capable of mending this deeply divided one nation, indivisible,[49] "public higher education . . . is increasingly structured to entrench rather than redress class trajectories, abjure the project of producing an educated public, and facilitate capital accumulation over all other values."[50]

For sure, all the rules and social dynamics are far more complex today than they were in the 1960s, but understanding history and the role black students played in deepening the spirit of democracy during the civil rights/black power movement is crucial to catalyzing a new campus revolution. Understanding the multiple and devastating disruptions that are being borne by today's black and brown youth is also crucial to being able to support a brave new generation of "intellectual freedom fighters"[51] in redefining an American democracy for the twenty-first century. Not surprisingly, some of the disruptions are occurring in those cities that played a leading role in America's era of spectacular industrial growth but are now experiencing massive population and job losses in its era of globalization. These cities offer visible proof of the decay of industrial society and the racist practices that produced its extraordinary material abundance "at the expense of other peoples all over the world."[52]

At the same time, a change has occurred in the long-standing geography of U.S. poverty, which began shifting in the 1990s from cities to the suburbs. "For the first time in U.S. history, poverty not only grew significantly in the suburbs, but it did so at a greater rate than in central cities," so that by the year 2000 almost half the poor were suburbanites.[53] In place of white middle-class families, "large numbers of poor, minority families in need of social services are living in neighborhoods characterized by deteriorating housing, failing schools, few social services, high crime, and few job opportunities."[54]

Whether living in cities, towns, or suburbs, too many young black and brown men and women are locked up in a racial caste system, caged by poor education, unemployment, and actual prison walls. Constituting a surplus labor force of corporate capitalism with its differing rules and legal protections for rich and poor, these disenfranchised youth "have been discarded as human refuse and are preyed upon by a legal system that criminalizes poverty."[55] Despite such icons of African American success as Barack Obama and Oprah Winfrey, conservatives have succeeded in turning back racial progress in America, and the criminal justice system is driving the reversal.[56] In a country that has the world's highest rate of incarceration, "the racial dimension of mass incarceration is its most striking feature. No other country in the world imprisons so many of its racial or ethnic minorities. The United States imprisons a larger percentage of its black population than South Africa did at the height of apartheid. In Washington, D.C., our nation's capital, it is estimated that three out of four young black men (and nearly all those in the poorest neighborhoods) can expect to serve time in prison. Similar rates of incarceration can be found in black communities across America."[57]

From the ashes of "mass unemployment, social neglect, economic abandonment, and intense police surveillance,"[58] a new young black militant is arising. Having rejected the electoral process, the legal system, the press, and especially the established black leaders, "this militant believes it is only in the streets and in acts of civil disobedience that change is possible."[59] Unlike the black youth of the 1960s, who saw access to education as their salvation, these militant young people eschew a system of higher education that has replaced its long-held mission of advancing the public good with one of providing job training for ambitious individuals.[60] In this system, "equity, fair play, and justice have given way to bureaucratic greed and unprincipled practices" as high-level administrators sweep up hefty compensation packages but refuse living wages to the workers who operate their campuses. And yet in these perilous times, higher education, with all its flaws, has a crucial role to play in assuring the long-term success of the rebellion that is simmering: "Rebellions are important because they represent the standing up of the oppressed. Rebellions break the threads that have been holding the system together. They shake up old values so that relations between individuals and groups within society are unlikely ever to be the same again."[61]

But rebellions, by themselves, cannot transform institutions of repression. Institutional transformation requires the kind of impassioned dialogue that occurred at the School of Architecture beginning in the summer of 1968—dialogue fueled by the unwavering chutzpah of youth. To turn the anger and outrage of rebellion into an emancipatory force, young people must have space to assume "responsibility for creating the new values, truths, infrastructures, and institutions that are necessary to build and govern a new society."[62] Institutions of higher education can provide that space. However, like the revolutionaries who reinvented education in Avery's shantytown, students graduate. Thus it is the faculty who are the honeybees charged with carrying forward the ideas for a new society from one class to the next. Not only are faculty society's scouts in signaling impending problems, but they can also be transgressors who resist the inevitable return to the status quo and provide continuity for young people to reorganize society.

Some Easy Wins

The School of Architecture's experiment resulted from a confluence of factors, some intended, others quite accidental. For sure, the passionate potency of insurrection would not have set fire to the bold recruitment effort narrated in this book had McGeorge Bundy not showed up in 1966 with $10 million for urban and minority affairs. And he and others only showed up because of an impending racial Armageddon that threatened national security. As Abigail Abruña noted, the school's support for affirmative action was more about having discovered a pot of gold than it was about commitment:

> There was affirmative action—I'm sure that was less because of the goodwill of the school and more because there was money available . . . because later on, the school turned around and, if you look at the configuration of the student body right now, it's clear that whatever looked like a commitment at the time has not been sustained.
>
> Abigail Abruña

Despite dubious motives, the school's experiment in educational equity has vital lessons for contemporary city-making education and practice. Above all, it demonstrates that equity is not about bringing historically marginalized populations into an *existing* institution; equity requires a fundamental structural change in the affairs of that institution. The curriculum has to change, who is included in decision making has to change, what is recognized as meritorious has to change, the school-community relationship has to change, how communities are planned and designed has to change. Opening the oak doors of opportunity to historically marginalized populations requires an institutional commitment to recognize—and transform—the structural conditions that underpin white privilege. To be sustainable, the commitment must be a moral one backed not only by financial resources but also by intellectual resources, including the vernacular knowledge that resides within disenfranchised communities of color.

To be sustainable, the commitment must consider the entire ladder of educational equity, not just the much-flaunted pipeline that channels historically marginalized populations one by one through the doors of opportunity. The availability of preprofessional and evening courses was essential in equipping the ethnic minority recruits with the technical skills to enter the Ivy League. Those courses were appropriately offered at community colleges and second-tier professional schools. Even Columbia had a pipeline to professional education through its college and general studies programs. However, once inside the oak doors, many recruits stayed only a year or two, quickly earning the Ivy League credentials that would set them apart for a lifetime. Later on, a few alumni returned to Columbia and elsewhere to layer on additional credentials. At the same time, a ladder of equity existed at the faculty level. Senior ethnic minority faculty advanced while assisting junior ones in their climb, their small numbers expanded by a blurry school/community boundary that brought ethnic minority professionals into the school from many different domains.

To be sustainable, the commitment must create an amazing, almost breathless sense of possibility while being brutally frank about the obstacles historically marginalized populations still face in this country. To persevere in the face of reluctant patrons, unsupportive majority firms, low pay, and outright racism—to not be among the many who drop out—ethnic minority recruits must be better equipped than their majority counterparts, technically, intellectually, and emotionally. A sustainable commitment would prepare its recruits on all those levels.

Finally, to be sustainable, the commitment to the alumni of a social experiment must be unfaltering. Just imagine if the School of Architecture had flaunted the extraordinary cadre of ethnic minority talent it happened to produce as a national model of educational equity (see Figure 25). Instead, amnesia set in as "the school turned around"; in-

Figure 25. This photo shows some members of the School of Architecture's extraordinary cadre of ethnic minority alumni (though not necessarily the members of the oral history cohort) at a private party in Max Bond's architecture office prior to GSAPP's 2007 annual alumni symposium. The symposium, which featured the ethnic minority alumni as speakers, was the first time that many of them had returned to the school. *Left to right (back)*: Charles Levonne Laughinghouse, David Hughes, Raymond C. Jackson, George Thomas Snead. *Left to right (front)*: J. Max Bond, Jr., Myles A. Stevens, Lloyd deSuze, Emmett B. Hagood, Sharon Egretta Sutton, Stanford R. Britt, Robert Arthur King. (Photo courtesy of Robert Arthur King.)

stead, the story remained hidden in folders filled with yellowing paper and disappearing onionskin copies. An unfaltering commitment would track and support ethnic minority alumni after graduation, feature them in historical accounts, hire them for professorships and lectures, and invite them to narrate their extraordinary life stories. Such a commitment would attract many other students from marginalized populations who would be convinced that architecture offers "a major professional opportunity for [them]."[63]

The School of Architecture's experiment in educational equity demonstrates that the continuing lack of cultural diversity in the city-making fields is not due to any of the many reasons found in strategic planning reports. It is due to the lack of will.

Epilogue

This book related a story about how the gift of an Ivy League education helped give my classmates and me the courage to behave like the wild buffalo that face a storm head-on. I spent a whole lot longer unraveling this story than I ever imagined, and even more time figuring out how to tell the story so anyone would be interested in reading it. One thing I realized during this incredibly long odyssey is that isolated acts of paying back privileges—saying a previously unsaid thank-you, establishing an endowed scholarship, even writing a book about a bold experiment—pale in comparison to the enormous storm that is coming into view.

The challenge is how to frame the lessons learned from this story so as to inspire transgressive action in today's terrain of unyielding racism and equally unyielding resistance to change. I am now seventy-five and the finish line is coming into view ever more clearly (an understatement since, according to one online retirement calculator, I only have enough money to live until I am eighty-four). How—and where—can I position myself to help others face the storm that is assuredly rolling in? How can I help the young people who have so inspired my own daredevil creativity see a way forward in their quest for revolutionary social change? Indeed, how can the legacy of Columbia's experiment help all my justice-oriented academic colleagues turn unblinking to face the storm? Before I address that question, let me engage you in taking stock of the terrain that so calls out for transformation.

Those of you with wild buffalo courage undoubtedly see a frightening scene on the horizon of burning cars and buildings, of people throwing rocks and bottles at police officers, and of police forces armed with military-style equipment. You know that these raucous uprisings reflect the nation's "history and maintenance of racist policies, through housing discrimination, divestment of black communities, and policing, all coming to a head."[1] You know that black and brown youth are rising up against these policies in Ferguson, Baltimore, Cleveland, Staten Island, North Charleston, Milwaukee, and countless other places. You know just how successful conservatives have been in turning back racial progress in America through the criminal justice system.[2] You know that representatives of millions of incarcerated black and brown human beings are surging into the streets to reject the status quo.[3] Knowing all this, how can you, through transgressive education and practice, give voice to these young black and brown militants by amplifying their story to non-believers?

Those of you with wild buffalo courage undoubtedly see a frightening scene coming into view in urban America. You know that many disinvested rust belt cities have a concentration of African Americans similar to that of the pre–civil rights era, with black populations totaling over 80 percent. You know that overinvested cities have a glut of healthcare and technology industries, as well as millennial-generation white employees whose hefty incomes fuel the housing market. You know that escalating housing costs have forced out low-income American-born and immigrant populations and even middle-class families, leaving these cities to the young, the super rich, and the homeless. You know that these swaps in geographic locales occur at tremendous cost to people and to the landscape as communities and infrastructure decay in one place while, in another, rapid overdevelopment destroys any semblance of authenticity. Knowing all this, how can you, through transgressive education and practice, intervene in this country's uneven development patterns in order to conserve the integrity of communities and the landscape?

Those of you with wild buffalo courage undoubtedly see a frightening scene coming into view not just in this country but around the world as the greatest wave of urbanization in history brings billions of people into cities in search of shelter who are unable to pay its escalating costs. You see a gap in housing affordability that is especially severe in larger cities and in poorer countries; you see that worldwide upward of 330 million urban families live in substandard housing or are paying an inordinate amount of their income toward housing.[4] You know that this affordability gap is widening; you know that just ten years from now—when I may have already passed the finish line—"440,000,000 urban households or as many as 1,600,000,000 individuals worldwide will face crowded, substandard housing."[5]

You know that finding the trillions of dollars needed to close the gap would not fix the global housing crisis because many rural migrants choose a traditional way of cooking, bathing, and washing clothes. You know that many so distrust the capriciousness of government-financed housing that they would rather reside on flood-prone land in homes constructed out of sheets of plastic, plywood, sheet metal, and even cardboard. You know that though solidarity may be strong in these spontaneous settlements, they lack the street grids to facilitate transportation and delivery of public services; are overcrowded, overpopulated, and without adequate jobs; are subject to rapidly spreading fires, disease, vermin, and crime among other socio-spatial problems. That is, you know they lack all the benefits of places planned according to modern codes and regulations, and that in many world cities the brutality of living in vermin-infested settlements occurs in the shadows of extreme wealth. Knowing all this, how can you, through transgressive education and practice, provide students with non-Eurocentric tools to redress these unsafe, unsanitary slum conditions, while also respecting slum dwellers' right to self-determination?

You know that these scenes have racialized, spatial dimensions; you know they call out for a bold generation of culturally diverse city-making professionals who, like the wild buffalo, can face the storm unblinking in order to reclaim a terrain that has been lost to corporate capitalism. As the differences between wealth and poverty become ever more extreme, how can you support young people in becoming that generation, capable of serving the world's most disenfranchised populations? How can you help young people fashion an experiment in democracy set afire by the spirit of revolutionary social change?

Last year, a D.C.-based journalist named Brentin Mock called me looking for ideas about how planners and designers can frame the racial-justice, police-reform discussions that current events are bringing into focus. Mock, who writes about race, civil rights, and voting rights, had just published a piece on the difficulty black students at Harvard Graduate School of Design have in leveraging design to bring about social change. The students complained that they were ill prepared to participate, as designers, in today's racial-justice and police-reform discussions because "their instruction has been based in the work of architects whose worldviews don't give heavy weight to social problems."[6] Challenged by the students' complaints, Mock decided to interview justice-oriented faculty to find out what design can—and cannot—do to increase safety in communities like Baltimore and Ferguson.

The ideas his interviews produced are well-worn ones that hardly seem up to overpowering the approaching storm. They include optimizing the surveillance potential of neighborhoods, working across disciplines to make incremental changes in residents' lives, bringing about professions that are representative of the communities they serve, facilitating the engagement of residents in making their own communities safer, and realizing that you cannot design your way out of violence[7]—strategies that were well-known to the revolutionaries in Columbia's experiment. But what attracted my attention in Mock's follow-up piece was his characterization of urban design as an instrument of power that the police use to impose violence upon others. He asserted that "some cops in Baltimore and Philadelphia know the bumpiest streets in their cities to take people they've arrested on 'rough rides' or 'nickel rides' . . . Some police in Chicago understand which buildings are most obscured from public view so they can be used as so-called 'black sites.'"[8]

In the face of such racialized spatial oppression, not taking positive action to counteract the oncoming storm—not being proactive—is simply untenable. For some time now, the question for me has been whether I and other transgressive faculty can take revolutionary action as outsiders within the mainstream? That is, can we help destroy the master's house while living in it, or do we have to step outside the frameworks of power that are driving the storm?

Surveying these extremely perilous times, I am compelled to take the position that "intellectual freedom fighters"[9] must operate both within and outside the frameworks of power—and they must operate interdependently, one supporting the other. Freedom fighters are needed in the streets, making visible the brutality of poverty and discrimination to whoever has the courage to face the entire scene unblinking. But they are equally needed within ivory towers to welcome those street fighters who can turn them black and brown again in a new and inclusive society.

Appendixes

Appendix A: Biographies of the Oral History Cohort
Listed Alphabetically in Order of Graduation Date

Biographies recorded, 2007–2009

John O. Phillips, American Institute of Architects (AIA)
Director of Planning for the Bronx (Retired)
Bachelor of Arts, *Columbia* 1962
Master of Architecture, *Columbia* 1966
Master of Hotel and Restaurant Management, City University of New
York

John O. Phillips enrolled in Columbia College as a premed student but, after meeting an architecture student, he decided "to go to architecture school because it looked interesting and it looked creative," even though the field lacked the role models that existed in medicine. Phillips earned a Master of Architecture degree in 1966 as one of the school's very few black students, and then he joined the Peace Corps. As a corps volunteer he designed low-cost housing and then returned to the United States to work in several New York City architecture firms before attaining licensure. However, he soon realized that he preferred community work to architecture and consequently accepted an urban design position in New York City's Planning Office. Phillips advanced through the ranks, eventually becoming deputy director for the Manhattan Office of City Planning. In 2001, he retired from the planning office, where his last position was as director of planning for the Bronx Office.

During his tenure as a city planner, Phillips served on the New York's Theatre Advisory Council, helping preserve the old theatres and vitality of the Times Square area. He was also involved in revitalizing subway stations in Midtown Manhattan, offering bonuses for development that improved stations. However, his major project was organizing the Ninth Avenue Festival in a derelict, multi-ethnic area that abutted the Theatre District. To promote Ninth Avenue merchants, Phillips designed festival shopping bags and even edited cookbooks—all as part of his urban planning assignment. The festival first attracted 250,000 people, growing to attract millions of people over a thirty-year period. Later, as director of the Bronx Office, Philips worked with community organizations to plan major projects, including the construction of 2,500 housing units and the revitalization of manufacturing areas.

Throughout his career, Phillips had extremely positive relationships with staff, having recruited and hired entry-level people whom he mentored into more advanced positions. Currently, he utilizes his love of mentoring in a program called Leading from the Middle, inspiring employees of nonprofit and public service organizations with his own experiences of personal and professional success. Phillips was born in New York City in 1940.

Carl C. Anthony
Founder, Urban Habitat Program; Formerly Deputy Director, Ford
    Foundation
Bachelor of Architecture, *Columbia* 1969

An African American attending Columbia's night school, Carl C. Anthony played a major role in the School of Architecture's recruitment efforts following the insurrection. He earned a Bachelor of Architecture degree in 1969 and subsequently traveled to West Africa to document indigenous villages—an experience that nurtured his respect for ecology and culture, and led to his becoming one of the founders of the environmental justice movement.

After working briefly in architecture and passing most of the licensing exam, Anthony redirected his attention to environmental issues. He founded Urban Habitat, an environmental and social justice organization in the San Francisco Bay Area and worked on numerous environmental initiatives in the area, including developing a livability compact for the region, raising funds for brownfield cleanup and sustainable development, and overseeing the conversion of military bases. Later, Anthony held leadership positions at the Ford Foundation in New York City, first as acting director and then as deputy director, supervising program officers in the foundation's global portfolio for environment and community development. While there, Anthony helped build new environmental leadership, promoted greater ecological integrity, and advocated for reducing the spatial isolation of disenfranchised communities.

Anthony has also held academic positions at UC Berkeley and Columbia University, and he has had fellowships at Harvard University and UC Berkeley. Anthony was publisher and editor of the only environmental justice journal in the country, *Race, Poverty, and Environment*. His most recent book is titled *The Earth, the City, and the Hidden Knowledge of a Race*, and he is also contributing to an eight-volume book series published by MIT Press that documents the work of his Ford Foundation grantees. In recognition of his contributions, PolicyLink, a national institute that advances economic and social equity, recently established the Carl Anthony Regional Equity Award to recognize outstanding environmental activists. Anthony was the first awardee. He was born in Philadelphia in 1939.

Luis Aponte-Parés, PhD

Associate Professor of Community Planning, Director of Latino Studies,
   University of Massachusetts Boston
Bachelor of Architecture, Catholic University
Master of Science (Architecture), *Columbia* 1970
PhD (Urban Planning), *Columbia* 1990

An activist Puerto Rican architecture student, Dr. Luis Aponte-Parés was recruited by Harry Quintana to participate in Columbia's Real Great Society Urban Planning Studio. Having studied the humanities at the Universidad de Puerto Rico and earned his Bachelor of Architecture degree from Catholic University, he attended Columbia for just one year, earning a Master of Science degree in 1970. Upon graduation, Aponte-Parés worked for the New York City Housing Authority, developing alternatives to urban renewal for Lower East Side community groups. He worked as a planner in New York and Boston, taught at Pratt Institute and City College of New York, and then returned to Columbia, earning his PhD in urban planning in 1990.

As a Rockefeller/Schomburg fellow at City College, Aponte-Parés investigated the appropriation of vacant land in East Harlem, the Lower East Side, the South Bronx, and Brooklyn. After decades of neglect by government officials, Puerto Rican squatters had taken over rubble-strewn lots where multistory buildings once stood, defying municipal ordinances to cultivate gardens and build small houses known as "casitas." Aponte-Parés traveled to Puerto Rico and Santo Domingo to document the casita typology as a cultural expression, and then produced videos for New

York's educational television station and for a Smithsonian Institution exhibition.

Aponte-Parés also studies Latino community development organizations in Boston and New York City as they attempt to reposition their communities within increasingly complex postindustrial environments. He has held academic positions at Boston Architectural College, Pratt Institute, and Universidad Interamericana in Puerto Rico, among others, and was founding director of the City College Architecture Center. Aponte-Parés served as director of the Northern Manhattan Planning Office in New York City and executive director of the Hispanic Office of Planning and Evaluation in Boston. In addition to being a professor and administrator at the University of Massachusetts Boston, he is president of the Puerto Rican Studies Association, and a board member on Boston's LGBT History Project. Aponte-Parés was born in Huma Cao, Puerto Rico, in 1945.

Jaime Luis Suarez
Sculptor and Architect
Professor, Director of Academic Affairs, Polytechnic University of
    Puerto Rico
Bachelor of Architecture, Catholic University
Master of Science (Architecture), *Columbia* 1970

Jaime Luis Suarez was another politically active Puerto Rican student that Harry Quintana recruited from Catholic University to participate in Columbia's Real Great Society Urban Planning Studio. After just one year he received a Master of Science degree in 1970, then returned to Puerto Rico to pursue his nascent interest in ceramics. While studying art at the Universidad de Puerto Rico, Suarez worked as an architect in a public housing agency and taught architecture at the Universidad de Puerto Rico. In 1980 he and several other ceramic artists opened a cooperative ceramic school and gallery called Casa Candina and Galleria Manos. Then, in 1995, Suarez became one of the founding members of the New School of Architecture at Polytechnic University, eventually becoming its director of academic affairs.

Suarez is alternately a sculptor, architect, and professor with architecture consuming the least of his attention. He has taught in public as well as private institutions, in architecture as well as art. Nevertheless, Suarez's distinction is as an artist. He has been commissioned for several large public installations in Puerto Rico, has ceramic sculpture in numerous collections in Europe and the United States, including at the Metropolitan Museum of Art, and has done set and costume design for Puerto Rico's national dance company.

Along with his own artistic endeavors, Suarez continues to run Casa Candina and Galleria Manos, and he serves on the boards of several non-profit organizations that advance Puerto Rican culture, including the Public School of Visual Arts. Suarez was born in 1946 in San Juan.

Emmett B. Hagood, AIA, National Organization of Minority Architects (NOMA)
Owner and Principal, EBH Inc. in Detroit, *Columbia* 1971

An African American, Emmett B. Hagood arrived at Columbia with sig-nificant experience as a draftsperson and having completed coursework in Philadelphia at Drexel University. Admitted with advanced standing, he graduated in just two years in 1971 and then returned home to Detroit, where he began teaching at the University of Detroit. Hagood worked in his father's construction company as well, renovating inner-city apart-ment buildings and single-family homes, including many in Detroit's Virginia Park and Highland Park neighborhoods. He became a registered architect in 1974 and opened a private practice in 1981. Hagood's firm has completed both single- and multifamily housing projects, and has designed several new and renovated elementary schools for the Detroit Board of Education.

Hagood is committed to working with nonprofit community develop-ment organizations. He aspires to help them fulfill their mission of pro-viding affordable housing to inner-city residents while also achieving a high level of design and professionalism. In addition to membership in AIA, Hagood belongs to NOMA and presently serves on the board of its Detroit chapter, where he chairs the membership committee. He is mar-ried and has two children, Emmett B. Hagood, III, and Mark A. Hagood. He was born in Columbia, South Carolina, in 1941.

Ghislaine M. P. Hermanuz
Professor of Architecture, Director of the Architectural Center, City
    College of New York
Principal, Hermanuz Ltd.
Diplôme d'Architecte, École Polytechnique de l'Université de Lausanne
Master of Science (Urban Planning), *Columbia* 1971

Identifying as a black woman, Ghislaine M. P. Hermanuz is actually French. She was born in Lausanne, Switzerland, her mother being from

Martinique in the French West Indies and her father being German. Hermanuz studied architecture at one of the world's leading universities, École Polytechnique de l'Université de Lausanne, which qualified her to practice architecture there. The Swiss program was supposed to encompass both architecture and urbanism, but Hermanuz felt that it fell short in exploring the civil unrest that was occurring not only in the United States but also in Europe. She left Switzerland to study the intersection of urbanism, design, people, and politics at Harvard University, where she had received a scholarship, but found the program unsuited to her interests.

Attracted to New York City's larger scale and to the United Nations, Hermanuz transferred to the urban planning program at Columbia in 1969, writing her thesis on the housing construction industry in the West Indies. After graduating in 1971, she joined the Architects Renewal Committee in Harlem for a couple of years and then returned to Columbia as assistant dean for minority affairs (1974–1979) and associate professor (1974–1986). During her tenure at Columbia, Hermanuz organized the Urban Technical Assistance Project, consulting on urban design guidelines for Frederick Douglass Boulevard in Harlem, among many other projects. Her teaching at City College and private practice address community development and design. She is concerned with issues of social justice and environmental quality in neighborhoods in despair, and with women's approaches to developing their neighborhoods. A widow, Hermanuz has a son and a stepson; she was born in 1942.

Roberta D. Washington, Fellow of the AIA (FAIA), NOMA

Principal, Roberta Washington Architects PC
Bachelor of Architecture, Howard University
Master of Science in Architecture (Hospital and Health Facility Design), *Columbia* 1971

Roberta D. Washington, FAIA, arrived at Columbia in 1970 with work experience and a Bachelor of Architecture degree from Howard University. She enrolled in a now-defunct program in hospital and health facility design, receiving a Master of Science in Architecture degree in 1971. Washington worked in New York City as a health facility planner and then spent four years directing an architecture design studio in the People's Republic of Mozambique. Discouraged by not seeing opportunities to advance into an associate position, and encouraged by a friend who had been an associate in a Hispanic firm, Washington struck out on her own. She formed Roberta Washington Architects PC in 1983, currently a ten-person firm that is the largest continuously operated, black-female-owned architecture firm in the country. Her portfolio features supportive housing for such constituents as the homeless, mentally ill, AIDS patients, ex-convicts, and recovering addicts.

Washington's portfolio additionally includes a hall of fame in Kansas City, a renovation of residential buildings in Harlem, a new condominium in Central Harlem, and a new subway station in Brooklyn. Of particular note is a recently finished school in New Haven, Connecticut, that Washington hopes will achieve a Leadership in Energy and Environmental Design Gold or Silver rating. However, one of her most significant projects is the African Burial Ground Interpretive Center in Lower Manhattan, to be situated within the lobby of a building adjacent to a newly discovered burial ground for fifteen thousand Africans.

Washington was the third black woman elevated to AIA fellowship and the second black woman elected as president of NOMA. She chaired the NYS Board of Architecture and a committee of the Central Harlem Community Planning Board. She serves on the New York City Landmarks Commission, is historian for the New York Coalition of Black Architects, and is on the board of the Architecture Foundation at the New York chapter of AIA. Washington was born in Greensborough, North Carolina.

Stanford R. Britt, FAIA, NOMA

President, Sulton, Campbell, Britt, Owens, and Associates in Maryland
Bachelor of Science, Drexel University
Master of Architecture, *Columbia* 1972
Master of Business Administration, Harvard University

Stanford R. Britt, FAIA, was widely recognized among his peers at Columbia as a leader of the black architecture students. Due to prior education and work experience, he earned his Master of Architecture degree in just three years in 1972. After graduation, Britt moved to Montreal to work with Moshe Safdie but then was offered a commission in Baltimore. Not yet licensed, he negotiated a career-long relationship with an established black architect, Leroy Campbell. In the ensuing years, Britt became an associate, then a principal, and finally the president of Sulton, Campbell, Britt, Owens, and Associates.

When Britt joined the firm, its commissions were mostly for housing and churches, which he was charged with expanding to include health-care. A contract for a community healthcare facility in Baltimore began his specialty in that area. In addition to housing and churches, his firm's portfolio now includes healthcare and educational facilities, with Britt spending most of his time on those commissions. A notable recent assignment was developing a master plan that allows Johns Hopkins Hospital to integrate an eighty-eight-acre research park into a derelict, low-income area in East Baltimore just north of the existing hospital. After completing the plan, Britt took a leave from his firm to initiate the first buildings, including an elderly housing project, a workforce condominium, and a research facility.

Britt has been active in both AIA and NOMA, where he served as the 1977–78 president. He was president of the Baltimore chapter of AIA, served on the AIA National Board, and was elevated to fellowship in 1989. Britt was a member and then president of the board of directors of a community school that serves gifted youth who are considered at-risk due to being in the foster care or juvenile justice system. Through his projects, Britt aspires to ensure that the low-income constituents of healthcare facilities are treated with dignity. He was born in Philadelphia in 1944.

Lloyd A. deSuze, Trinidad and Tobago Institute of Architects

Director, Gillespie and Steel Limited in Trinidad and Tobago
Bachelor of Architecture, *Columbia* 1972

Lloyd deSuze was admitted to Columbia in 1969. Born in Trinidad, West Indies, deSuze migrated to Brooklyn in 1960 at age thirteen to join his parents, who were Trinidadian but naturalized as U.S. citizens. Previously, he had worked as a drafting technician and taken evening classes in architecture at Pratt Institute and the Cooper Union. Given this prior exposure, deSuze completed his Bachelor of Architecture degree in just three years, graduating in 1972. Using a Kinne Award, deSuze traveled in the East African countries of Kenya, Tanzania, and Uganda, where he conducted field surveys of tribal architecture with two other classmates. Subsequently, he was employed at Bond Ryder and Associates in New York City, doing production work for the Schomburg Center for Research in Black Culture in Harlem and the Martin Luther King, Jr., Memorial Center in Atlanta.

In 1978 deSuze returned to Trinidad, and he has been employed ever since at Gillespie and Steel Associates, a Barbadian company that provides comprehensive planning, design, and project management services throughout the eastern Caribbean and Florida. He began as a project architect and climbed the ladder to manager, associate director, and finally director of interior design. deSuze's portfolio includes major interior projects, much of it commercial. He also integrates interior design with corporate visions to create recognizable brand buildings. deSuze managed a significant renovation of the Central Bank of Trinidad and Tobago, and has completed several projects for the RBTT Bank, including the rebranding of its branch banks. He excels in delivering high-quality products on time and on budget.

deSuze is licensed to practice architecture by the Board of Architecture of Trinidad and Tobago, and he is a member of the Trinidad and Tobago Institute of Architects. He lists as his life accomplishments receiving financial support from Columbia, graduating from the program, and having a family that includes a wife and two daughters. deSuze was born in 1947.

Charles Levonne Laughinghouse

Principal and Sole Owner, Laughinghouse Consultants LLC
Bachelor of Arts (Architecture), *Columbia* 1972
Master of Architecture, UC Berkeley

Charles Levonne Laughinghouse entered Columbia College a year before the insurrection in 1967. He graduated in 1972 with a Bachelor of Arts degree, having taken courses in the Division of Architecture while also participating in varsity track and football. Laughinghouse subsequently earned a Master of Architecture degree from UC Berkeley and studied international affairs and African culture at the Kwame Nkrumah University of Science and Technology in Ghana. After apprenticeships in San Francisco and New York, and an adjunct position at Pratt Institute, Laughinghouse moved to New Orleans to teach at Louisiana State University, Tulane University, and Southern University. Subsequently, he became assistant dean at the University of Wisconsin–Milwaukee.

While still in New Orleans, Laughinghouse launched a consulting firm after a Columbia classmate recommended him for a commission in a historic district of Washington, D.C. His firm has completed several hundred projects, ranging from master planning a mixed-use development for an unincorporated black settlement to executing construction management contracts. In addition, Laughinghouse has endeavored to raise public awareness of design, reaching out to elected officials who make decisions affecting the designed environment and also to nontraditional students. For example, Laughinghouse implemented a curriculum in Landry High School in New Orleans that exposed predominantly black students and staff to the design process. After New Orleans Public Schools published the curriculum, other schools and organizations adopted it, including the Milwaukee Urban League and National Association of Minority Contractors.

Laughinghouse also instigated a number of conferences at the University of Wisconsin to raise awareness of urban issues related to housing, historic preservation, and energy conscious design. These activities led to funding from the National Endowment for the Arts to create a video about black communities in the United States. Working alongside a professional filmmaker, Laughinghouse produced—and raised funds for—*Black Communities in the USA*, a documentary exploring how people of African descent have influenced the nation's land planning, physical development, and design aesthetics, which was aired on an NBC affiliate station in Milwaukee. Laughinghouse cherishes the label "jack of many trades." He was born in 1949 in Greenville, North Carolina.

Myles A. Stevens, AIA, NOMA

Principal, Stevens & Associates in San Francisco
Bachelor of Architecture, University of Illinois at Chicago
Master of Science in Architecture, *Columbia* 1972

When Myles A. Stevens enrolled in Columbia, he had a Bachelor of Architecture degree from the University of Illinois at Chicago and teaching experience from the University of Kansas. After receiving his Master of Architecture degree a year later in 1972, he went to work for landscape architect Lawrence Halprin, first in his New York City office and then in San Francisco. To develop expertise in landscape architecture, Stevens enrolled in site planning courses at UC Berkeley, where he also taught for five years.

Since 1978, Stevens has headed a multidisciplinary design firm that provides services for public and private clients throughout the San Francisco Bay Area. His firm has benefited from San Francisco's liberal business climate, yielding a portfolio of projects ranging from $100,000 to $71 million in construction value, including several major transportation projects. Among the firm's most notable projects are the South San Francisco Bay Area Rapid Transit Station and Parking Structure, a $40 million project; the 40-story St. Regis Museum Tower and Condominiums; the Water Treatment Plant Campus Facilities Operations Center in San Mateo, California; and the rooftop photovoltaic retrofit for Moscone Convention Center, which is the second-largest such installation in the world.

Stevens's work is guided by a belief "that new futures can be shaped by applying architectural design in the service of environmental quality and community benefit." He is a member of NOMA, the Black Chamber of Commerce in San Francisco, and a neighborhood planning association in San Francisco; formerly he was a member of AIA. Stevens is the father of two children, a physician who has her own practice and a civil engineer who works in his firm. He was born in 1944 in Kansas City. One of his early role models of entrepreneurship was his Aunt Zelma, who ran a thriving restaurant and motel serving black clientele during segregation.

Maybelle Bennett Taylor

Director, Howard University Community Association in Washington, D.C.
Artium Baccalaureus (Black Studies), Vassar College
Master of Science (Urban Planning), *Columbia* 1972

Maybelle Bennett Taylor entered Columbia in 1970 after graduating cum laude from Vassar College with a major in black studies. She completed her Master of Science degree in urban planning in 1972 and then took a position as a town planner in Lagos, Nigeria. Returning to her hometown, Washington D.C., Taylor held several positions involving public policy planning, most notably as director of research at the Coalition on Human Needs, and was also zoning commissioner for the District of Columbia. Then, in 1991, Taylor accepted a position as assistant for community relations in the president's office at Howard University, which evolved into her current job as director of the Howard University Community Relations Association. This position draws upon the breadth of Taylor's experience in physical, public policy, and regulatory planning, and her knowledge of university expansion plans gained during her tenure as zoning commissioner.

The association seeks to improve the university's relationship with the surrounding neighborhoods by engaging residents in dialogue and by helping them access university programs. According to Taylor, these relationships have turned from confrontation to cautious hopefulness. Among the wide range of initiatives she has overseen, the LeDroit Park Initiative stands out as a success in reversing neighborhood disinvestment. With its home ownership opportunities for low- and moderate-income families and its combination of market-rate and subsidized housing, LeDroit Park is a mixed-income, culturally diverse neighborhood that exemplifies community reinvestment.

In addition to her planning work, Taylor provides instruction in fiber arts at the New Community ArtSpace and the Emergence Community Arts Collective, programs that offer affordable arts and crafts classes as an alternative to the destructive pursuits that often plague low-income communities. Together, her planning and artistic involvements help Taylor realize her commitment to not displacing the historical residents of a community, while bringing back the arts to hardworking people who have lost their ability to find joy in creative pursuits. She was born in 1950.

Richard Thomas
Manager of Operations, New York City School Construction
    Authority
Bachelor of Architecture, *Columbia* 1972

Richard Thomas was the son of Blackfoot and Mohawk Indians. He attended community college and took evening courses in building design at Pratt Institute before entering Columbia in 1969. Due to his prior exposure, Thomas completed the five-year program in just three years, graduating in 1972 with a Bachelor of Architecture degree.

Early in his career, Thomas worked with Bond Ryder and Associates on the Lionel Hampton Houses in Harlem and with Mitchell/Giurgola Associates on dormitories at Yale University. Subsequently, he designed Faith United Methodist Church, where he was a member, making it the first Americans with Disabilities Act–compliant church in Staten Island. Currently, Thomas is manager of operations in the facilities division for New York City School Construction Authority. He is also designing a museum for his tribe in honor of a slain tribe member and is running for political office. Thomas serves on a tribal council to understand "the ways of the Native Americans, the indigenous people that we are," which is very important in his life.

Thomas's four children are all in the arts: one daughter is an actress, a son is in the entertainment world, another son is in animation, and a daughter is in the film industry. As he explained, "I took a different road," prioritizing raising his children as "good citizens." Thomas was born in Staten Island in 1942.

Anonymous
Formerly Project Manager, Smithsonian Office of Design and
    Construction
Bachelor of Arts (Fine Arts), Wesleyan University
Master of Architecture, *Columbia* 1973

Robert A. Bennett, AIA
Associate Vice President for Capital Planning, William Paterson
    University of New Jersey
Bachelor of Architecture, Howard University
Master of Science (Urban Planning), *Columbia* 1973

African American architect/planner Robert A. Bennett completed the
two-year Master of Science degree over a period of three years in 1973,
having arrived from Howard University with a Bachelor of Architecture
degree. After graduating, Bennett relocated to West Africa, where he
practiced in private firms, taught urban design and planning, and conducted government-sponsored research. He completed a host of master
plans overseas before returning to the United States, most notably a master plan for a region in postwar Nigeria.

Though he was once principal of a design firm, Bennett more often
has had positions running capital programs for large institutions that are
going through critical stages in their physical growth and development.
While living in Cleveland, his work reoriented to community design
and developing projects that were eventually incorporated into the city's
master plan. During that time, he also helped organize a corps of volunteer colleagues to serve underprivileged communities in the Cleveland
metropolitan area.

In his current position as associate vice president for capital planning,
design, and construction at William Paterson University in Wayne, New
Jersey, Bennett completed a master plan that has been cited as a best
practice in community-engaged campus planning. A 2003 award from
the *American School and University* magazine noted as the plan's strengths
"using existing space with an eye toward future development, a strong
commitment to preserving the remaining open space on campus, and
using information garnered from [a] campus-wide charrette," which Bennett facilitated. In all his work, Bennett seeks to develop succinct programs for planning and design projects, to create credible budgets and

timelines that can be met in the field, to provide excellent client services for the institutions he assists, and to engage individuals at those institutions in the planning and design process. He was born in New York City in 1948.

Raymond C. Jackson, NOMA

Project Executive, Savin Engineers PC in Hauppauge, New York
Bachelor of Architecture, *Columbia* 1973

Raymond C. Jackson started out as an office boy in an architectural firm where he picked up drafting skills and was soon promoted to draftsman. Prior to entering Columbia, Jackson took evening courses at Pratt Institute, which allowed him to earn a Bachelor of Architecture degree by 1973. After graduation, he accumulated experience in both public and private work, developing a specialty in hospital construction. Jackson's largest assignment was the $250 million Elmhurst Hospital in Queens, New York, where he dealt with environmental issues related to an accessory garage, supervised construction of an office management building and an ambulatory care facility, and also oversaw the rehire of employees for a six-hundred-bed hospital. His duties were similar at the Health and Hospitals Corporation and at the Harlem Hospital Ambulatory Care facility.

However, Jackson most enjoyed working early in his career on the Schomburg Library and the Lionel Hampton Houses for his former professor Max Bond at Bond Ryder and Associates. A highlight of this job was having an opportunity to meet personally with Mr. Hampton. Another highlight was contributing to the firm's initial design for the Martin Luther King, Jr., Center in Atlanta, which he presented personally to Coretta Scott King. He is particularly proud of being able to meet Mrs. King and considers that his work with Bond was "the most fun."

In addition to being involved with NOMA and mentoring minority students on a firsthand basis, Jackson volunteers for organizations that provide affordable housing in New York City's ethnic minority communities. He believes that working with architects and engineers in these communities is a way of giving back and addressing some of the needs he experienced in his boyhood. Jackson was born in Greenville, South Carolina in 1948.

George Thomas Snead, AIA

President and CEO, CSGS Inc. in California
Associate in Construction Technology, City College of New York
Bachelor of Architecture, *Columbia* 1973

An African American, George Thomas Snead is the son of an architect and had earned an associate's degree in construction technology from City College of New York before hearing about Columbia's outreach efforts. He received his Bachelor of Architecture degree in 1973 and set out on what he describes as "a very circuitous route" to his current position as president and CEO of CSGS Inc., which provides architecture consulting services with a specialty in project, program, and construction management.

After graduation, Snead spent about twelve years working as an architect for the U.S. Department of Housing and Urban Development. He takes great pride in being part of an agency that provided housing for low-income urbanites and in completing thousands of residential units throughout California and Arizona. Subsequently, Snead developed a CSGS portfolio that includes project administration (e.g., a recreation center in New Orleans and low-rise, high-density housing in Brownsville, New York) as well as design (e.g., educational facilities for the New York City Board of Education, residential renovations in California, and restaurants in Beverly Hills and Santa Monica). Snead is currently working with Construction Controls Group, where he is assistant project director, managing a construction bond program for Los Angeles Community College District.

Snead is a registered architect in the state of California and a member of AIA and NOMA, where he mentors young people with an interest in the building industry. He also volunteers with nonprofit and religious groups, helping them work through the design process for their facilities. In addition to serving as commissioner on California's Board of Architectural Examiners, Snead has photographed historic sites in Japan, China, Brazil, and many European urban centers, gaining insights into urban growth and development. Snead also enjoys demystifying architecture for his clients so they can unravel all the details that make projects successful. He was born in Brooklyn in 1948.

Sharon Egretta Sutton, PhD, FAIA

Professor of Architecture and Urban Design, Adjunct Professor of
  Social Work, Director of the Center for Environment Education and
  Design Studies, University of Washington in Seattle
Fine Artist and Former Musician
Bachelor of Music, University of Hartford
Master of Architecture, *Columbia* 1973
Master of Philosophy, Hunter College
Master of Arts and PhD (Psychology), City University of New York

Dr. Sharon Egretta Sutton, FAIA, was introduced to professional life
at age sixteen when she was hired to play French horn in the Dayton
Symphony Orchestra. After moving to New York City and obtaining
a Bachelor of Music degree, she spent a summer at Tanglewood Music
Center and then went to work for the renowned impresario Sol Hurok.
As a young black woman she was thrilled to perform in the orchestras of
the Bolshoi, Leningrad, Royal, and Moiseyev ballet companies in such
concert halls as New York City's old Metropolitan Opera House, San
Francisco's War Memorial, and Philadelphia's Academy of Music. Sutton
later performed in the New World Symphony Orchestra, in Radio City
Music Hall, and on Broadway with *Fiddler on the Roof*, *A Funny Thing
Happened on the Way to the Forum*, and *Man of La Mancha*.

Her shift into architecture began in the early 1960s when she rede-
veloped a rooming house on Manhattan's West Side as rent-controlled
apartments. With a renovation completed, she began studying interior
design at Parsons School of Design while still working as a musician.
After receiving a Master of Architecture degree from Columbia in 1973
that included a year studying art and architecture in Florence, Italy, Sutton apprenticed in several New York City offices and received her license
in 1976. That same year, in addition to teaching at Pratt Institute and in
two public schools, she began doctoral studies in psychology at the City
University of New York.

Since 1975, Sutton has served on the faculties of Pratt Institute, Columbia University, the University of Cincinnati, and the University of
Michigan—where she became the first African American woman in the
United States to be promoted to full professor of architecture—before accepting her current position at the University of Washington. She writes
books and articles aimed at both scholarly and general audiences, and she
lectures internationally at colleges and universities, in community settings,
and at professional meetings in several disciplines. Sutton's fine art is in

private and public collections, including at the Library of Congress. These endeavors have resulted in numerous awards, among them a Life Recognition Award from the Michigan Women's Hall of Fame, fellow status in AIA, a Distinguished Professor Award from the Association of Collegiate Schools of Architecture, an AIA Whitney Young, Jr., Award, and an AIA Seattle Medal of Honor.

In conferring the Regents Award for Distinguished Public Service, James J. Duderstadt, then president of the University of Michigan, characterized Sutton's contributions as follows: "Whether she is teaching architectural design, helping elementary school children to improve their community, or raising public awareness of environmental issues, Sharon Sutton connects knowledge with action in pursuit of social progress. She is a national advocate for reinvigorating urban America and its youth, and is a socially conscious—and conscientious—teacher and community worker. Professor Sutton engages her students in service to low-income communities as she teaches them professional skills . . . [and she] is also a tireless local advocate for the role of the environment in human development." Sutton was born in Cincinnati in 1941.

David Hughes, AIA
Professor, Kent State University
Bachelor of Architecture, *Columbia* 1974
Master of Arts in Planning, City College of New York

An African American, David Hughes arrived at Columbia with academic credits from Hofstra University and some work experience. Widely recognized as a leader among the ethnic minority recruits, he earned a Bachelor of Architecture degree in 1974 and then went on to graduate study, first at Princeton University and then at City College of New York, where he earned a Master of Arts degree in planning. Hughes worked in the Mayor's Policy and Development Office in Newark and was eventually recruited to Cleveland to work for a planning agency there. After receiving his architecture license in 1979, he opened a practice in Cleveland and began a collaboration with Robert P. Madison International Inc., a large, black-owned architecture firm, which led to a tenure-track position at Kent State University. Hughes is currently one of twenty-two African American full professors of architecture.

A world traveler, Hughes has toured throughout Europe and in Egypt. As a Fulbright Scholar, he undertook a two-year journey across the African continent, teaching in Uganda and Zambia, and conducting research for a book that provides a theoretical framework for the design, critique, and analysis of architecture derived from Africa. The book represents the culmination of Hughes's endeavors to contribute to knowledge about the contributions of Africans and African Americans to the world of architecture. In addition to Fulbright funding, the research had support from the Graham Foundation, the Cooper Hewitt Smithsonian Design Museum, and Kent State University.

Gaining recognition for the contributions of African and African American architects is part of Hughes's life mission "to inspire, encourage, and mentor black students, faculty, and practitioners to enter, persevere, and prosper in architecture." Hughes is a member of AIA and NOMA, and is proud to have maintained an architecture practice. Yet he notes that he does not have "a work of substance" to his name and, with that observation, leaves open the possibility of completing a signature piece. Hughes was born in Brooklyn in 1948.

George Peterson Meadows
Owner and Principal, George Meadows RA in New Jersey
Bachelor of Architecture, *Columbia* 1974

George Peterson Meadows graduated in 1974, having earned a Bachelor of Architecture degree in just four years. Unable to find employment in architecture, he worked as a planner, advancing from an entry-level position to planning officer for the city of Newark. Meadows then began accepting jobs in different architecture firms, gaining experience in residential, commercial, and institutional buildings. With early training completed in two fields, he took licensing exams to practice as both a professional planner and an architect, and then opened a private practice in planning and architecture.

Meadows served as architect for school districts in both Irvington and Paterson, New Jersey. He designed several churches, childcare centers, a municipal plaza, and a catering facility in a historic district of Paterson and is currently converting an industrial building there into housing. In describing these projects, Meadows notes that while they are driven by clients, he turns their requirements into something that serves the broader community. His goals as a planner/architect are to help community clients develop as entrepreneurs by assisting them through the process of creating facilities that meet given spatial requirements. Meadows also tries to bring a high level of design sensitivity to his projects, particularly his schools, subsidized housing, and childcare centers. Because he cares more about the occupants of his buildings than would a mainstream architect/ planner, Meadows believes he brings more to the table and is more willing to seek adventurous solutions.

Meadow also cares deeply about mentoring the next generation. According to his firm résumé, "He is committed to the deliberate and active recruitment, hiring, and training of ethnic minority design professionals to . . . ensure that they are adequately prepared to become independent practitioners of the professions of architecture and planning."

In addition to mentoring young professionals, Meadows spends significant time with students from kindergarten through college, encouraging them to consider architecture as a career. He has judged the National Association for the Advancement of Colored People ACT-SO program and taught pre-architecture courses at Passaic County Technical Institute. Because of his own trouble gaining entry-level experience, Meadows takes great joy in reaching out to young people "to pass along whatever [he's] learned." He was born in Newark in 1948.

Robert Arthur King, FAIA
Owner and Principal, Robert Arthur King Architect
Adjunct Professor, New York School of Interior Design
Associate's Degree (Engineering), Academy of Aeronautics
Bachelor of Architecture, *Columbia* 1975
Diploma, Architectural Association in London

Robert Arthur King, FAIA, arrived a Columbia having earned an associate's degree in engineering at the Academy of Aeronautics in New York and taken additional engineering coursework at the City University of New York. A Harlem-born West Indian, he graduated in 1975 with a Bachelor of Architecture degree and then earned a diploma from the prestigious Architectural Association in London. Returning to the United States at the height of the 1970s recession, King was unable to find work in architecture, so he took construction jobs. However, with the one-on-one mentoring of black architect John Louis Wilson (*Columbia* 1928), King was able to get his architecture license. He is currently a registered architect in New York and nine other states, and is also a certified interior designer in New York State.

King's specialty is the restoration and preservation of historic buildings, where his objective is not to make a design statement but to create spaces that are in harmony with what already exists. Most of the buildings he restores were built in the 1800s—for example, he once adapted an 1883

mansion to accommodate multiple apartments. Because of his construction experience, King often serves a mediator for the American Arbitra-
tion Association, especially on disputes between clients and contractors.

In addition to his work as an architect and interior designer, King is an
avid photographer and has published photographic essays documenting
the stone sculptures contained in New York's historic building facades.
He has also self-published a book on building codes to support a course
he teaches as an adjunct professor at the New York School of Interior Design, and he is a popular guest critic and lecturer in the New York metropolitan area. King was formerly a member of the New York State Board
for Interior Design, has been elected treasurer of the New York chapter
of the American Society of Interior Designers, and currently serves on
the board of directors of New York's Brownstone Revival Committee.
He was born in 1945.

Mark G. Barksdale

Owner and Principal, M. G. Barksdale, Architects and Planners
Bachelor of Science (Architecture), City College of New York
Master of Science (Urban Planning), *Columbia* 1976
Master of Science (Health Services), *Columbia* 1984
Juris Doctor (Law), Yale University

An African American, Mark G. Barksdale has a deep love for music,
having performed as a percussionist for the Dance Theatre of Harlem, the
Queens Festival Orchestra, and various orchestras and rhythm and blues
bands. He entered Columbia having worked at ARCH while earning
an undergraduate architecture degree from City College of New York;
as a graduate student he continued interning with the Harlem office of
New York City's Department of City Planning. Barksdale graduated in
1978 with a Master of Science degree in urban planning and subsequently
earned a Master of Science degree in health services planning and design
from Columbia and a Juris Doctor degree from Yale University.

Licensed to practice both architecture and planning in the state of
New Jersey, Barksdale has held several influential positions in Newark,
serving variously as a planner, historic preservationist, and architect. Most
notably, he was hired to update the city's master plan, including its overall land use patterns as well the specific redevelopment plans for wards
and neighborhoods throughout the city. Barksdale has also been involved
with a number of architecture projects in Newark, New York City, and
elsewhere, and briefly worked for a law firm.

Barksdale's broad academic and professional experiences inform his community engagement commitments. He has served as vice chairman of a Manhattan community planning board, was on the board of an ambulatory care network that manages neighborhood healthcare centers, was an officer with the New York Coalition of Black Architects, and has been a trustee for the Emanuel Pieterson Historical Society, a historic preservation group that disseminates information about African American contributions to the history of New York State and the nation as a whole. Barksdale was born in Washington, D.C., in 1952 and grew up in New York City.

Victor G. Alicea

Bachelor of Science (Experimental Psychology), *Columbia* 1963
Master of Social Work, *Columbia* 1966
Master of Philosophy, *Columbia* 1977
PhD in Urban Planning, *Columbia* 1978

Dr. Victor G. Alicea was born in Ponce, Puerto Rico, and spent his childhood in New York City in Harlem and East Harlem in the "El Barrio" neighborhood. He entered City College of New York in 1956 as a pre-engineering student, transferring to Columbia University after several semesters. Alicea earned four degrees from Columbia between 1963 and 1978, culminating in a PhD in urban planning, followed by postgraduate training at the Gestalt Psychotherapy Institute. He has participated in numerous institutes in public administration, group dynamics, community development, and healthcare service, and has received awards for his contributions in the field of education.

Alicea has held posts as a social worker, educator, and planner and served as consultant in various community development programs. He was lecturer and acting chairman of the Division of Planning during his doctoral studies. After graduation, Alicea was appointed director of the Puerto Rican Research and Resources Center in Washington, D.C., and from that position became chief planner, founder, and president of Boricua College in 1974, making him the longest-serving president of a private college in New York State.

Throughout his professional career, Alicea has maintained a deep commitment to the Puerto Rican community and to the city of New York. He has served on commissions and committees for Mayors Wagner, Lindsay, Koch, Dinkins, and Giuliani. In 1990, Alicea was appointed to the New York City Planning Commission by Mayor Dinkins and re-appointed in 1995 by Mayor Giuliani. He was elected to the Governing Board of the Hispanic Association of Colleges and Universities in 1994 and, in 1996, he became a fellow and trustee of the New York Academy of Medicine. In 1998, he was reelected to another term as secretary of the Board of Trustees. Alicea has two sons and five grandchildren. He was born in 1939.

Frank W. Peterson, Jr.
Architect, U.S. Army Corps of Engineers in Alabama
Bachelor of Science (Architecture), Tennessee State University
Bachelor of Architecture, *Columbia* 1978

A southern-born, African American Vietnam veteran, Frank W. Peterson, Jr., arrived at Columbia in 1969 with some work experience and a non-professional degree in architecture. He completed the Bachelor of Architecture degree in 1978 and worked briefly in New York City. Peterson relocated first to Washington, D.C., and then he settled in Mobile, Alabama, where he established a practice designing low-income housing and black churches. During an economic downturn, Peterson accepted a position as an architect with the U.S. Army Corps of Engineers in the Mobile District, where he was able continue his commitment to designing housing. Presently, he is a private negotiator for the Corps, but he has also been a design architect and a construction manager.

Peterson's milestones to attaining his current position were receiving a Columbia degree, working for New York–area architects, and being mentored by senior African American architects. During the late 1970s, he received a presidential design award from Jimmy Carter for his work on Herbert Field, and he recently completed the architecture and interior design for an administrative building at MacDill Air Force Base. However, Peterson is most interested in working on military housing projects. Because the type of enlisted and officer personnel on military bases has changed radically over the years, he has had the unique challenge of designing new approaches to military housing.

Peterson is also invested in mentoring aspiring architects and has undertaken a variety of mayoral appointments in the city of Mobile. He is married, plays golf, and has five children. Peterson was born in Atlanta in 1945.

Appendix B: Academic Credentials of All Ethnic Minority Recruits Attending the School of Architecture, 1965–1976

In the list below, an asterisk marks the names of members of the oral history cohort.

All Degrees the Recruits Earned from Columbia University

John O. Phillips★
    Bachelor of Arts, *Columbia* 1962
    Master of Architecture, *Columbia* 1966
Victor G. Alicea★
    Bachelor of Science (Experimental Psychology), *Columbia* 1963
    Master of Social Work, *Columbia* 1966
    Master of Philosophy, *Columbia* 1977
    PhD in Urban Planning, *Columbia* 1978
Robert L. Wilson (deceased)
    Bachelor of Architecture, *Columbia* 1963
    Master of Science in Architecture, *Columbia* 1970
David C. Singler
    Master of Architecture, *Columbia* 1966
Carl C. Anthony★
    Bachelor of Architecture, *Columbia* 1969
William Garrison McNeil
    Master of Architecture, *Columbia* 1969

Luis Aponte-Parés★
    Master of Science (Architecture), *Columbia* 1970
    PhD (Urban Planning), *Columbia* 1990
Manuel Otero
    Columbia 1970
Jaime Luis Suarez★
    Master of Science (Architecture), *Columbia* 1970
James Richard Doman (deceased)
    Master of Architecture, *Columbia* 1971
James M. Francis
    Columbia 1971
Emmett B. Hagood★
    Columbia 1971
Robert Henry
    Columbia 1971
Ghislaine M. P. Hermanuz★
    Master of Science (Urban Planning), *Columbia* 1971
Harry J. Quintana (deceased)
    Columbia 1971
Roberta D. Washington★
    Master of Science in Architecture (Hospital and Health Facility
        Design), *Columbia* 1971
Stanford R. Britt★
    Master of Architecture, *Columbia* 1972
Lloyd A. deSuze★
    Bachelor of Architecture, *Columbia* 1972
Charles Levonne Laughinghouse★
    Bachelor of Arts (Architecture), *Columbia* 1972
Myles A. Stevens★
    Master of Science in Architecture, *Columbia* 1972
James A. Strawder, Jr.
    Bachelor of Architecture, *Columbia* 1972
Maybelle Bennett Taylor★
    Master of Science (Urban Planning), *Columbia* 1972
Richard Thomas★
    Bachelor of Architecture, *Columbia* 1972
Francis Lee Turner
    Bachelor of Architecture, *Columbia* 1972
Anonymous★
    Master of Architecture, *Columbia* 1973

Robert A. Bennett★
  Master of Science (Urban Planning), *Columbia* 1973
Rudolph Dupuy
  Master of Architecture, *Columbia* 1973
Shirley A. Graves
  Master of Science (Urban Planning), *Columbia* 1973
Hiram E. Jackson, III
  Master of Science (Urban Planning), *Columbia* 1973
Raymond C. Jackson★
  Bachelor of Architecture, *Columbia* 1973
Rolando Laveist
  Bachelor of Architecture, *Columbia* 1973
Errol A. Rhoden
  Bachelor of Architecture, *Columbia* 1973
George Thomas Snead★
  Bachelor of Architecture, *Columbia* 1973
Sharon Egretta Sutton★
  Master of Architecture, *Columbia* 1973
Stephen J. P. P. Beaumont
  Master of Architecture, *Columbia* 1974
Marilyn Henry Howell
  Master of Science (Urban Planning), *Columbia* 1974
David Hughes★
  Bachelor of Architecture, *Columbia* 1974
Stanley S. McIntosh
  Master of Science (Urban Planning), *Columbia* 1974
George Peterson Meadows★
  Bachelor of Architecture, *Columbia* 1974
Robert J. Harmon
  Master of Architecture, *Columbia* 1975
Robert Arthur King★
  Bachelor of Architecture, *Columbia* 1975
Mark G. Barksdale★
  Master of Science (Urban Planning), *Columbia* 1976
  Master of Science (Health Services), *Columbia* 1984
Terry D. Plater
  Master of Architecture, *Columbia* 1976
Albert Smith, III
  Master of Architecture, *Columbia* 1976

Lillian L. Thompson
  Master of Architecture, *Columbia* 1976
Richard Gerald Shaw
  Master of Architecture, *Columbia* 1977
Frank W. Peterson, Jr.★
  Bachelor of Arts (Architecture), *Columbia* 1978
Adé Omowale
  Master of Architecture, *Columbia* 1981
James P. Wooten
  PhD (Urban Planning) *Columbia* 1982

Advanced Degrees the Recruits Earned from Other Universities

Mark G. Barksdale★
  Juris Doctor (Law), Yale University
Stanford R. Britt★
  Master of Business Administration, Harvard University
Marilyn Henry Howell
  Juris Doctor (Law), New York University
David Hughes★
  Master of Arts in Planning, City College of New York
Robert Arthur King★
  Diploma, Architectural Association in London
Charles Levonne Laughinghouse★
  Master of Architecture, UC Berkeley
John O. Phillips★
  Master of Hotel and Restaurant Management, City University of
    New York
Sharon Egretta Sutton★
  Master of Philosophy, Hunter College
  Master of Arts and PhD (Psychology), City University of New York

The Recruits Who Did Not Graduate

Carmen Gloria Baba-Dijois
Martin Bowman
Tony Brown
Iris Concepción
Felix Cosme

Myrta Cruz
Elizabeth Davilla
David Kirkwood
Rodney D. Parker
Juan Santana

Notes

Introduction

1. Frances Fox Piven and Richard A. Cloward, *Poor People's Movements: Why They Succeed, How They Fail* (New York: Vintage Books, 1979), 8.

2. Robert B. Goldmann, *Money in Search of a Mission* (New York: Ford Foundation Division of National Affairs Project Evaluation, 1970), 2.

3. Piven and Cloward, *Poor People's Movements.*

4. Cornel West, "Foreword," in Michelle Alexander, *The New Jim Crow: Mass Incarceration in the Age of Colorblindness*, Kindle ed. (New York: New Press, 2012), n. pag.

5. Chris Hedges, "Rise of the New Black Radicals," *Truthdig*, 26 April 2015, http://www.truthdig.com/report/item/rise_of_the_new_black_radicals_20150426/, quoting T-Dubb-O, one of the founders of Hands Up United.

6. Grace Lee Boggs and Scott Kurashige, *The Next American Revolution: Sustainable Activism for the Twenty-First Century* (Berkeley: University of California Press, 2011), 67.

7. John Eligon, "Racial Violence in Milwaukee Was Decades in the Making, Residents Say," *New York Times*, 14 August 2016.

8. Thomas J. Sugrue, *The Origins of the Urban Crisis: Race and Inequality in Postwar Detroit* (Princeton, N.J.: Princeton University Press, 1996).

9. Goldmann, *Money in Search of a Mission.*

10. My research assistant, Elizabeth A. Circo, was enrolled in the University of Washington's Doctoral Program in Social Welfare. She was of mixed-race African American heritage and held undergraduate and graduate degrees from Howard University. Her training as a researcher and interviewer outweighed her unfamiliarity with the idiosyncrasies of architecture and planning; I

coached her as did the first few interviewees, and she soon learned the jargon and traditions of these fields.

11. The study, titled "Forty Years after the Insurrection: A Study of African American and Puerto Rican Students at Columbia University's School of Architecture, 1964–1973," was conducted in strict accordance with procedures specified in University of Washington IRB application #32054. Elizabeth collected the oral histories by telephone, the average session lasting one hour and forty-five minutes, with the shortest being forty minutes and the longest being two hours and forty-five minutes.

12. I reviewed each transcript and provided it to the interviewee, inviting changes in wording or corrections of fact, which only two people did. Elizabeth's interview transcriptions totaled 353 single-spaced pages.

13. Edited by Richard Oliver and published by Rizzoli in 1981.

14. I asked Polshek, the former dean who oversaw this publication, why the Division of Planning was not included in the centennial publication. He responded that at the time of the publication, the division was in a disastrous state and that architecture was, at any rate, a more glamorous profession. He did not remember considering including the planning division in the book.

15. My primary archival data includes over 1,200 pages of documents from Columbia University's Rare Book and Manuscript Library and Avery Library: Department of Drawings and Archives. From the former, I reviewed the Central Files (Faculty of Architecture Meeting Minutes, School of Architecture: 1931–1973, and Miscellaneous); the GSAS Collection (School of Architecture 1969–1984); and the Office of the Provost Records (1953–2006). From the latter, I reviewed the Max Bond Papers, various centennial notes, and selected school catalogs. In addition, I searched the ProQuest Historical Newspapers: *New York Times* archive for articles related to race, housing, urban renewal, Robert Wagner, John Lindsay, and Columbia University during the period of time under investigation. Finally, I reviewed materials from the AIA Library and American Planning Association Division of Rare and Manuscript Collections at Cornell University.

16. One of the cohort members was earning a nonprofessional B Arts degree through Columbia College but taking classes alongside the professional degree students.

17. Almost five years had elapsed between the time I completed the interviews and my discovery in the archives of additional names of ethnic minority students. Due to this passage of time and the need for moving the project forward, I decided against attempting to expand the study population. Though it represents a smaller proportion of the total cohort, I believe the study population's views are representative, and they are supported by the archival data.

18. The AIA College of Fellows has only about one hundred African American fellows; that four are from this one group of recruits is amazing.

19. I use the term "at least" because I have drawn this information from the *1984 Alumni Directory, Columbia University Graduate School of Architecture and*

Planning (GSAPP), the *2004 Columbia University Directory* (Purchase, N.Y.: Bernard C. Harris Publishing), and the *2014 Columbia University Alumni Directory* (Harris Connect, 2013). These sources are inconsistent and likely incomplete.

20. According to a 2007 study, 35 percent of African American architects graduated from just seven HBCUs, with 65 percent spread among the remaining 117 majority schools. At the time of the study, Columbia ranked first among majority schools in producing African American architects. See Dennis Mann and Brad Grant, "African American Architects and Their Education: A Demographic Study" (working paper, University of Cincinnati Center for the Study of Practice, Cincinnati, Ohio, 2007). However, by 2009, Columbia had fallen to third place behind Pratt Institute and the City University of New York, both of which began expanding their enrollment of black students.

21. That is, in its 134-year history, Columbia's School of Architecture produced seven African American alumni who are fellows in the American Institute of Architects, with four graduating during the arc of insurgency.

22. West, "Foreword."

1. Pre-1965 Context

1. Manning Marable, *Race, Reform, and Rebellion: The Second Reconstruction and Beyond in Black America, 1945 to 2006*, 3rd ed. (Jackson: University Press of Mississippi, 2007).

2. Steven Gregory, *Black Corona: Race and the Politics of Place in an Urban Community* (Princeton, N.J.: Princeton University Press, 1998).

3. Marable, *Race, Reform, and Rebellion*.

4. Mindy Thompson Fullilove, *Root Shock: How Tearing Up City Neighborhoods Hurts America, and What We Can Do about It* (New York: Random House, 2004), 121.

5. Thomas J. Sugrue, *Sweet Land of Liberty: The Forgotten Struggle for Civil Rights in the North* (New York: Random House, 2008).

6. Fullilove, *Root Shock*.

7. Ibid.

8. Benjamin P. Bowser, *The Black Middle Class: Social Mobility—and Vulnerability* (Boulder, Colo.: Lynne Rienner, 2007).

9. Marable, *Race, Reform, and Rebellion*, 37.

10. Claire Gilbert and Donald Heller, "The Truman Commission and Its Impact on Federal Higher Education Policy from 1947 to 2010" (working paper, Pennsylvania State University, Center for the Study of Higher Education, University Park, 2010), 1–21.

11. Ibid.

12. Stefan M. Bradley, *Harlem vs. Columbia University: Black Student Power in the Late 1960s* (Urbana: University of Illinois Press, 2009), 64.

13. Laura Kalman, *Yale Law School and the Sixties* (Chapel Hill: University of North Carolina Press, 2005).

14. James J. Farrell, *The Spirit of the Sixties: Making Postwar Radicalism* (New York: Routledge, 1997).

15. Anthony M. Orum, *Black Students in Protest: A Study of the Origins of the Black Student Movement* (Washington, D.C.: American Sociological Association, 1972).

16. Ibram H. Rogers, *The Black Campus Movement: Black Students and the Racial Reconstitution of Higher Education, 1965–1972*, Kindle ed. (New York: Palgrave Macmillan, 2012), 2.

17. Bowser, *Black Middle Class*.

18. Martha Biondi, *The Black Revolution on Campus*, Kindle ed. (Berkeley: University of California Press, 2012).

19. Rogers, *Black Campus Movement*, 3.

20. Ibid.

21. Bradley, *Harlem vs. Columbia*.

22. Linda Perkins, "The African American Female Elite: The Early History of African American Women in the Seven Sister Colleges, 1880–1960," *Harvard Educational Review* 67, no. 4 (1997): 718–56.

23. Rogers, *Black Campus Movement*, 5.

24. St. Claire Drake, "What Happened to Black Studies?" *New York University Educational Quarterly* 10, no. 3 (1979): 15, as quoted in Biondi, *Black Revolution on Campus*, 3.

25. Sugrue, *Sweet Land of Liberty*, 13.

26. Ada Louise Huxtable, "600 Acres of Trouble: Morningside, City's Top Renewal Area, Is a Crucible of Crime and Creativity," *New York Times*, 30 September 1964.

27. Bradley, *Harlem vs. Columbia*.

28. Huxtable, "600 Acres of Trouble."

29. Charles Grutzner, "Renewal on the Way for Morningside: City Preparing to Ask U.S. for Funds to Draw a Plan for Heights Quickly," *New York Times*, 11 September 1960.

30. Huxtable, "600 Acres of Trouble."

31. Bradley, *Harlem vs. Columbia*, 34.

32. Huxtable, "600 Acres of Trouble."

33. Editor, "Need for Housing Vexes Columbia: University in Conflict with Tenants," *New York Times*, 25 August 1957.

34. Fred M. Hechinger, "Columbia Plans Huge Expansion: Buildings to Cost 68 Million," *New York Times*, 9 April 1961.

35. Craig Steven Wilder, *Ebony and Ivy: Race, Slavery, and the Troubled History of America's Universities*, Kindle ed. (New York: Bloomsbury, 2013), 265.

36. Ibid., 9.

37. Ibid.

38. Jerome Karabel, *The Chosen: The Hidden History of Admission and Exclusion at Harvard, Yale, and Princeton* (New York: Houghton Mifflin, 2005), 2.

39. Editor, "Bias at Columbia Denied at Hearing: Two Officials Defend

College of Surgeons on Racial Charges before Council Group," *New York Times*, 18 May 1946.

40. Grace Lee Boggs and Scott Kurashige, *The Next American Revolution: Sustainable Activism for the Twenty-First Century*, Kindle ed. (Berkeley: University of California Press, 2012).

41. Ibid.

42. Jerome Karabel, "How Affirmative Action Took Hold at Harvard, Yale, and Princeton," *Journal of Blacks in Higher Education* 48 (Summer 2005): 67.

43. Editor, "Search for Negro Students," *New York Times*, 20 October 1963.

44. Bradley, *Harlem vs. Columbia*, 140, citing Kalman, *Yale Law School and the Sixties*.

45. Karabel, "How Affirmative Action Took Hold at Harvard, Yale, and Princeton," 62.

46. Ibid.

47. Burton J. Bledstein, *The Culture of Professionalism: The Middle Class and the Development of Higher Education in America* (New York: Norton, 1978).

48. Marta Gutman and Richard Plunz, "Anatomy of Insurrection," in *The Making of an Architect, 1881–1981*, ed. Richard Oliver (New York: Rizzoli, 1981), 183–210.

49. Sharon E. Sutton, "The Progress of Architecture," *Progressive Architecture*, October 1993, 77.

50. The specific titles changed over the years as the university administration expanded and roles were redefined.

51. Gutman and Plunz, "Anatomy of Insurrection."

52. This evolution progressed from being a required course in the architecture curriculum (1912), to being a planning studio (1935), to becoming a specialization within the M Architecture program, to becoming a program that admitted students who earned the MS in Planning and Housing degree (1941), to offering a PhD in Urban Planning (1953), to offering a BA in Planning (1961), which was later eliminated. These dates are from an accreditation report dated December 1969 (Central Files, School of Architecture: 1956–1971, Box 618, Folder 8) and from the school's current website, http://old.arch.columbia.edu/programs/urban-planning/mission-history. Where the dates did not agree, I have listed the ones found in the archives.

53. Correspondence dated 20 January 1964 (Provost Records: 1963–2006, Box 80, Barzum to Kirk).

54. Correspondence dated 22 June 1965 (Central Files: Miscellaneous, Box 457, Folder 17, Barzum to Smith).

55. Ada Louise Huxtable, "Expansion at Columbia: A Restricted Vision and Bureaucracy Seen as Obstacles to Its Development," *New York Times*, 5 November 1966.

56. Richard Oliver, "History VI: 1959–1968," in *The Making of an Architect, 1881–1981*, ed. Richard Oliver (New York: Rizzoli, 1981), 167–82.

57. Judith Oberlander, "History IV: 1933–1935," in *The Making of an Architect, 1881–1981*, ed. Richard Oliver (New York: Rizzoli, 1981), 119–26.

58. Gutman and Plunz, "Anatomy of Insurrection."

59. Oliver, "History VI," 172.

60. Gutman and Plunz "Anatomy of Insurrection," p. 190.

61. Oliver, "History VI."

62. "Stenographic Transcript of Proceedings: Meeting of Faculty and Staff of the School of Architecture, Columbia University, Held at Avery Hall, 22 March 1963" (Central Files: School of Architecture, 1956–1971, Box 618, Folder 4).

63. Correspondence dated 3 March 1963 (Central Files: School of Architecture, 1956–1971, Box 618, Folder 2, Chamberlain to Kirk).

64. Correspondence dated 20 March 1963 (Central Files: School of Architecture, 1956–1971, Box 618, Folder 3, Colbert to Salvadori).

65. "Stenographic Transcript of Proceedings."

66. Ibid.

67. Oliver, "History VI," 176.

68. Correspondence dated 20 January 1965 (Barzun to Kirk), n. pag.

69. Ibid., n. pag.

70. Oliver, "History VI," 178.

2. 1965–1967 Context

1. Thomas J. Sugrue, *Sweet Land of Liberty: The Forgotten Struggle for Civil Rights in the North* (New York: Random House, 2008).

2. Ibid.

3. Minutes of the Fall Meeting of the AIA Board of Directors in Chatham, Cape Cod, Mass., 26–28 September 1967 (Document no. 446, American Institute of Architects Library).

4. Document no. 353 dated 30 April 1967 (American Institute of Architects Library, entered 3 May 1967).

5. Minutes of the Fall Meeting of the AIA Board of Directors.

6. Document no. 353.

7. Document no. 365 dated 30 November 1967 (American Institute of Architects Library, entered 6 December 1967).

8. Minutes of the Fall Meeting of the AIA Board of Directors, 25.

9. Ibid., 26.

10. Ibid., 25.

11. Document no. 375 dated 7 May 1968 (American Institute of Architects Library).

12. Henry Sanoff, "Origins of Community Design," *Progressive Planning Magazine*, 2 January 2006, http://www.plannersnetwork.org/2006/01/origins-of-community-design/.

13. Ada Louise Huxtable, "Planning for Cities in Chaos," *New York Times*, 16 October 1967.

14. Walter Thabit, "The History of Planners for Equal Opportunity" (PEO Archives, Rare and Manuscript Collections, University Library, Carl A. Kroch Library, Cornell University, May 1999), 26.

15. Ibid., 11.

16. Correspondence dated 18 May 1965 (Provost Records: 1953–2006, Box 98, Carter to Jemmott).

17. Thabit, "History of Planners for Equal Opportunity," 12.

18. Ibid., 16.

19. Huxtable, "Planning for Cities in Chaos."

20. Roger Starr, "Advocators of Planners," *American Society of Planning Officials* 33, no. 2 (1967): n. pag.

21. Thabit, "History of Planners for Equal Opportunity."

22. Charles G. Bennett, "Wagner Defends City as a 'Model': Studied by Nation, He Says in Summing Up Tenure," *New York Times*, 19 October 1965.

23. Ibid.

24. Lawrence O'Kane, "Morningside Tenants Protest Renewal at City Hall Hearing," *New York Times*, 12 March 1965.

25. Ben A. Franklin, "East Side Group Assails Renewal: Pickets in Capital against Plan for Cooper Square," *New York Times*, 13 October 1965.

26. Ibid.

27. George Dugan, "City Aid Promised to East Harlem: 3 New Commissioners Make a Rehabilitation Tour," *New York Times*, 3 January 1966.

28. Michael Stern, "Lindsay's Office Has First Sit-In: East Harlem Tenants Seek Action on Apartments," *New York Times*, 15 January 1966.

29. Ibid.

30. Ada Louise Huxtable, "Project, Planned 10 Years, Has Been Called Unsound: Work Starts on Total Renewal Project," *New York Times*, 21 October 1966.

31. Ibid.

32. Steven V. Roberts, "Decisions Nearing on Renewal Projects Planned under Mayor Wagner," *New York Times*, 3 May 1966.

33. Ibid.

34. Huxtable, "Project, Planned 10 Years, Has Been Called Unsound."

35. Ada Louise Huxtable, "New Era for Parks: Hoving and Young Appointees Hope to Scrap the Traditional and Try the New," *New York Times*, 10 February 1966.

36. Steven V. Roberts, "Renewal Backed in Williamsburg: Plans Approved but Puerto Ricans Make Protest," *New York Times*, 28 July 1967; Editor, "2 Groups Protest High Cost of Slum Renovation: It Results in Increased Rents," *New York Times*, 21 July 1966.

37. Charles G. Bennett, "Estimate Board Scene of Uproar: Crowd Is in Argumentative Mood at Regular Meeting," *New York Times*, 11 June 1966.

38. Lynn Haney, "Training of Blacks as Architects Increasing: Training Black Architects," *New York Times*, 15 March 1970.

39. Editor, "Negro Architects Helping Harlem Plan Its Future," *New York Times*, 16 March 1969.

40. Ibid.

41. David K. Shipler, "Coalition 'Appoints' 3 Nonwhites to City Plan Group as a Protest," *New York Times*, 13 August 1969.

42. Haney, "Training of Blacks as Architects Increasing."

43. Notes by Richard Rinzler dated 22 January 1969 (Avery Archive: Max Bond Professional Papers, Architects Renewal Committee in Harlem: 1968–1973, Box 7, Folder 8), 7.

44. Luis Aponte-Parés, "Lessons from el Barrio—The East Harlem Real Great Society/Urban Planning Studio: A Puerto Rican Chapter in the Fight for Urban Self-Determination," in *Latino Social Movements: Historical and Theoretical Perspectives*, ed. Rodolfo D. Torres and George Katsiaficas (New York: Routledge, 1999), 52, quoting Richard W. Poston, *Action Now! A Citizen's Guide to Better Communities* (Carbondale: Southern Illinois University Press, 1976), 106.

45. Aponte-Parés, "Lessons from el Barrio," 53.

46. Roger Starr, "The Case of the Columbia Gym," in "The Universities," special issue, *National Affairs* 13 (Fall 1968): 106.

47. O'Kane, "Morningside Tenants Protest Renewal at City Hall Hearing."

48. Robert E. Price, "Columbia: Turning the University Around," in *The University and the City: Eight Cases of Involvement*, ed. George Nash (New York: McGraw-Hill, 1973), 67.

49. Stefan M. Bradley, "'This Is Harlem Heights': Black Student Power and the 1968 Columbia University Rebellion," *Afro-Americans in New York Life and History* 32 no. 1 (2008): 99–122.

50. Kai Bird, *The Color of Truth: McGeorge Bundy and William Bundy, Brothers in Arms* (New York: Simon & Schuster, 1998), 377.

51. Price, "Columbia."

52. Robert B. Goldmann, *Money in Search of a Mission* (New York: Ford Foundation Division of National Affairs Evaluation Report, 1970), 2.

53. Bird, *Color of Truth*.

54. Goldmann, *Money in Search of a Mission*, 3.

55. Ibid., 3.

56. Price, "Columbia," 105.

57. Goldmann, *Money in Search of a Mission*.

58. Marta Gutman and Richard Plunz, "Anatomy of Insurrection," in *The Making of an Architect, 1881–1981*, ed. Richard Oliver (New York: Rizzoli, 1981), 183–210.

59. Stefan M. Bradley, *Harlem vs. Columbia University: Black Student Power in the Late 1960s* (Urbana: University of Illinois Press, 2009).

60. Jeff Ueland and Barney Warf, "Racialized Topographies: Altitude and Race in Southern Cities," *Geographical Review* 96, no. 1 (2006): 50–78.

61. Editor, "10-Year Harlem Plan Is Questioned," *New York Times*, 2 May 1965.

62. Ralph Blumenthal, "Harlem Awaits Use of 1964 Plan: Renewal Proposal Resulted from Study by Columbia," *New York Times*, 23 March 1972.

63. Ibid.

64. Ada Louise Huxtable, "The State Office Building Dilemma," *New York Times*, 2 November 1969.

65. Ibid.

66. Charles Abrams, "The City," lecture at the "On the Uses of Knowledge: the University and the Community" symposium at the University of Chicago, 25 September 1967, n. pag.

67. Charles Abrams, "Present Labor Pains in Planning Education," *American Society of Planning Officials* 34, no. 1 (1968): 1–2.

3. 1968 Insurgency

1. Charles Kaiser, *1968 in America: Music, Politics, Chaos, Counterculture, and the Shaping of a Generation*, Kindle ed. (New York: Grove/Atlantic, 2012), loc. 119.

2. Ibid.

3. Ibid.

4. Douglas Robinson, "Group Backs Two in Draft Protest: Critic and Author Support Registration Card," *New York Times*, 12 January 1968.

5. Fred P. Graham, "The Law: Case against Spock et al.," *New York Times*, 14 January 1968. A Boston court convicted Spock, Coffin, and two of the defendants of conspiracy, but the conviction was overturned the following year by the U.S. Court of Appeals for insufficient evidence (see Eric Page, "Benjamin Spock, World's Pediatrician, Dies at 94," *New York Times*, 17 March 1998).

6. An online project at the University of Washington describes the antiwar activity that racked college campuses. See the contribution by Jessie Kindig, "Draft Resistance in the Vietnam Era," *Antiwar and Radical History Project*, 2008, http://depts.washington.edu/antiwar/vietnam_draft.shtml.

7. "Tet Offensive: Vietnam War," *History.com*, 2009, http://www.history.com/topics/vietnam-war/tet-offensive.

8. Kaiser, *1968 in America*.

9. "Tet Offensive."

10. Kaiser, *1968 in America*.

11. Ibid., loc. 2942, 3197.

12. Ibid.

13. Ibid., loc. 3248–55.

14. Richard Reeves, "Lindsay Renews Criticism of War: Tells Columbia Group He Hopes for Rockefeller Race," *New York Times*, 26 March 1968.

15. Ibid.

16. Editor, "Dr. Kirk Urges U.S. to Leave Vietnam: Columbia Head Finds War Delays Nation's Advance," *New York Times*, 13 April 1968.

17. B. Drummond Ayres, Jr., "A Target of Campus Protesters Is a 'Think Tank': Institute of Defense Analysis," *New York Times*, 26 April 1968.

18. J. Anthony Lucas, "Faculty Warns Columbia on Its Expansion Policy: 70 Members Find It Would Worsen Racial Tensions in Morningside Heights," *New York Times,* 27 March 1968.

19. Editor, "Columbia Seeks Master Planner: I. M. Pei Is Expected to Get Major Expansion Job," *New York Times*, 15 April 1968.

20. Kaiser, *1968 in America*, loc. 780–81.

21. Ada Louise Huxtable, "Hard Questions for Harlem," *New York Times*, 11 February 1968.

22. Ibid.

23. Steven V. Roberts, "Negro-Latin Feud Hurting Harlem: Groups Fighting for Control of Area Renewal Projects," *New York Times*, 25 February 1968.

24. Seth S. King, "Sewage Plant Voted over Harlem Protest, *New York Times*, 26 April 1968.

25. Ibid.

26. C. Gerald Fraser, "12 Arrested at Site of Gym in Morningside Park," *New York Times*, 21 February 1968.

27. Ibid.

28. Editor, "13 Held in Protest over Columbia Gym," *New York Times*, 29 February 1968.

29. Edith Evans Asbury, "Protesters Boo Shriver at Talk on 'Struggle for Urban Power,'" *New York Times*, 3 March 1968.

30. Peter Millones, "Community Discontent and an Increase in Protests Sow the Seeds of Concern at Columbia University," *New York Times*, 3 March 1968.

31. Editor, "New Columbia Gym Is Opposed," *New York Times*, 16 April 1968.

32. Marta Gutman and Richard Plunz, "Anatomy of Insurrection," in *The Making of an Architect, 1881–1981*, ed. Richard Oliver (New York: Rizzoli, 1981), 183–210.

33. Martin Gansberg, "3,500 Join Columbia Boycott," *New York Times*, 14 March 1968.

34. Jocelyn Wilk, "1968: Columbia in Crisis," *Columbia University Libraries: Information Services*, nd, https://exhibitions.cul.columbia.edu/exhibits/show/1968.

35. Ibid.

36. Alan Feigenberg as quoted by Richard Rosenkranz in *Across the Barricades* (New York: J. B. Lippincott, 1971), 16–17.

37. Wilk, "1968."

38. Stefan M. Bradley, "'This Is Harlem Heights': Black Student Power and the 1968 Columbia University Rebellion," *Afro-Americans in New York Life and History* 32, no. 1 (2008): 100–101.

39. Stefan M. Bradley, "'Gym Crow Must Go': Black Student Activism at

Columbia University, 1967–1968," *Journal of African American History* 88 no. 2 (2003): 203.

40. Ibid., 175.

41. Steven V. Roberts, "Sit-in Spectrum Has a Wide Range: But All Students Agree on Voice in Key Decisions," *New York Times*, 25 April 1968.

42. Millones, "Community Discontent and an Increase in Protests Sow the Seeds of Concern at Columbia University."

43. Wilk, "1968."

44. Ibid.

45. Michael Stern, "Teachers at Columbia Risk Violence as Mediators," *New York Times*, 30 April 1968.

46. Jack Gould, "Radio: Keeping Abreast of the Turmoil at Columbia: Students' WKCR Gives a Lesson in Reporting," *New York Times*, 27 April 1968.

47. Ibid.

48. Wilk, "1968."

49. John Kifner, "Students Run Columbia Protest along Principles of Democracy," *New York Times*, 27 April 1968.

50. My description of Avery Hall's occupiers is based upon correspondence dated 19 September 1968 noting "the inability of some thirty suspended students to register due to last spring's demonstrations" (Provost Records: 1953–2006, Lipson to Cordier). In addition, my information comes from Rosenkranz, *Across the Barricades*, who reported that many other students joined the architecture and urban planning students to create a group of "more than eighty who were there the last night" (Epilogue 2). None of the twenty-four School of Architecture students listed by Rosencrantz as participants in the occupation was black; just two were urban planning students.

51. Tony Schuman as quoted in Rosenkranz, *Across the Barricades*, 5.

52. Rolf Busch as quoted in ibid., 29.

53. Alan Feigenberg as quoted in ibid., Log 5.

54. Rosenkranz, *Across the Barricades*, 88.

55. Ken Greenberg as quoted in ibid., 34–35.

56. Ray Lifchez as quoted in ibid., 89.

57. Rosenkranz, *Across the Barricades*, 47.

58. Gutman and Plunz, "Anatomy of Insurrection."

59. Ibid., 204.

60. David Burnham, "Police Guarding Gates to Campus: Also Occupy All Buildings Not Held by Students," *New York Times*, 27 April 1968.

61. Ibid.

62. Ibid.

63. Wilk, "1968."

64. Bradley, "This Is Harlem Heights."

65. Martin Arnold, "Lindsay Orders Report on Police: Leary Will Study Charges of Brutality at Columbia," *New York Times*, 1 May 1968.

66. Wilk, "1968."

67. Ibid.

68. Wilk's "1968," created to mark the fortieth anniversary of the student insurgency, reported that, at 2:30 a.m. on April 30, 1968, "police entered Avery Hall through the main doors to clear the building of occupying students. The police met moderate resistance, and some students received injuries. The police made forty-two arrests." The exhibition also reported that of the 4,993 letters received from parents, students, alumni, and the public, 4,082 supported the university's decision to call in the police.

69. Joel Silverberg as quoted in Rosenkranz, *Across the Barricades*, 218.

70. Helen Niebert (a fictitious name) as quoted in ibid., 226.

71. Kitty Brewster as quoted in ibid., 228.

72. Silverberg as quoted in ibid., 231.

73. Fred Parker as quoted in ibid., Log 11–12.

74. Arnold, "Lindsay Orders Report on Police."

4. 1968–1971 Experimentation

1. Ibram H. Rogers, *The Black Campus Movement: Black Students and the Racial Reconstitution of Higher Education, 1965–1972*, Kindle ed. (New York: Palgrave Macmillan, 2012).

2. Jocelyn Wilk, "1968: Columbia in Crisis," *Columbia University Libraries: Information Services*, nd, https://exhibitions.cul.columbia.edu/exhibits/show/1968.

3. C. Gerald Fraser, "Negroes Keep Campaign on Gym: 'Still the Major Issue' Says Head of Black Students," *New York Times*, 2 May 1968.

4. Ibid.

5. Wilk, "1968."

6. A. Scott Henderson, *Housing and the Democratic Ideal: The Life and Thought of Charles Abrams* (New York: Columbia University Press, 2000).

7. Ibid., 11. Though even some of the most progressive turn-of-the century social reformers presumed that, whereas immigrants were capable of being Americanized, Negros were innately inferior to the white race. See Khalil Gibran Muhammad, *The Condemnation of Blackness: Race, Crime, and the Making of Modern Urban America*, Kindle ed. (Cambridge, Mass.: Harvard University Press, 2010).

8. Henderson, *Housing and the Democratic Ideal*.

9. Ibid.

10. Correspondence dated 8 May 1968 (Provost Records: 1953–2006, Box 240, SOA Faculty, Urban Planning, May 8, 1968–October 26, 1971, Abrams to Rustin).

11. Ibid.

12. Correspondence dated 9 May 1968 (Provost Records: 1953–2006, Box 240, SOA Faculty, Urban Planning, May 8, 1968–October 26, 1971, Abrams to Truman).

13. This recommendation came to pass the following year when Milton Moran Weston II (*Columbia* 1954) became the first African American to serve on Columbia's Board of Trustees. See "Columbia 250: Milton Moran Weston, II," *Columbia 250*, nd, http://c250.columbia.edu/c250_celebrates/remarkable_columbians/milton_weston.html.

14. Correspondence dated 9 May 1968 (Abrams to Truman).

15. Minutes of the Fifty-Second Meeting of the Faculty of Architecture, 28 April 1968 (Central Files, Columbia University Minutes of the Faculty of Architecture).

16. Minutes of the Fifty-Third Meeting of the Faculty of Architecture, 5 May 1968 (Central Files).

17. Ibid.

18. Minutes of the Fifty-Fifth Meeting of the Faculty of Architecture, 17 May 1968 (Central Files).

19. Minutes of the Sixty-First Meeting of the Faculty of Architecture, 25 April 1969 (Central Files).

20. Ibid.

21. Minutes of the Fifty-Seventh Meeting of the Faculty of Architecture, 26 November 1968 (Central Files).

22. Minutes of the Sixtieth Meeting of the Faculty of Architecture, 18 April 1969 (Central Files).

23. Minutes of the Sixty-First Meeting of the Faculty of Architecture.

24. "A Statement of Urgency," 1 October 1968 (Central Files: School of Architecture 1956–1971, Box 618, Folder 7), 7.

25. Wilk, "1968."

26. "Statement of Urgency," 12.

27. "Architectural Divisional Council Position Paper on Faculty," 16 September 1968 (Central Files: School of Architecture 1956–1971, Box 618, Folder 7).

28. "Resolution on Aid to Minority Students," 11 September 1968, attached to "First Report of the Executive Council," 25 September 1968 (Central Files: School of Architecture 1956–1971, Box 618, Folder 6).

29. Minutes of the Forty-Eighth Meeting of the Faculty of Architecture, 9 May 1967 (Central Files).

30. Robert B. Goldmann, *Money in Search of a Mission* (New York: Ford Foundation Division of National Affairs Project Evaluation, 1970).

31. Correspondence dated 15 June 1970 (Central Files: School of Architecture 1956–1971, Box 618, Folder 7, McClure to Cordier).

32. Marta Gutman and Richard Plunz, "Anatomy of Insurrection," in *The Making of an Architect, 1881–1981*, ed. Richard Oliver (New York: Rizzoli, 1981), 183–210.

33. "Architectural Divisional Council Position Paper on Faculty," 2.

34. Ibid., 206.

35. Ibid.

36. Minutes of the Sixty-Second Meeting of the Faculty of Architecture, 13 May 1969 (Central Files, Columbia University Minutes of the Faculty of Architecture).

37. Gutman and Plunz, "Anatomy of Insurrection."

38. Memo from Albert Mayer based upon earlier divisional discussions, 8 December 1967 (Provost Records: 1953–2006, Box 80), n. pag.

39. Ibid.

40. Of the school's six degree programs, just three were implicated in the experimental operation's democratic learning and service efforts: the B Architecture degree program, offered as both a five-year day program and a six-year evening program; the two-year MS in Urban Planning degree program; and the MS in Urban Design degree program, a new degree offered in the Division of Architecture that had just been extended from one to two years.

41. Sharon E. Sutton and Susan P. Kemp, "Introduction: Place as Marginality and Possibility," in *The Paradox of Urban Space: Inequality and Transformation in Marginalized Communities*, ed. Sharon E. Sutton and Susan P. Kemp (New York: Palgrave Macmillan, 2011), 2.

42. Tracy M. Soska, "University and Communities in Partnership: Exploring the Roots and Current Trends of Higher Education Community Engagement in the United States," in *Community Engagement in Higher Education: Policy Reforms and Practice*, ed. W. James Jacob, Stewart E. Sutin, John Weidman, and John L. Yeager (Rotterdam: Sense Publishers, 2015), 105–26.

43. Ms. Moore became an educational planner.

44. "To Whom It May Concern," 10 February 1969 (Central Files: School of Architecture 1956–1971, Box 618, Folder 7).

45. Ibid.

46. Ibid., 1–2.

47. Ibid., 2.

48. Ibid., 4.

49. Ada Louise Huxtable, "600 Acres of Trouble: Morningside, City's Top Renewal Area, Is a Crucible of Crime and Creativity," *New York Times*, 30 September 1964.

50. Document no. 588, "Exhibit 7: Long Range Plan for AIA Scholarships," Minutes, Fall Meeting of the AIA Board of Directors, 20–21 September 1982 (AIA Archives).

51. Rogers, *Black Campus Movement*, 157.

52. "Mellon Fellowship Questionnaire," February 1969, Response to Question #17 (Provost Records: 1953–2006, Box 98, Folder Architecture: General), n. pag.

53. Gutman and Plunz, "Anatomy of Insurrection," 207.

54. Goldmann, *Money in Search of a Mission*, 75.

55. Harold K. Bell and Vernon Ben Robinson, "Appendix IV: A Consortium Venture for Student Field Training," in *A Partnership of Equals: An Action Research Report for Urban Affairs Executives of Universities, Corporations, Govern-*

ments, and Community Organizations (New York: Columbia University Urban Action and Experimentation Program, 1971), n. pag.

5. 1969–1971 Transgression

1. Charles McClintock, "Spanning Boundaries of Knowledge and Organization: Collaborations for Mind and Management in Higher Education," *Organization* 8, no. 2 (2001): 350.

2. Ibram H. Rogers, *The Black Campus Movement: Black Students and the Racial Reconstruction of Higher Education, 1965–1972*, Kindle ed. (New York: Palgrave Macmillan, 2012), 96.

3. Ibid., 121.

4. Ibid., 92.

5. Ibid., 128–29.

6. Ibid.

7. Ibid. This is a paraphrase of Rogers quoting Paula Giddings, who was describing her experiences as a protester at Howard University.

8. St. Claire Drake, "What Happened to Black Studies?" *New York University Educational Quarterly* 10, no. 3 (1979): 15, as quoted in Martha Biondi, *The Black Revolution on Campus*, Kindle ed. (Berkeley: University of California Press, 2012), 3.

9. Jacqueline S. Mithun, "Black Power and Community Change: An Assessment," *Journal of Black Studies* 7, no. 3 (1977), quoting John Hope Franklin and Isidore Starr, eds., *The Negro in Twentieth-Century America: A Reader on the Struggle for Civil Rights* (New York: Vintage Books, 1967), 180.

10. Minutes of the Sixty-Seventh Meeting of the Faculty of Architecture, 4 May 1971 (Provost Records: 1953–2006, Box 240).

11. William G. Bowen and Derek Bok, *The Shape of the River: Long-Term Consequences of Considering Race in College and University Admissions* (Princeton, N.J.: Princeton University Press, 1998), 129.

12. Ibid.

13. Ibid., 130.

14. "History," *Columbia University in the City of New York*, nd, http://www.columbia.edu/content/history.html.

15. Correspondence dated 15 June 1970 (Central Files: SOA 1956–1971, Box 618, Folder 9, McClure to Cordier), 9.

16. Ibid.

17. Linda N. Groat and Sherry Ahrentzen, "Reconceptualizing Architectural Education for a More Diverse Future: Perceptions and Visions of Architectural Students," *Journal of Architectural Education* 49, no. 3 (1996): 166–83.

18. Brad Grant, "Cultural Invisibility: The African American Experience in Architectural Education," in *Voices in Architectural Education: Cultural Politics and Pedagogy*, ed. Tomas A. Dutton (New York: Bergin and Garvey, 1991), 151.

19. Lynn Haney, "Training of Blacks as Architects Increasing: Training Black Architects," *New York Times*, 15 March 1970.

20. "History," *National Organization of Minority Architects*, nd, http://www .noma.net/article/46/organization/about/history.

21. This organization had several names, but here and throughout I use its last one.

22. Harold K. Bell and Vernon Ben Robinson, "Appendix IV: A Consortium Venture for Student Field Training," in *A Partnership of Equals: An Action Research Report for Urban Affairs Executives of Universities, Corporations, Governments, and Community Organizations* (New York: Columbia University Urban Action and Experimentation Program, 1971), n. pag.

23. Ibid.

24. Sharon E. Sutton, "Seeing the Whole of the Moon," in *Multicultural Teaching in the University*, ed. David Schoem, Linda Frankel, Ximena Zúñiga, and Edith Lewis (Westport, Conn.: Praeger Press, 1993), 161.

25. Kathryn H. Anthony, "Private Reactions to Public Criticism: Students, Faculty, and Practicing Architects State Their Views on Design Juries in Architectural Education," *Journal of Architectural Education* 40, no. 3 (1987): 2–11.

26. Ibid.

27. See, for example, Kathryn H. Anthony, *Designing for Diversity: Gender, Race, and Ethnicity in the Architectural Profession* (Urbana: University of Illinois Press, 2001); Andrew S. Caplan and Jamie Gilham, "Included against the Odds: Failure and Success among Minority Ethnic Built-Environment Professionals in Britain," *Construction Management and Economics* 23 (December 2005): 1007–15; and Dana Cuff, *Architecture: The Story of Practice* (Cambridge, Mass.: MIT Press, 1991).

28. Memo from Albert Mayer based on earlier divisional discussions, 8 December 1967 (Provost Records: 1953–2006, Box 80).

29. Ibid., n. pag.

30. Ibid.

31. Editor, "Columbia Students Give Slum Aid Hints," *New York Times*, 29 April 1969.

32. Robert B. Goldmann, *Money in Search of a Mission* (New York: Ford Foundation Division of National Affairs Project Evaluation, 1970), 77.

33. Correspondence dated 13 December 1967 (Provost Records: 1953–2006, Box 80, Abrams to Truman); correspondence dated 15 March 1968 (Central Files: Miscellaneous, Abrams to Kirk).

34. Notes by Richard Rinzler dated 22 January 1969 (Avery Archive: Max Bond Professional Papers, Architects Renewal Committee in Harlem: 1968–1973, Box 7, Folder 8), 3.

35. Luis Aponte-Parés, "Lessons from el Barrio—The East Harlem Real Great Society/Urban Planning Studio: A Puerto Rican Chapter in the Fight for Urban Self-Determination," in *Latino Social Movements: Historical and Theoretical*

Perspectives, ed. Rodolfo D. Torres and George Katsiaficas (New York: Routledge, 1999), 43–77.

36. Notes by Rinzler dated 22 January 1969, 1.

37. Harlem Core and the Architects Renewal Committee in Harlem
Inc., "The Case for a Harlem High School, Committee for a Harlem High
School," February 1969 (Avery Archives: Max Bond Papers, 1951–2009, Box
7: Professional Papers, Architects Renewal Committee in Harlem, 1968–1973,
Folder 7).

38. "Position Paper on Reclamation Site #1," prepared by ARCH, submitted at the Community Hearing Reclamation Site No. 1, 8 August 1969 (Avery
Archives: Max Bond Papers).

39. Harlem Core and the Architects Renewal Committee in Harlem Inc.,
"Case for a Harlem High School, Committee for a Harlem High School," n.
pag.

40. West Harlem Platform, "Morningside Educational Park, Preliminary
Report," nd (Avery Archives: Max Bond Papers).

41. Tom Angotti, Cheryl Doble, and Paula Horrigan, eds., *Service-Learning
in Design and Planning: Education at the Boundaries* (Oakland, Calif.: New Village
Press, 2011), 3.

42. Sharon E. Sutton, "Review Essay: Can Service-Learning Help Restore
the Public University's Role in Safeguarding American Democracy?" *Michigan
Journal of Community Service Learning* 19, no. 1 (2012): 70.

6. 1969–1971 Unraveling

1. Martha Biondi, *The Black Revolution on Campus*, Kindle ed. (Berkeley:
University of California Press, 2012), 3.

2. Correspondence dated 15 June 1970 (Central Files: SOA 1956–1971,
Box 618, Folder 9, McClure to Cordier), 14.

3. Ada Louise Huxtable, "The State Office Building Dilemma," *New York
Times*, 2 November 1969.

4. Lynn Haney, "Training Blacks as Architects Increasing," *New York Times*,
15 March 1970.

5. David K. Shipler, "Small Plant Taking Big Step in Prefabs," *New York
Times*, 27 October 1970.

6. Editor, "Romney Hails Prefab in Yonkers," *New York Times*, 18 May 1971.

7. Robert B. Goldmann, *Money in Search of a Mission* (New York: Ford
Foundation Division of National Affairs Project Evaluation, 1970).

8. Minutes of the Sixty-Seventh Meeting of the Faculty of Architecture,
4 May 1971 (Central Files, Columbia University Minutes of the Faculty of
Architecture).

9. Matthew Dallek, "The Conservative 1960s," *Atlantic Monthly*, December
1995, 130–35.

10. Barbara Ehrenreich, *Fear of Falling: The Inner Life of the Middle Class* (New York: Harper Perennial, 1990), 3.

11. Ibid., 39–40.

12. U.S. Department of State, "Years of Change: The 1960s and 1970s," *About Education*, nd, http://economics.about.com/od/useconomichistory/a/change.htm.

13. Bill Kovach, "Mayor, in Albany, Warns on Budget," *New York Times*, 13 February 1969.

14. Kai Bird, *The Color of Truth: McGeorge Bundy and William Bundy, Brothers in Arms* (New York: Simon & Schuster, 1998).

15. Walter Thabit, "The History of Planners for Equal Opportunity" (PEO Archives, Rare and Manuscript Collections, University Library, Carl A. Kroch Library, Cornell University, May 1999).

16. Minutes of the Sixty-Fifth Meeting of the Faculty of Architecture, 20 November 1970 (Central Files, Columbia University Minutes of the Faculty of Architecture).

17. Minutes of the Fifty-Sixth Meeting of the Faculty of Architecture, 12 November 1968 (Central Files, Columbia University Minutes of the Faculty of Architecture).

18. Correspondence dated December 1968 (Central Files: Miscellaneous, Box 457, Folder 17, Cordier to Smith).

19. Correspondence dated 9 December 1970 (Central Files, Columbia University Minutes of the Faculty of Architecture, Salvadori to Fitch).

20. "Comments re: Architecture School Proposal for 'Restructuring' from Dr. Halford" (Central Files: School of Architecture 1956–1971, Box 618, Folder 7).

21. Correspondence dated 5 May 1969 (Central Files: School of Architecture 1956–1971, Box 618, Folder 7, Smith to Plaut, Jr.).

22. Correspondence dated 31 December 1969 (Provost Records: 1953–2006, Box 240, Office of Minority Affairs, Kenen to Smith).

23. Correspondence dated 15 October 1970 (Central Files: School of Architecture 1956–1971, Box 618, Folder 12, Office of the Provost to Smith).

24. Correspondence dated 15 June 1970 (McClure to Cordier).

25. Correspondence dated 28 August 1970 (Central Files: School of Architecture 1956–1971, Box 618, Folder 12, Emerson to Kenen).

26. Correspondence dated 5 March 1970 (Central Files: School of Architecture 1956–1971, Box 618, Folder 12, Smith to Kenen).

27. Correspondence dated 14 November 1969 (Provost Records: 1953–2006, Box 239, File 1: 15 June 1970–19 December 1973, Williams to Smith).

28. Correspondence dated 19 March 1971 (Central Files: School of Architecture 1956–1971, Box 618, Folder 14, Berg to McGill).

29. Correspondence dated 3 April 1969 (Provost Records: 1953–2006, Box 98, Architecture: General to June 30, 1969, Williams to Smith), n. pag.

30. Correspondence dated 31 January 1969 (Provost Records: 1965–2006, Box 98, Architecture: General, Brookhart to Truman).

31. Correspondence dated 21 April 1969 (Provost Records: 1965–2006, Box 98, Architecture: General, Kusch to Smith).

32. Correspondence dated 16 May 1969 (Provost Records: 1965–2006, Box 98, Architecture: General, Kusch to Smith).

33. Correspondence dated 10 January 1972 (Provost Records: 1953–2006, Box 234, School of Architecture Institute of Urban Environment, Rapkin to Young).

34. Correspondence dated 7 April 1971 (Provost Records: 1953–2006, Box 234, School of Architecture Institute of Urban Environment, Rapkin to Johnson).

35. Correspondence dated 12 December 1969 (Provost Records: 1953–2006, Box 240, School of Architecture Faculty, Urban Planning, Berg to Kusch).

36. Correspondence dated 17 December 1969 (Provost Records: 1953–2006, Box 168, Folder 6: Urban Center, Berg to Cordier), 2.

37. Ibid., 3.

38. Ibid.

39. Ibid.

40. Ibid., 11.

41. Memo from Albert Mayer dated 8 December 1967 (Provost Records: 1953–2006, Box 80), n. pag.

42. Correspondence dated 17 December 1969 (Berg to Cordier), 14.

43. Ibid., 15–16.

44. Correspondence dated 15 June 1970 (McClure to Cordier).

45. Correspondence dated 18 August 1970 (Central Files: School of Architecture 1956–1971, Box 618, Folder 12, Gjertsen to Cordier).

46. Correspondence dated 10 September 1970 (Provost Records: 1953–2006, Box 239, File 1: 15 June 1970–19 December 1973, Kusch to McGill).

47. Marta Gutman and Richard Plunz, "Anatomy of Insurrection," in *The Making of an Architect, 1881–1981*, ed. Richard Oliver (New York: Rizzoli, 1981), 208.

48. Ibid.

49. Correspondence dated 22 January 1970 (Provost Records: 1953–2006, Box 239, File 1: 15 June 1970–19 December 1973, Berg to Cordier and Kusch), 1.

50. Correspondence dated 11 January 1971(Central Files: School of Architecture, 1956–1971, Box 618, Folder 14, Newman to Giurgola).

51. Registered letter dated 5 February 1971 (Central Files: School of Architecture, 1956–1971, Box 618, Folder 14, Newman to Smith).

52. Correspondence dated 17 April 1973 (Provost Records: 1953–2006, Box 240, School of Architecture Faculty, 1968–1972, Smith to Brookhart).

53. Ibid.

54. Correspondence dated 19 December 1969 (Central Files: School of Architecture 1956–1971, Box 618, Folder 8, Bond, Doman, Glasser, Goldberg, Jackson, Karmi, Kliment, MacNeil, and Williams to Kenen).

55. Ibid.

56. "Charles Rieger: Associate Professor of Architecture, Academic Record 1946–1967," nd (Provost Records: 1953–2006, Box 98, Architecture: General).

57. Correspondence dated 6 March 1963 (Central Files: School of Architecture 1956–1971, Box 618, Folder 3, Halse to Barzum).

58. Correspondence dated 6 May 1971 (Provost Records: 1953–2006, Box 239, File 1: 15 June 1970–19 December 1973, Berg to McGill).

59. Minutes of the Sixty-Fifth Meeting of the Faculty of Architecture.

60. Brad Grant, "Cultural Invisibility: The African American Experience in Architectural Education," in *Voices in Architectural Education: Cultural Politics and Pedagogy*, ed. Tomas A. Dutton (New York: Bergin and Garvey, 1991), 151.

61. Marilyn Gittell, "The Illusion of Affirmative Action," *Change* 7, no. 8 (1975): 40.

62. "Selection of William Kinne Awards," Appendix B, Minutes of the Seventy-First Meeting of the Faculty of Architecture (Christ-Janer to William Kinne Fellowship Committee).

63. Correspondence dated 16 February 1971 (Central Files: School of Architecture 1956–1971, Box 618, Folder 14, Black Student-Faculty Organization to McGill).

64. Correspondence dated 26 February 1971 (Central Files: School of Architecture 1956–1971, Box 618, Folder 14, Black Student-Faculty Organization to McGill), 1.

65. Correspondence dated 16 February 1971 (Central Files: School of Architecture 1956–1971, Box 618, Folder 14, Black Student-Faculty Organization to McGill).

66. Correspondence dated 19 February 1971 (Central Files: School of Architecture 1956–1971, Box 618, Folder 14, McGill to Black Student-Faculty Organization).

67. Correspondence dated 26 February 1971 (Central Files: School of Architecture 1956–1971, Box 618, Folder 14, Black Student-Faculty Organization to McGill).

68. Correspondence dated 16 April 1971 (Central Files: SOA 1956–1971, Box 618, Folder 12, McGill to the Search Committee).

69. Wilbur C. Rich, "From Muskogee to Morningside Heights: Political Scientist Charles V. Hamilton," *Living Legacies: Great Moments and Leading Figures in the History of Columbia University*, nd, http://www.columbia.edu/cu/alumni/Magazine/Spring2004/hamilton.html.

70. "Job Description: Assistant to the Dean for Minority Affairs," nd (Provost Records: 1953–2006, Box 240, Office of Minority Affairs).

71. Correspondence dated 29 June 1971 (GSAS Collection, Box 1, File 13, November 1969–November 1971, Jackson to McGill).

72. Ibid.

73. Correspondence dated 30 July 1971 (GSAS Collection, Box 1, File 13, November 1969–November 1971, McGill to Jackson).

74. Correspondence dated 9 July 1971 (GSAS Collection, Box 1, File 13, November 1969–November 1971, Frankel to Young).

75. Correspondence dated 28 September 1971 (Provost Records: 1953–2006, Box 240, Office of Minority Affairs, Admissions Committee to Smith).

76. Correspondence dated 5 October 1971 (Provost Records: 1953–2006, Box 240, Office of Minority Affairs, Smith to Brookhart).

77. Though university administrators rejected Smith's proposal, they later approved an exception that allowed Jackson to be simultaneously an administrator and a student after he threatened legal action.

78. Minutes of the Sixty-Fifth Meeting of the Faculty of Architecture.

79. "Appendix E: Stated Rules of the Faculty of Architecture (Adopted by the Faculty 12 May 1971)" in Minutes of the Sixty-Seventh Meeting of the Faculty of Architecture, 4 May 1971 (Central Files: Columbia University Minutes of the Faculty of Architecture), n. pag.

80. Ibid., n. pag.

81. Minutes of the Sixty-First Meeting of the Faculty of Architecture, 25 April 1969 (Provost Records: 1953–2006, Box 240), 2.

82. William J. McGill, address delivered at commencement exercises of Columbia University's 219th academic year on 16 May 1973, released by the Office of Public Information on the same date. Obtained from the Office of the President, 5 January 2011, 3.

7. 1972–1976 Extinction

1. A dean search committee would typically receive a charge letter from the president or be summoned to a meeting to address the sorts of issues Kouzmanoff raised. With his carefully worded questions, Kouzmanoff seems to have been calling the president's bluff to either commit to the school's future or simply shut it down.

2. Correspondence dated 11 May 1971 (Central Files: SOA 1956–1971, Box 618, Folder 14, Kouzmanoff to McGill).

3. Susan M. Strauss, "History VII: 1968–1981," in *The Making of an Architect, 1881–1981*, ed. Richard Oliver (New York: Rizzoli, 1981), 243–63.

4. Ibid., 247, quoting correspondence from Young to McGill and deBary, 24 January 1972 (Central Files).

5. Minutes of the Seventy-Second Meeting of the Faculty of Architecture, 25 April 1972 (Provost Records: 1953–2006, Box 240), 2.

6. In academic parlance, a "dowry" consists of the perks the university provides to an incoming dean to advance his or her vision of a school.

7. Strauss, "History VII."

8. Minutes of the Sixty-Seventh Meeting of the Faculty of Architecture,

4 May 1971 (Central Files: Columbia University Minutes of the Faculty of
Architecture), n. pag.

9. Correspondence dated 15 June 1970 (Central Files: SOA 1956–1971,
Box 618, Folder 9, McClure to Cordier), 9.

10. Correspondence dated 12 April 1972 (Provost Records: 1953–2006,
Box 240, Architecture Meeting, 19 April 1972, Bond, Chan, and Lewis to
Polshek).

11. Correspondence dated 6 November 1972 (Office of the Provost, School
of Architecture: General, Box 239, File 1, Interdepartment Memorandum from
David Evan Glasser), n. pag.

12. Minutes of the Seventy-Fifth Meeting of the Faculty of Architecture,
20 February 1973 (Provost Records: 1953–2006, Box 240).

13. Correspondence dated 13 February 1973 (GSAS Collection, Box 1, File
12, January 1972–December 1974, Mintz to Fraenkel).

14. Correspondence dated 2 April 1971 (Provost Records: 1953–2006,
Box 234, School of Architecture Institute of Urban Environment, Johnson to
Rapkin).

15. Correspondence dated 26 October 1972 (Provost Records: 1953–2006,
Box 239, File 1: 15 June 1970–19 December 1973, Rapkin to Polshek), n. pag.

16. Correspondence dated 4 January 1972 (Provost Records: 1953–2006,
Box 234, School of Architecture Institute of Urban Environment, Bassett to
McGill, deBary, and Carter), n. pag.

17. Ibid.

18. Minutes of the Seventy-Eighth Meeting of the Faculty of Architecture,
25 April 1973 (Avery Archives: Plunz Papers).

19. Correspondence dated 13 April 1972 (Provost Records: 1953–2006,
Box 240, Architecture Meeting, 4.19.1972, Graduate Architecture Students to
the Dean et al.), n. pag.

20. Correspondence dated 18 July 1974 (GSAS Collection, Box 1, File 12,
January 1972–December 1974, Friedman to Polshek).

21. Correspondence dated 15 May 1973 (Provost Records: 1953–2006, Box
239, File 1: 15 June 1970–19 December 1973, Kahn to Polshek).

22. Correspondence dated 9 May 1974 (GSAS Collection, Box 1, File 12,
January 1972–December 1974, Mintz to PhD Students).

23. Correspondence dated 15 May 1973 (Kahn to Polshek), n. pag.

24. "Avery Grows," *University Record*, 12 September 1974 (GSAS Collection,
Box 1, File 12, January 1972–December 1974), 5.

25. Correspondence dated 13 October 1971 (GSAS Collection, Box 1, File
13, November 1969–November 1971, Grava to Young), 2.

26. Appendix B of the Minutes of the Eightieth Meeting of the Faculty of
Architecture, 8 October 1974 (Richard Plunz Papers, 1935–1999, Avery Drawings and Archives).

27. Appendix A of the Minutes of the Sixty-Eighth Meeting of the Faculty

of Architecture, 12 October 1971 (Provost Records: 1953–2006, Box 239, File 1: 15 June 1970–19 December 1973).

28. Five-Year Plan for the Graduate School of Architecture and Planning, Confidential Draft Copy (Provost Records: 1953–2006, Box 117, 1975–1976 SOA Budget, 24 July 1974), 30.

29. Correspondence dated 18 May 1973 (Provost Records: 1953–2006, Box 239, Black and Puerto Rican Organization, Graves to the BPRSFAO).

30. "Fred Samuel Playground," *Historical Signs Project on the Official Website of the New York City Department of Parks and Recreation*, nd, http://www.nycgovparks.org/parks/M160/history.

31. Correspondence dated 6 December 1973 (Provost Records: 1953–2006, Box 239, Black and Puerto Rican Organization, Thompson and McIntosh to Polshek), 1.

32. Ibid.

33. Correspondence dated 6 December 1973 (Provost Records: 1953–2006, Box 239, Black and Puerto Rican Organization, Polshek to Thompson and McIntosh).

34. Correspondence dated 11 January 1974 (Provost Records: 1953–2006, Box 239, Black and Puerto Rican Organization, Polshek to Thompson and McIntosh), n. pag.

35. Ibid.

36. Correspondence dated 25 June 1973 (Provost Records, 1953–2006, Box 239, Black and Puerto Rican Organization, Polshek to McGill).

37. Five-Year Plan for the Graduate School of Architecture and Planning.

38. Correspondence dated 13 May 1975 (Provost Records: 1953–2006, Box 239, Dean's Office, Marcuse to Polshek), 1.

39. I attempted to interview Marcuse to get his account of this story, but he did not respond.

40. Correspondence dated 13 May 1975 (Marcuse to Polshek).

41. Five-Year Plan for the Graduate School of Architecture and Planning, 1.

42. Correspondence dated 21 March 1975 (GSAS Collection, Box 1, File 12, January 1972–December 1974, Diamond to Mintz), n. pag.

43. Correspondence dated 22 March 1975 (GSAS Collection, Box 1, File 12, January 1972–December 1974, deBary to Diamond), 2.

44. "AICP Code of Ethics and Professional Conduct," *American Planning Association*, adopted 19 March 2005, revised 13 October 2009, n. pag., https://www.planning.org/ethics/ethicscode.htm.

45. Correspondence dated 20 March 1975 (GSAS Collection, Box 1, File 12, January 1972–December 1974, Polshek to deBary).

46. Ibid., 1.

47. "Urban Planning PhD," *Columbia Daily Spectator*, 6 October 1975, n. pag. (GSAS Collection, Box 1, File 12, January 1972–December 1974).

48. Correspondence dated 13 May 1975 (Marcuse to Polshek), 1.

49. I also attempted to contact Piven; however, like Marcuse, she did not respond.

50. Correspondence dated 13 May 1975 (Marcuse to Polshek).

51. Correspondence dated 26 February 1975 (Max Bond Papers: 1951–2009, Box 5: Personal Papers, Folder 15, deBary to Bond, Jr.), n. pag.

52. Correspondence dated 17 March 1975 (GSAS Collection, Box 1, File 12, January 1972–December 1974, Passin to deBary), 3.

53. Correspondence dated 12 March 1975 (GSAS Collection, Box 1, File 12, January 1972–December 1974, Skinner to deBary), 1.

54. Correspondence dated 16 May 1975 (Provost Records: 1953–2006, Box 239, Dean's Office, Polshek to deBary).

55. Correspondence dated 16 May 1975 (Provost Records: 1953–2006, Box 239, Dean's Office, deBary [Draft] to Polshek), 3.

56. "Urban Planning PhD."

57. Editor, "Excerpts from the Message by Governor Rockefeller on the State of the State," *New York Times*, 19 January 1972.

58. Ibid.

59. Ibid.

60. Howard J. Samuels, "New York City and the Oil Problem," *New York Times*, 29 November 1974.

61. Paul Goldberger, "Women Architects Building Influence in a Profession That Is 98.8 Percent Male," *New York Times*, 18 May 1974.

62. Michelle Alexander, *The New Jim Crow: Mass Incarceration in the Age of Colorblindness*, Kindle ed. (New York: New Press, 2012), 45.

63. Paul Delaney, "Coalition Fears Reported Housing Cut: Fears a Reaction," *New York Times*, 6 January 1973.

64. Martin Tolchin, "Mayors Decry Nixon Housing Proposal: Lindsay Warns Senators That Cities Are Caught in Middle in Struggle," *New York Times*, 4 October 1973.

65. Ada Louise Huxtable, "The Housing Crisis," *New York Times*, 18 November 1975.

66. Jonathan Kozol, *Rachel and Her Children: Homeless Families in America* (New York: Fawcett Columbine, 1988).

67. M. A. Farber, "Columbia's New Freshmen Seem Passive, Not Active," *New York Times*, 4 November 1970.

68. William J. McGill, address delivered at commencement exercises of Columbia University's 219th academic year on 16 May 1973, released by the Office of Public Information on the same date. Obtained from the Office of the President, 5 January 2011, 2–3.

69. Paul Goldberger, "Students in City, despite Slump, Work on What Might Be," *New York Times*, 16 May 1976.

70. Ibid.

71. Ibid.

72. Ibid.

73. Alexander, *New Jim Crow*, 46.

74. McGill, address delivered at commencement exercises, 2.

8. Alumni Years

1. Victoria Kaplan quoting David Norman, a pseudonym for a participant in a study reported in *Structural Inequality: Black Architects in the United States* (Lanham, Md.: Rowman & Littlefield, 2006), 53.

2. Richard P. Nathan, "A Retrospective on Richard M. Nixon's Domestic Policies," *Presidential Studies Quarterly* 26, no. 1 (1996): 155–64.

3. Bradford C. Grant and Dennis Alan Mann, eds., *Directory of African American Architects* (Cincinnati, Ohio: Center for the Study of Practice, 1995), 8.

4. Kaplan, *Structural Inequality*.

5. Ibid., 81.

6. Ibid., 19.

7. U.S. Census Bureau, *Statistical Abstract of the United States* (Washington, D.C.: Government Publishing Office, 2001).

8. Stephen A. Kliment, "Diversity: What the Numbers Tell Us," *AIArchitect*, 13 October 2006, http://info.aia.org/aiarchitect/thisweek06/1013/1013rc_face.htm.

9. Ibid.

10. Corporate Diversity Counseling Group at Holland & Knight, "Demographic Diversity Audit, 2005, confidential unpublished report.

11. Used in this context, the term "only one" refers to someone whose demographics are singular in an organization (e.g., the only woman or the only African American).

12. Andrew S. Caplan and Jamie Gilham, "Included against the Odds: Failure and Success among Minority Ethnic Built Environment Professionals in Britain," *Construction Management and Economics* 23 (December 2005): 1013.

13. For a black property owner to hire a black architect is simply an added liability, given long-standing biases of banks against black-owned property. The legendary John H. Johnson, publisher and founder of *Ebony* and *Jet* magazines, was one patron who challenged these biases. Using the threat of media exposure, he boldly hired black architect John Moutoussamy to design his company's office building in Chicago. See Kliment, "Diversity."

14. Kaplan, *Structural Inequality*, 91.

15. Kliment, "Diversity."

16. Melvin Mitchell, *The Crisis of the African American Architect: Conflicting Cultures of Architecture and (Black) Power* (Lincoln, Neb.: Writers Advantage, 2001), 122–23.

17. Alan Mallach, "Introduction," in *Rebuilding America's Legacy Cities: New Directions for the Industrial Heartland*, ed. Alan Mallach (New York: American Assembly, Columbia University, 2012), xv.

18. U.S. Census Bureau, *2010 United States Census* (Washington, D.C.: Government Publishing Office, 2010).

19. Sharon E. Sutton and Susan P. Kemp, "Place: A Site of Social and Environmental Inequity," in *The Paradox of Urban Space: Inequality and Transformation in Marginalized Communities*, ed. Sharon E. Sutton and Susan P. Kemp (New York: Palgrave Macmillan, 2011), 18.

20. Ibid.

21. Kliment, "Diversity."

22. Sam Roberts, "Infamous 'Drop Dead' Was Never Said by Ford," *New York Times*, 28 December 2006.

23. Dana Cuff, *Architecture: The Story of Practice* (Cambridge, Mass.: MIT Press, 1991), 130.

24. Ibid.

25. Ibid., 129.

26. Ibid., 141, 137.

27. Ibid., 140.

28. Caplan and Gilham, "Included against the Odds," 1012.

29. "Jimmy Carter: Assistance for Minority and Disadvantaged Small Businesses Statement on Signing H.R. 11318 into Law," *American Presidency Project*, 25 October 1978, http://www.presidency.ucsb.edu/ws/?pid=30042.

30. Sharon E. Sutton, *Learning through the Built Environment: An Ecological Approach to Child Development* (New York: Irvington, 1985), 15–16.

31. "George H. W. Bush: Domestic Affairs," *University of Virginia Miller Center*, nd, http://millercenter.org/president/biography/bush-domestic-affairs.

32. "Bill Clinton: Domestic Affairs," *University of Virginia Miller Center*, nd, http://millercenter.org/president/biography/clinton-domestic-affairs.

33. Cuff, *Architecture*, 149.

34. I have changed some of the places and institutions in these biographical sketches to maintain the confidentiality of the oral history cohort.

35. Frances Stanley, "Town and Gown: LeDroit Park and Howard University," *Marketwise* 1 (2001): 2–3.

36. Ibid., 3.

37. "A Sacred Space in Manhattan," *National Park Service*, nd, https://www.nps.gov/afbg/learn/news/newsreleases.htm.

38. Thomas Fisher, *In the Scheme of Things: Alternative Thinking on the Practice of Architecture* (Minneapolis: University of Minnesota Press, 2000), 93.

39. Ibid., 97.

40. Ibid., 100.

41. Kai Bird, *The Color of Truth: McGeorge Bundy and William Bundy, Brothers in Arms* (New York: Simon & Schuster, 1998), 377.

42. Gordon Lafer, "Land and Labor in the Post-industrial University Town: Remaking Social Geography," *Political Geography* 22, no. 1 (2003): 101.

43. Larry Keating and David L. Sjoquist, "The Use of an External Organization to Facilitate University-Community Partnerships," *Cityscape* 5, no. 1 (2000): 141.

44. Margaret E. Dewar and Claudia B. Isaac, "Learning from Difference: The Potentially Transforming Experience of Community-University Collaboration," *Journal of Planning Education and Research* 17, no. 4 (1998): 346.

45. Ibid.

46. Sharon E. Sutton, "Review Essay: Can Service-Learning Help Restore the Public University's Role in Safeguarding American Democracy?" *Michigan Journal of Community Service Learning* 19, no. 1 (2012): 69, citing Wendy Brown, "The End of Educated Democracy," *Representations* 116, no. 1 (2011): 19–41.

47. Olon F. Dotson, "Fourth World Theory: The Evolution of . . . ," *Buildings* 4, no. 2 (2014): 1.

48. Ibid, 2.

49. Parker Palmer, "The Politics of the Brokenhearted: On Holding the Tensions of Democracy," in *Deepening the American Dream: Reflections on the Inner Life and Spirit of Democracy*, ed. Mark Nepo (San Francisco: Jossey-Bass, 2005), 231–57.

50. Brown, "End of Educated Democracy," 24.

51. Cornel West, "Foreword," in Michelle Alexander, *The New Jim Crow: Mass Incarceration in the Age of Colorblindness*, Kindle ed. (New York: New Press, 2012), n. pag.

52. Grace Lee Boggs and Scott Karashige, *The Next American Revolution: Sustainable Activism for the Twenty-First Century*, Kindle ed. (Berkeley: University of California Press, 2011), 72.

53. Alexandra K. Murphy, "The Symbolic Dilemmas of Suburban Poverty: Challenges and Opportunities Posed by Variations in the Contours of Suburban Poverty," *Sociological Forum* 25, no. 3 (2010): 541–42.

54. Ibid., 543.

55. Chris Hedges, "Rise of the New Black Radicals," *Truthdig*, 26 April 2015, http://www.truthdig.com/report/item/rise_of_the_new_black_radicals_20150426/.

56. Alexander, *New Jim Crow.*

57. Ibid., 6–7.

58. West, "Foreword," n. pag.

59. Hedges, "Rise of the New Black Radicals."

60. Brown, "End of Educated Democracy."

61. Boggs and Karashige, *Next American Revolution*, 67.

62. Ibid., 68.

63. Lynn Haney, "Training Blacks as Architects Increasing," *New York Times*, 15 March 1970.

Epilogue

1. John Eligon and Robert Gebeloff, "Affluent and Black, and Still Trapped by Segregation," *New York Times*, 20 August 2016.

2. Michelle Alexander, *The New Jim Crow: Mass Incarceration in the Age of Colorblindness*, Kindle ed. (New York: New Press, 2012).

3. Chris Hedges, "Rise of the New Black Radicals," *Truthdig*, 26 April 2015, http://www.truthdig.com/report/item/rise_of_the_new_black_radicals _20150426/.

4. Richard Florida, "Solving the Global Housing Crisis," *Atlantic CityLab*, 24 October 2014, http://www.citylab.com/housing/2014/10/solving-the -global-housing-crisis/381891.

5. Ibid.

6. Brentin Mock, "There Are No Courses on Race and Justice, So We Made Our Own Syllabus," *Atlantic CityLab*, 14 May 2014, http://www.citylab .com/design/2015/05/there-are-no-urban-design-courses-on-race-and -justice-so-we-made-our-own-syllabus/393335/.

7. Brentin Mock, "What Urban Design Can Actually Do to Address Police Violence," *Atlantic CityLab*, 14 May 2014, http://www.citylab.com/design/ 2015/05/what-urban-design-can-actually-do-to-address-police-violence/ 393845/.

8. Ibid.

9. Cornel West, "Foreword," in Alexander, *New Jim Crow*.

Bibliography

Archives

Archives and Records, American Institute of Architects, Washington, D.C.

Central Files Miscellaneous, University Archives, Rare Book and Manuscript Library, Columbia University, New York.

Columbia University Minutes of the Faculty of Architecture, University Archives, Rare Book and Manuscript Library, Columbia University, New York.

Graduate School of Architecture Planning and Preservation Centennial Archives, Avery Archives, Columbia University, New York.

Graduate School for Arts and Sciences Collection, School of Architecture, 1969–1984, University Archives, Rare Book and Manuscript Library, Columbia University, New York.

Historical Photograph Collection, University Archives, Rare Book and Manuscript Library, Columbia University, New York.

Max Bond Papers, 1951–2009, Avery Archives, Columbia University, New York.

Office of Public Affairs Photograph Collection, University Archives, Rare Book and Manuscript Library, Columbia University, New York.

Office of the Provost Records, 1953–2006, University Archives, Rare Book and Manuscript Library, Columbia University, New York.

Planners for Equal Opportunity Archives, Rare and Manuscript Collections, University Library, Carl A. Kroch Library, Cornell University, Ithaca, N.Y.

School of Architecture, 1956–1971, University Archives, Rare Book and Manuscript Library, Columbia University, New York.

University Protest and Activism Collection, University Archives, Rare Book and Manuscript Library, Columbia University, New York.

Books and Articles

Abrams, Charles. "Present Labor Pains in Planning Education." *American Society of Planning Officials* 34, no. 1 (1968): 1–2.

"AICP Code of Ethics and Professional Conduct." *American Planning Association*, adopted 19 March 2005, revised 13 October 2009, https://www.planning.org/ethics/ethicscode.htm.

Alexander, Michelle. *The New Jim Crow: Mass Incarceration in the Age of Colorblindness.* Kindle ed. New York: New Press, 2012.

Angotti, Tom, Cheryl Doble, and Paula Horrigan, eds. *Service-Learning in Design and Planning: Education at the Boundaries.* Oakland, Calif.: New Village Press, 2011.

Anthony, Kathryn H. *Designing for Diversity: Gender, Race, and Ethnicity in the Architectural Profession.* Urbana: University of Illinois Press, 2001.

———. "Private Reactions to Public Criticism: Students, Faculty, and Practicing Architects State Their Views on Design Juries in Architectural Education." *Journal of Architectural Education* 40, no. 3 (1987): 2–11.

Aponte-Parés, Luis. "Lessons from el Barrio—The East Harlem Real Great Society/Urban Planning Studio: A Puerto Rican Chapter in the Fight for Urban Self-Determination." In *Latino Social Movements: Historical and Theoretical Perspectives*, edited by Rodolfo D. Torres and George Katsiaficas, 43–77. New York: Routledge, 1999.

Arnold, Martin. "Lindsay Orders Report on Police: Leary Will Study Charges of Brutality at Columbia." *New York Times*, 1 May 1968.

Asbury, Edith Evans. "Protesters Boo Shriver at Talk on 'Struggle for Urban Power.'" *New York Times*, 3 March 1968.

Ayres, B. Drummond, Jr. "A Target of Campus Protesters Is a 'Think Tank': Institute of Defense Analysis." *New York Times*, 26 April 1968.

Bell, Harold K., and Vernon Ben Robinson. "Appendix IV: A Consortium Venture for Student Field Training." In *A Partnership of Equals: An Action Research Report for Urban Affairs Executives of Universities, Corporations, Governments, and Community Organizations.* New York: Columbia University Urban Action and Experimentation Program, 1971.

Bennett, Charles G. "Estimate Board Scene of Uproar: Crowd Is in Argumentative Mood at Regular Meeting." *New York Times*, 11 June 1966.

———. "Wagner Defends City as a 'Model': Studied by Nation, He Says in Summing Up Tenure." *New York Times*, 19 October 1965.

"Bill Clinton: Domestic Affairs." *University of Virginia Miller Center*, nd, http://millercenter.org/president/biography/clinton-domestic-affairs.

Biondi, Martha. *The Black Revolution on Campus.* Kindle ed. Berkeley: University of California Press, 2012.

Bird, Kai. *The Color of Truth: McGeorge Bundy and William Bundy, Brothers in Arms*. New York: Simon & Schuster, 1998.

Bledstein, Burton J. *The Culture of Professionalism: The Middle Class and the Development of Higher Education in America*. New York: Norton, 1978.

Blumenthal, Ralph. "Harlem Awaits Use of 1964 Plan: Renewal Proposal Resulted from Study by Columbia." *New York Times*, 23 March 1972.

Boggs, Grace Lee, and Scott Kurashige. *The Next American Revolution: Sustainable Activism for the Twenty-First Century*. Kindle ed. Berkeley: University of California Press, 2012.

Bowen, William G., and Derek Bok. *The Shape of the River: Long-Term Consequences of Considering Race in College and University Admissions*. Princeton, N.J.: Princeton University Press, 1998.

Bowser, Benjamin P. *The Black Middle Class: Social Mobility—and Vulnerability*. Boulder, Colo.: Lynne Rienner, 2007.

Bradley, Stefan. "'Gym Crow Must Go': Black Student Activism at Columbia University, 1967–1968." *Journal of African American History* 88, no. 2 (2003): 163–81.

———. *Harlem vs. Columbia University: Black Student Power in the Late 1960s*. Urbana: University of Illinois Press, 2009.

———. "'This Is Harlem Heights': Black Student Power and the 1968 Columbia University Rebellion." *Afro-Americans in New York Life and History* 32, no. 1 (2008): 99–122.

Burnham, David. "Police Guarding Gates to Campus: Also Occupy All Buildings Not Held by Students." *New York Times*, 27 April 1968.

Bush, George W. "Presidential Proclamation 7984: Establishment of the African Burial Ground National Monument." *National Park Service*, 27 February 2006, http://www.nps.gov/afbg/learn/management/presidential -proclamation.htm.

Caplan, Andrew S., and Jamie Gilham. "Included against the Odds: Failure and Success among Minority Ethnic Built-Environment Professionals in Britain." *Construction Management and Economics* 23 (December 2005): 1007–15.

Cuff, Dana. *Architecture: The Story of Practice*. Cambridge, Mass.: MIT Press, 1991.

Dallek, Matthew. "The Conservative 1960s." *Atlantic Monthly*, December 1995, 130–35.

Delaney, Paul. "Coalition Fears Reported Housing Cut: Fears a Reaction." *New York Times*, 6 January 1973.

Dewar, Margaret E., and Claudia B. Isaac. "Learning from Difference: The Potentially Transforming Experience of Community-University Collaboration." *Journal of Planning Education and Research* 17, no. 4 (1998): 334–47.

Dotson, Olon F. "Fourth World Theory: The Evolution of . . . " *Buildings* 4, no. 2 (2014): http://www.mdpi.com/2075-5309/4/2/155/pdf.

Drake, St. Claire. "What Happened to Black Studies?" *New York University Educational Quarterly* 10, no. 3 (1979): 9–16.

Dugan, George. "City Aid Promised to East Harlem: 3 New Commissioners Make a Rehabilitation Tour." *New York Times*, 3 January 1966.

Editor. "2 Groups Protest High Cost of Slum Renovation: It Results in Increased Rents." *New York Times*, 21 July 1966.

———. "10-Year Harlem Plan Is Questioned." *New York Times*, 2 May 1965.

———. "13 Held in Protest over Columbia Gym." *New York Times*, 29 February 1968.

———. "Bias at Columbia Denied at Hearing: Two Officials Defend College of Surgeons on Racial Charges before Council Group." *New York Times*, 18 May 1946.

———. "Columbia Seeks Master Planner: I. M. Pei Is Expected to Get Major Expansion Job." *New York Times*, 15 April 1968.

———. "Columbia Students Give Slum Aid Hints." *New York Times*, 29 April 1969.

———. "Excerpts from the Message by Governor Rockefeller on the State of the State." *New York Times*, 19 January 1972.

———. "Dr. Kirk Urges U.S. to Leave Vietnam: Columbia Head Finds War Delays Nation's Advance." *New York Times*, 13 April 1968.

———. "Need for Housing Vexes Columbia: University in Conflict with Tenants." *New York Times*, 25 August 1957.

———. "Negro Architects Helping Harlem Plan Its Future." *New York Times*, 16 March 1969.

———. "New Columbia Gym Is Opposed." *New York Times*, 16 April 1968.

———. "Romney Hails Prefab in Yonkers." *New York Times*, 18 May 1971.

———. "Search for Negro Students." *New York Times*, 20 October 1963.

Ehrenreich, Barbara. *Fear of Falling: The Inner Life of the Middle Class*. New York: Harper Perennial, 1990.

Farber, M. A. "Columbia's New Freshmen Seem Passive, Not Active." *New York Times*, 4 November 1970.

Farrell, James J. *The Spirit of the Sixties: Making Postwar Radicalism*. New York: Routledge, 1997.

Fisher, Thomas. *In the Scheme of Things: Alternative Thinking on the Practice of Architecture*. Minneapolis: University of Minnesota Press, 2000.

Florida, Richard. "Solving the Global Housing Crisis." *Atlantic CityLab*, 24 October 2014, http://www.citylab.com/housing/2014/10/solving-the -global-housing-crisis/381891.

Franklin, Ben A. "East Side Group Assails Renewal: Pickets in Capital against Plan for Cooper Square." *New York Times*, 13 October 1965.

Franklin, John Hope, and Isidore Starr, eds. *The Negro in Twentieth-Century America: A Reader on the Struggle for Civil Rights*. New York: Vintage Books, 1967.

Fraser, C. Gerald. "12 Arrested at Site of Gym in Morningside Park." *New York Times*, 21 February 1968.

———. "Negroes Keep Campaign on Gym:'Still the Major Issue' Says Head of Black Students." *New York Times*, 2 May 1968.

"Fred Samuel Playground." *Historical Signs Project on the Official Website of the New York City Department of Parks and Recreation*, nd, http://www .nycgovparks.org/parks/M160/history.

Fullilove, Mindy Thompson. *Root Shock: How Tearing Up City Neighborhoods Hurts America, and What We Can Do about It*. New York: Random House, 2004.

Gansberg, Martin. "3,500 Join Columbia Boycott." *New York Times*, 14 March 1968.

"George H. W. Bush: Domestic Affairs." *University of Virginia Miller Center*, nd, http://millercenter.org/president/biography/bush-domestic-affairs.

Gilbert, Claire, and Donald Heller. "The Truman Commission and Its Impact on Federal Higher Education Policy from 1947 to 2010." Working paper, Pennsylvania State University, Center for the Study of Higher Education, University Park.

Gittell, Marilyn. "The Illusion of Affirmative Action." *Change* 7, no. 8 (1975): 39–43.

Goldberger, Paul. "Students in City, despite Slump, Work on What Might Be." *New York Times*, 16 May 1976.

———. "Women Architects Building Influence in a Profession That Is 98.8 Percent Male." *New York Times*, 18 May 1974.

Goldmann, Robert B. *Money in Search of a Mission*. New York: Ford Foundation Division of National Affairs Project Evaluation, 1970.

Gould, Jack. "Radio: Keeping Abreast of the Turmoil at Columbia: Students' WKCR Gives a Lesson in Reporting." *New York Times*, 27 April 1968.

Graham, Fred P. "The Law: Case against Spock et al." *New York Times*, 14 January 1968.

Grant, Bradford C. "Cultural Invisibility: The African American Experience in Architectural Education." In *Voices in Architectural Education: Cultural Politics and Pedagogy*, edited by Tomas A. Dutton, 149–64. New York: Bergin and Garvey, 1991.

Grant, Bradford C., and Dennis Alan Mann, eds. *Directory of African American Architects*. Cincinnati, Ohio: Center for the Study of Practice, 1995.

Gregory, Steven. *Black Corona: Race and the Politics of Place in an Urban Community*. Princeton, N.J.: Princeton University Press, 1998.

Groat, Linda N., and Sherry Ahrentzen. "Reconceptualizing Architectural Education for a More Diverse Future: Perceptions and Visions of Architectural Students." *Journal of Architectural Education* 49, no. 3 (1996): 166–83.

Grutzner, Charles. "Renewal on the Way for Morningside: City Preparing to Ask U.S. for Funds to Draw a Plan for Heights Quickly." *New York Times*, 11 September 1960.

Gutman, Marta, and Richard Plunz. "Anatomy of Insurrection." In *The Making of an Architect, 1881–1981*, edited by Richard Oliver, 183–210. New York: Rizzoli, 1981.

Haney, Lynn. "Training of Blacks as Architects Increasing: Training Black Architects." *New York Times*, 15 March 1970.

Hechinger, Fred M. "Columbia Plans Huge Expansion: Buildings to Cost 68 Million." *New York Times*, 9 April 1961.

Hedges, Chris. "Rise of the New Black Radicals." *Truthdig*, 26 April 2015, http://www.truthdig.com/report/item/rise_of_the_new_black_radicals_20150426/.

Henderson, A. Scott. *Housing and the Democratic Ideal: The Life and Thought of Charles Abrams*. New York: Columbia University Press, 2000.

Huxtable, Ada Louise. "600 Acres of Trouble: Morningside, City's Top Renewal Area, Is a Crucible of Crime and Creativity." *New York Times*, 30 September 1964.

———. "Expansion at Columbia: A Restricted Vision and Bureaucracy Seen as Obstacles to Its Development." *New York Times*, 5 November 1966.

———. "Hard Questions for Harlem." *New York Times*, 11 February 1968.

———. "The Housing Crisis." *New York Times*, 18 November 1975.

———. "New Era for Parks: Hoving and Young Appointees Hope to Scrap the Traditional and Try the New." *New York Times*, 10 February 1966.

———. "Planning for Cities in Chaos." *New York Times*, 16 October 1967.

———. "Project, Planned 10 Years, Has Been Called Unsound: Work Starts on Total Renewal Project." *New York Times*, 21 October 1966.

———. "The State Office Building Dilemma." *New York Times*, 2 November 1969.

"Jimmy Carter: Assistance for Minority and Disadvantaged Small Businesses Statement on Signing H.R. 11318 into Law." *American Presidency Project*, 25 October 1978, http://www.presidency.ucsb.edu/ws/?pid=30042.

Kaiser, Charles. *1968 in America: Music, Politics, Chaos, Counterculture, and the Shaping of a Generation*. Kindle ed. New York: Grove/Atlantic, 2012.

Kalman, Laura. *Yale Law School and the Sixties*. Chapel Hill: University of North Carolina Press, 2005.

Kaplan, Victoria. *Structural Inequality: Black Architects in the United States*. Lanham, Md.: Rowman & Littlefield, 2006.

Karabel, Jerome. *The Chosen: The Hidden History of Admission and Exclusion at Harvard, Yale, and Princeton*. New York: Houghton Mifflin, 2005.

———. "How Affirmative Action Took Hold at Harvard, Yale, and Princeton." *Journal of Blacks in Higher Education* 48 (Summer 2005): 58–77.

Keating, Larry, and David L. Sjoquist. "The Use of an External Organization to Facilitate University-Community Partnerships." *Cityscape* 5, no. 1 (2000): 141–57.

Kifner, John. "Students Run Columbia Protest along Principles of Democracy." *New York Times*, 27 April 1968.

Kindig, Jessie. "Draft Resistance in the Vietnam Era." *Antiwar and Radical*

History Project, 2008, http://depts.washington.edu/antiwar/vietnam_draft
.shtml.

King, Seth S. "Sewage Plant Voted over Harlem Protest." *New York Times*,
26 April 1968.

Kliment, Stephen A. "Diversity: What the Numbers Tell Us." *AIArchitect*,
13 October 2006, http://info.aia.org/aiarchitect/thisweek06/1013/1013rc
_face.htm.

Kovach, Bill. "Mayor, in Albany, Warns on Budget." *New York Times*, 13 February
ary 1969.

Kozol, Jonathan. *Rachel and Her Children: Homeless Families in America*. New
York: Fawcett Columbine, 1988.

Lafer, Gordon. "Land and Labor in the Post-industrial University Town:
Remaking Social Geography." *Political Geography* 22, no. 1 (2003): 89–117.

Lucas, J. Anthony. "Faculty Warns Columbia on Its Expansion Policy: 70
Members Find It Would Worsen Racial Tensions in Morningside Heights."
New York Times, 27 March 1968.

Mallach, Alan. "Introduction." In *Rebuilding America's Legacy Cities: New
Directions for the Industrial Heartland*, edited by Alan Mallach, xiii–xx. New
York: American Assembly, Columbia University, 2012.

Mann, Dennis, and Brad Grant. "African American Architects and Their
Education: A Demographic Study." Working paper, University of Cincinnati
Center for the Study of Practice, Cincinnati, Ohio, 2007.

Marable, Manning. *Race, Reform, and Rebellion: The Second Reconstruction and
Beyond in Black America, 1945 to 2006*. 3rd ed. Jackson: University Press of
Mississippi, 2007.

McClintock, Charles. "Spanning Boundaries of Knowledge and Organization:
Collaborations for Mind and Management in Higher Education." *Organization*
zation 8, no. 2 (2001): 349–57.

Millones, Peter. "Community Discontent and an Increase in Protests Sow the
Seeds of Concern at Columbia University." *New York Times*, 3 March 1968.

Mitchell, Melvin. *The Crisis of the African American Architect: Conflicting Cultures
of Architecture and (Black) Power*. Lincoln, Neb.: Writers Club, 2001.

Mithun, Jacqueline S. "Black Power and Community Change: An Assessment."
Journal of Black Studies 7, no. 3 (1977): 263–80.

Mock, Brentin. "There Are No Courses on Race and Justice, So We Made
Our Own Syllabus." *Atlantic CityLab*, 14 May 2014, http://www.citylab
.com/design/2015/05/there-are-no-urban-design-courses-on-race-and
-justice-so-we-made-our-own-syllabus/393335/.

———. "What Urban Design Can Actually Do to Address Police Violence."
Atlantic CityLab, 14 May 2014, http://www.citylab.com/design/2015/05/
what-urban-design-can-actually-do-to-address-police-violence/393845/.

Murphy, Alexandra K. "The Symbolic Dilemmas of Suburban Poverty: Challenges
lenges and Opportunities Posed by Variations in the Contours of Suburban
Poverty." *Sociological Forum* 25, no. 3 (2010): 541–69.

Nathan, Richard P. "A Retrospective on Richard M. Nixon's Domestic Policies." *Presidential Studies Quarterly* 26, no. 1 (1996): 155–64.

O'Kane, Lawrence. "Morningside Tenants Protest Renewal at City Hall
Hearing." *New York Times*, 12 March 1965.

Oliver, Richard. "History VI: 1959–1968." In *The Making of an Architect,
1881–1981*, edited by Richard Oliver, 167–82. New York: Rizzoli,
1981.

Orum, Anthony M. *Black Students in Protest: A Study of the Origins of the Black
Student Movement*. Washington, D.C.: American Sociological Association,
1972.

Palmer, Parker. "The Politics of the Brokenhearted: On Holding the Tensions
of Democracy." In *Deepening the American Dream: Reflections on the Inner
Life and Spirit of Democracy*, edited by Mark Nepo, 231–57. San Francisco:
Jossey-Bass, 2005.

Perkins, Linda. "The African American Female Elite: The Early History of
African American Women in the Seven Sister Colleges, 1880–1960."
Harvard Educational Review 67, no. 4 (1997): 718–56.

Piven, Frances Fox, and Richard A. Cloward. *Poor People's Movements: Why
They Succeed, How They Fail*. New York: Vintage Books, 1979.

Price, Robert E. "Columbia: Turning the University Around." In *The University and the City: Eight Cases of Involvement*, edited by George Nash, 119–43.
New York: McGraw-Hill, 1973.

Reeves, Richard. "Lindsay Renews Criticism of War: Tells Columbia Group
He Hopes for Rockefeller Race." *New York Times*, 26 March 1968.

Rich, Wilbur C. "From Muskogee to Morningside Heights: Political Scientist
Charles V. Hamilton." *Living Legacies: Great Moments and Leading Figures in
the History of Columbia University*, nd, http://www.columbia.edu/cu/alumni/
Magazine/Spring2004/hamilton.html.

Roberts, Sam. "Infamous 'Drop Dead' Was Never Said by Ford." *New York
Times*, 28 December 2006.

Roberts, Steven V. "Decisions Nearing on Renewal Projects Planned under
Mayor Wagner." *New York Times*, 3 May 1966.

———. "Negro-Latin Feud Hurting Harlem: Groups Fighting for Control of
Area Renewal Projects." *New York Times*, 25 February 1968.

———. "Renewal Backed in Williamsburg: Plans Approved but Puerto Ricans
Make Protest." *New York Times*, 28 July 1967.

———. "Sit-in Spectrum Has a Wide Range: But All Students Agree on Voice
in Key Decisions." *New York Times*, 25 April 1968.

Robinson, Douglas. "Group Backs Two in Draft Protest? Critic and Author
Support Registration Card." *New York Times*, 12 January 1968.

Rogers, Ibram H. *The Black Campus Movement: Black Students and the Racial
Reconstitution of Higher Education, 1965–1972*. Kindle ed. New York:
Palgrave Macmillan, 2012.

Rosenkranz, Richard. *Across the Barricades*. New York: J. B. Lippincott, 1971.

Samuels, Howard J. "New York City and the Oil Problem." *New York Times*, 29 November 1974.

Sanoff, Henry. "Origins of Community Design." *Progressive Planning Magazine*, 2 January 2006, http://www.plannersnetwork.org/2006/01/origins-of -community-design/.

Shipler, David K. "Coalition 'Appoints' 3 Nonwhites to City Plan Group as a Protest." *New York Times*, 13 August 1969.

———. "Small Plant Taking Big Step in Prefabs." *New York Times*, 27 October 1970.

Soska, Tracy M. "University and Communities in Partnership: Exploring the Roots and Current Trends of Higher Education Community Engagement in the United States." In *Community Engagement in Higher Education: Policy Reforms and Practice*, edited by W. James Jacob, Stewart E. Sutin, John Weidman, and John L. Yeager, 105–26. Rotterdam: SensePublishers, 2015.

Stanley, Frances. "Town and Gown: LeDroit Park and Howard University." *Marketwise* 1 (2001): 1–11.

Starr, Roger. "Advocators of Planners." *American Society of Planning Officials* 33, no. 2 (1967): n. pag.

———. "The Case of the Columbia Gym." In "The Universities," special issue, *National Affairs* 13 (Fall 1968): 102–21.

Stern, Michael. "Lindsay's Office Has First Sit-In: East Harlem Tenants Seek Action on Apartments." *New York Times*, 15 January 1966.

———. "Teachers at Columbia Risk Violence as Mediators." *New York Times*, 30 April 1968.

Strauss, Susan M. "History VII: 1968–1981." In *The Making of an Architect, 1881–1981*, edited by Richard Oliver, 243–63. New York: Rizzoli, 1981.

Sugrue, Thomas J. *The Origins of the Urban Crisis: Race and Inequality in Postwar Detroit*. Princeton, N.J.: Princeton University Press, 1996.

———. *Sweet Land of Liberty: The Forgotten Struggle for Civil Rights in the North*. New York: Random House, 2008.

Sutton, Sharon E. *Learning through the Built Environment: An Ecological Approach to Child Development*. New York: Irvington, 1985.

———. "The Progress of Architecture." *Progressive Architecture*, October 1993, 69–79.

———. "Review Essay: Can Service-Learning Help Restore the Public University's Role in Safeguarding American Democracy?" *Michigan Journal of Community Service Learning* 19, no. 1 (2012): 69–73.

———. "Seeing the Whole of the Moon." In *Multicultural Teaching in the University*, edited by David Schoem, Linda Frankel, Ximena Zúñiga, and Edith Lewis, 161–71. Westport, Conn.: Praeger, 1993.

Sutton, Sharon E., and Susan P. Kemp. "Introduction: Place as Marginality and Possibility." In *The Paradox of Urban Space: Inequality and Transformation in Marginalized Communities*, edited by Sharon E. Sutton and Susan P. Kemp, 1–9. New York: Palgrave Macmillan, 2011.

———. "Place: A Site of Social and Environmental Inequity." In *The Paradox of Urban Space: Inequality and Transformation in Marginalized Communities*, edited by Sharon E. Sutton and Susan P. Kemp, 13–28. New York: Palgrave Macmillan, 2011.

"Tet Offensive: Vietnam War." *History.com*, 2009, http://www.history.com/topics/vietnam-war/tet-offensive.

Tolchin, Martin. "Mayors Decry Nixon Housing Proposal: Lindsay Warns Senators That Cities Are Caught in Middle in Struggle." *New York Times*, 4 October 1973.

Ueland, Jeff, and Barney Warf. "Racialized Topographies: Altitude and Race in Southern Cities." *Geographical Review* 96, no. 1 (2006): 50–78.

U.S. Census Bureau, *2010 United States Census*. Washington, D.C.: Government Publishing Office, 2010.

———. *Statistical Abstract of the United States*. Washington, D.C.: Government Publishing Office, 2001.

U.S. Department of State. "Years of Change: The 1960s and 1970s." *About Education*, nd, http://economics.about.com/od/useconomichistory/a/change.htm.

West, Cornel. "Foreword." In Michelle Alexander, *The New Jim Crow: Mass Incarceration in the Age of Colorblindness*. Kindle ed. New York: New Press, 2012.

Wilder, Craig Steven, *Ebony and Ivy: Race, Slavery, and the Troubled History of America's Universities*. Kindle ed. New York: Bloomsbury, 2013.

Wilk, Jocelyn. "1968: Columbia in Crisis." *Columbia University Libraries: Information Services*, nd, https://exhibitions.cul.columbia.edu/exhibits/show/1968.

Index

125th Street, 79, 80; location in Harlem, *61*; SAS march and, 76; State Office Building project, 51, 59–60, 122; student proposals for transforming, 49, 142

Abrams, Charles, 166; background of, 2, 48–49; Derrick Burrows and, 96; community-service learning and, 88; death of, 133; effect on the Division of Planning, 2, 52–53; eliminating community engagement and, 159; ethnic minority recruitment in the Planning Division and, 93; launching of UAEP and, 86; leave of absence from Columbia, 5, 79, 85, 132; negotiation of a joint Columbia/Harlem peacemaking deal, 78–80; NYC luncheon speech on urban problems, 39; Planning Division's community-service learning and, 88; response to the Harlem/Morningside urban renewal crisis, 52–53; university–community restructuring and, 89, 90

Abruña, Abigail, 110, 113, 145, 165, 200

Adams, Alverna, 110–11

Ad Hoc Faculty Group (AHFG), 65–66, 69, 71, 76, 80

administrators: August André Baker, 190–91; Bruce Fenderson, 189–90

advocacy planning: Architects Renewal Committee in Harlem, 42–43; opponents of, 39–40; Planners for Equal Opportunity and, 38–40; RGS/Uptown, 42, 43

Afro-American Society, 100–1

AHFG. *See* Ad Hoc Faculty Group

AIA. *See* American Institute of Architects

AIP. *See* American Institute of Planners

Alicea, Victor G., 229–30, 231

American Association of Planning Officials, 38

American Institute of Architects (AIA): Architecture in the Neighborhoods program and, 43; Artists in Schools program and, 185; black architects, 110; black empowerment in the 1970s and, 128–29; ethnic minority recruitment and, 91; response to the urban crisis of 1965–1976, 37–38

American Institute of Certified Planners, 179

American Institute of Planners (AIP), 38, 39–40

American Planning Association, 179

amnesty, 131

of 1971–1972 and, 148–49, 154,
155; Dean Polshek's encounters with
race and, 163–65; racial struggles in
the School of Architecture and, 6,
148–50; support for ethnic minority
recruits, 112; transforming the status
quo, 113–14
black architects: in academia, 178; the
drawbacks of government work for,
180; female firm principals, 191–92;
number graduated by Columbia
University, 11–12; underrepresentation
in the profession, 110, 178–79, 180
black community: insurgency of 1968 at
Columbia and, 64, 65, 76–77
black mentors, 110
black migrants/migration, 17–19, 25
Black Panthers, 22
"black sites," 206
Black Student Movement, 99–101
black students: activism in the 1960s,
20–25; Black Student Movement and
ethnic minority recruits, 99–101; the
challenges of social transformation
and, 205–6; insurgency of 1968 and,
64–65; militancy and the importance
of rebellion in today's world, 199–200;
pre-1965 Ivy League schools and,
27–29; underrepresentation in
architecture and planning in the 2000s,
178, 179. See also Black and Puerto
Rican Student-Faculty-Administrators
Organization; Society for Afro-
American Students
black urbanization: pre-1965, 17–20, 35
black women: firm principals, 191–92;
professors of architecture and planning,
194–95; students, Dean Polshek's
encounters with race and, 163–65
Bond, J. Max, Jr., 202
Bond, Max: Architects Renewal Committee in Harlem and, 121; backlash
from the Ghana trip, 143–44; ethnic
minority alumni and, 202; ethnic
minority recruitment and, 95; ethnic
minority recruits on being taught
by, 107; as a mentor, 110; James
Polshek and, 154–55; promoted to
professorship, 129; sponsoring of

community-service platforms, 88;
study abroad in Ghana and, 104, 105
Bowles, Kirk: civil rights activism and, 75;
on the conflict between Columbia
and Harlem/Morningside, 46–47; on
discrimination against women in the
School of Architecture, 146; on the
ethnic minority cohort leadership
in exploring alternative professional
roles, 196; on ethnic minority recruits
transforming the status quo, 114;
middle career years, 187; on New York
and Harlem in 1968, 58; on passing the
Architecture Registration Exam, 183,
184; on shortcomings of the platform
system, 136, 137; on staff member Loes
Schiller, 111; on student internships,
120–21; success as a student, 126; on
working as a high school student with
the Black Panthers, 22
Bowman, Martin, 234
BPRSFAO. See Black and Puerto Rican
Student-Faculty-Administrators
Organization
Britt, Marva, 105
Britt, Stanford R., 97, 202, 215–16, 232,
234
Brown, H. Rap, 64
Brown, Tony, 234
Brown University, 27
Brown v. Board of Education, 18, 21
Bundy, McGeorge, 44–45, 200
Burrows, Derrick, 47, 96, 146
Busch, Rolf, 67
Bush, George W. H., 188

Campus Walk, 63, 70
career trajectories of the ethnic minority
cohort: advanced career years in the
1990s and 2000s, 188–95; early career
years in the 1970s, 181–84; effect
of racial underrepresentation in the
professions on, 178–80; effect of the
dark age for social progress on, 176–80;
leadership in exploring alternative roles
in the city-making professions, 196;
middle years in the 1980s, 184–88;
passing the Architecture Registration
Exam, 181–82, 183–84

ESE SELECT TITLES FROM EMPIRE STATE EDITIONS

Allen Jones with Mark Naison, *The Rat That Got Away: A Bronx Memoir*

Janet Grossbach Mayer, *As Bad as They Say? Three Decades of Teaching in the Bronx*

William Seraile, *Angels of Mercy: White Women and the History of New York's Colored Orphan Asylum*

Andrew J. Sparberg, *From a Nickel to a Token: The Journey from Board of Transportation to MTA*

New York's Golden Age of Bridges. Paintings by Antonio Masi, Essays by Joan Marans Dim, Foreword by Harold Holzer

Daniel Campo, *The Accidental Playground: Brooklyn Waterfront Narratives of the Undesigned and Unplanned*

Gerard R. Wolfe, *The Synagogues of New York's Lower East Side: A Retrospective and Contemporary View, Second Edition.* Photographs by Jo Renée Fine and Norman Borden, Foreword by Joseph Berger

Howard Eugene Johnson with Wendy Johnson, *A Dancer in the Revolution: Stretch Johnson, Harlem Communist at the Cotton Club.* Foreword by Mark D. Naison

Joseph B. Raskin, *The Routes Not Taken: A Trip Through New York City's Unbuilt Subway System*

Phillip Deery, *Red Apple: Communism and McCarthyism in Cold War New York*

North Brother Island: The Last Unknown Place in New York City. Photographs by Christopher Payne, A History by Randall Mason, Essay by Robert Sullivan

Richard Kostelanetz, *Artists' SoHo: 49 Episodes of Intimate History*

Stephen Miller, *Walking New York: Reflections of American Writers from Walt Whitman to Teju Cole*

Tom Glynn, *Reading Publics: New York City's Public Libraries, 1754–1911*

Greg Donaldson, *The Ville: Cops and Kids in Urban America, Updated Edition.* With a new epilogue by the author, Foreword by Mark D. Naison

David Borkowski, *A Shot Story: From Juvie to Ph.D.*

Craig Saper, *The Amazing Adventures of Bob Brown: A Real-Life Zelig Who Wrote His Way Through the 20th Century*

R. Scott Hanson, *City of Gods: Religious Freedom, Immigration, and Pluralism in Flushing, Queens.* Foreword by Martin E. Marty

Dorothy Day and the Catholic Worker: The Miracle of Our Continuance. Edited, with an Introduction and Additional Text by Kate Hennessy, Photographs by Vivian Cherry, Text by Dorothy Day

Pamela Lewis, *Teaching While Black: A New Voice on Race and Education in New York City*

Mark Naison and Bob Gumbs, *Before the Fires: An Oral History of African American Life in the Bronx from the 1930s to the 1960s*

Robert Weldon Whalen, *Murder, Inc., and the Moral Life: Gangsters and Gang-busters in La Guardia's New York*

Joanne Witty and Henrik Krogius, *Brooklyn Bridge Park: A Dying Waterfront Transformed*

For a complete list, visit www.empirestateeditions.com.